OXFORD Business English

Jon Naunton

Additional material by James Greenan

ProFile 3

Upper-Intermediate

Student's Book

OXFORD
UNIVERSITY PRESS

	1 **Target markets** p6	2 **Triumph and disaster** p16	3 **Prioritizing** p26
LISTENING	An advertising agency	Debt advice	Scheduling large projects
READING	Generation Y	An entrepreneur	Time management
GRAMMAR	The present	The past	The future
LANGUAGE FOR	Giving opinions	Apologies, criticism, and deductions	Requests and offers
SPEAKING	Advertising controls	Assessing blame	Delegating tasks
CASE STUDY	The Boston Matrix	Making career decisions	Critical path analysis
WRITING	Advertising copy	Abbreviations	Letters requesting payment
CD-ROM	Managing Director, marketing agency	A designer	A project manager, model-making

	4 **Globalization** p36	5 **Company culture** p46	6 **Supply and demand** p56
LISTENING	Globalization	Organizational cultures	Elasticity of demand
READING	Western companies in China	Social responsibility in business	Commodity prices
GRAMMAR	Routines and habits	Modals	Conjunctions
LANGUAGE FOR	Speaking with conviction	Obligation and necessity	Participating in meetings
SPEAKING	One-minute arguments	Intranet rulebook	Roles within teams
CASE STUDY	The marketing mix	Motivating staff	Marketing policy
WRITING	Summarizing arguments	An email to all staff	Describing trends
CD-ROM	European Sales Manager	A webmaster	An importer of gardenware

	7 Negotiations p66	8 Staying competitive p76	9 International business p86
LISTENING	Negotiating	A management consultant	Export documentation
READING	Negotiating strategies	International competition	Transporting goods
GRAMMAR	Conditionals	Verb patterns	Passives
LANGUAGE FOR	Dealing with customer complaints	Making presentations	Welcoming visitors
SPEAKING	Dealing with call centre complaints	Rescuing sales	Describing a process
CASE STUDY	Red and blue stylists	Rules of competition	Moving production overseas
WRITING	Responding to customer complaints	Reports	A poster presentation
CD-ROM	A headhunter	A business consultant	A research scientist

	10 Human resources p96	11 Business start-up p106	12 Reputations p116
LISTENING	Getting a job interview	Franchises	Repairing a reputation
READING	Company loyalty	Family businesses	Recovering a reputation
GRAMMAR	Phrasal verbs	Adjective and adverb patterns	The definite article
LANGUAGE FOR	Handling interview questions	Responding to requests / suggestions	Clarifying
SPEAKING	Different types of interview	Starting up a business	Checking and clarifying information
CASE STUDY	Choosing a candidate for a job	A franchise opportunity	Court cases
WRITING	Job application letters	A letter requesting financial support	A press release
CD-ROM	An employment and training adviser	A family business	A senior PR consultant

Information files p126 **Grammar guide** p135 **Listening script** p146 **CD-ROM Answer key** p159 **Glossary** p164

Target markets

TALKING BUSINESS

1 Read about OGO. Then work in groups to design an advertising strategy for the product. Think about:
- which consumers you would target
- how you could advertise the product.

> Two Dutch entrepreneurs are trying to sell oxygen in a can. The product, called OGO, costs about £8.99 and gives five minutes' worth of oxygen. Richard Hammond of Spirit, the advertising agency appointed to handle OGO's launch in the UK, is confident of success. He says that bottled water was once considered unmarketable because water was freely available from the tap. He points out:
>
> 'The mineral water market didn't exist fifteen years ago and now it is worth $25bn worldwide.'
>
> The Independent

LISTENING

1 🔊 Joan Howard works for a top British advertising company. She is being interviewed about her job. Listen to part A.

  1 Joan mentions the following advertising roles. What does she say about each one?
    - copywriters
    - account managers.
  2 What stressful event is Joan dealing with?

2 🔊 Listen to part B.

  1 What important information does an advertising agency need from its client?
  2 How does it help the agency to create an advertising strategy?

3 🔊 Joan discusses two ways of finding out if an advertising campaign has been successful. Listen to part C and summarize it using these notes to help you.

Tracking studies let agencies know ¹............................. .
One way you can find out if a campaign has been successful is by using before ²............................. . This tells the agency if the target audience's attitudes ³............................. .

4 Study listening script 1.1 on page 146 and add words to do with advertising to the spidergram.

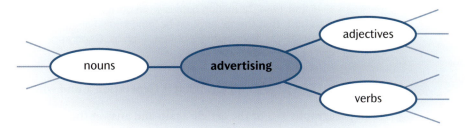

GRAMMAR
The present

1 Match the sentences a–d with the definitions of use 1–4.

1 a repeated action starting in the past and continuing up to the present ......
2 a routine action ......
3 an activity in progress in the present ......
4 something that happened in an unfinished time period ......

a We plan the campaigns with the client.
b She has worked with some major clients during her career.
c She is currently working at the organization's New York office.
d We've been looking for a replacement.

2 Identify the tenses in a–d in **1** above.

3 Turn to part A of listening script 1.1 on page 146. Find other examples of each tense and say why they are used in each case.

4 Discuss the difference in meaning between the pairs of sentences below.

1 a What do you do?
  b What are you doing?
2 a What do you think?
  b What are you thinking?
3 a He's impossible!
  b He's being impossible!
4 a We have lost market share.
  b We've been losing market share.

See page 142 of the grammar guide.

5 Complete the sentences by choosing the correct form in *italics*.

1 Your advertising plan *sounds / is sounding* great.
2 High wages generally *cause / are causing* inflation.
3 They've *been interviewing / interviewed* new copywriters all morning.
4 Fiona usually *is working / works* in London, but she *is working / works* in Ohio for a few months.
5 How long has she *written / been writing* the report?
6 I *don't know / 'm not knowing* what these survey results *mean / are meaning*.
7 I can't come on Friday, I'm *going / go* to Madrid.
8 How many times have you *visited / been visiting* the Brazilian market?

Target markets 1

READING

> Between 1946 and 1964, 72 million babies were born in the USA. There were so many children born that this generation became known as 'the Baby Boomers'. Since then other generations have been identified, such as 'Generation X', the 17 million children born between 1965 and 1978.

1 Read the text on page 9 quickly. What is Generation Y and why is it important?

2 Read paragraphs 1–3 of the article again and answer the questions.
1. What do Laura Schaefer and Lori Silverman tell us about changes in fashions between generations?
2. How has this affected companies like Nike and Pepsi?
3. How is Generation Y different from Generation X? In what way are they more important?
4. How is Generation Y different from the Baby Boomer generation?

3 Now read paragraphs 4–6 of the article again and answer the questions.
1. Decide if the statements a–f are true (*T*) or false (*F*). Find evidence to support your answers. Generation Yers:
   a. like celebrity endorsements. ......
   b. enjoy humour and irony in advertisements. ......
   c. distrust slogans and image-building campaigns. ......
   d. aren't brand conscious. ......
   e. belong to different ethnic groups. ......
   f. rely on TV to find out about fashion. ......
2. How are some brand leaders trying to find out what Generation Yers want?

4 The following words (1–8) appear in bold in the text. Match them with the definitions a–h on the right.

1	over	a	very stylish
2	to shape tastes	b	a long period of advertising
3	rival	c	all the same, used to describe a group
4	slick	d	finished, no longer fashionable
5	irony	e	a sentence like a slogan, used in advertising
6	tagline	f	a kind of humour where the meaning is hidden
7	homogenous	g	to create / change consumer interests
8	campaign	h	competing, used for a business opponent

5 Work in groups and discuss these questions.
1. Do you think you have the same kind of marketing generations in your country?
2. Do you think that the Internet and cable / satellite TV have become more important than national TV for advertising products?
3. What do you think is the best way of discovering the tastes and interests of teenage consumers?
4. You can now buy electronic boxes which remove the commercials from TV programmes. How will firms continue to reach and influence their consumers?

Generation Y

All across America a new generation of consumers is making its presence felt. In one shopping mall, clerk Laura Schaefer has been handling returned goods. 'They say "My mom and dad got me these".' Parents in Nikes sit quietly while their teenage daughters try on massive platform shoes. Asked what brands are cool, these teens give a list of names their parents have never heard of. Which brands are **over**? Now the names are familiar: Levi's, Converse, Nike. 'They just went out of style,' shrugs Lori Silverman, 13. Labels that have **shaped popular tastes** since the Baby Boomers were young simply aren't producing the same excitement with today's kids. PepsiCo. Inc. has struggled to build loyalty among teens, Nike Inc.'s sales are tumbling as the brand sinks in teen popularity polls, while Levi Strauss & Co. is fighting falling market share. Meanwhile, newcomers in entertainment, sports equipment and fashion have become hot names.

Today's kids aren't Baby Boomers. They're part of Generation Y which rivals the baby boom in size and will soon rival it in buying power. Generation Y is the 60 million children born between 1979 and 1994. Marketers haven't been given an opportunity like this since the baby boom. Yet for a lot of established brands, Generation Y presents huge risks. Boomer brands flopped in their attempts to reach Generation X, but with only 17 million that was tolerable. This is the first generation to hurt a Boomer brand simply by ignoring it – and big enough to launch **rival** brands.

Companies unable to connect with Generation Y will lose out on a vast new market. Along with cynicism, Generation Y is marked by a distinctly practical worldview. Raised in dual income and single-parent families, they've already been given substantial financial responsibility. Surveys show they are deeply involved in family purchases, be they groceries or a new car. Most expect to have careers and are already thinking about home ownership.

Nike has found out the hard way that Generation Y is different. Although still popular among teens, the brand has lost its tight hold on the market in recent years. Nike's **slick** national ad campaigns, emphasizing image and celebrity, helped build the brand among Boomers, but they have backfired with Generation Y. 'It doesn't matter to me that Michael Jordan has endorsed Nikes,' says Ben Dukes, 13. Instead Generation Yers respond to humour, **irony**, and the truth. Sprite has scored with ads that make fun of celebrity endorsers and carry the **tagline** 'Image is nothing. Obey your thirst.'

This doesn't mean that Generation Yers aren't brand-conscious. But marketing experts say they form a less **homogeneous** market than their parents. One factor is their racial and ethnic diversity. Another is the breaking up of media, with network TV being replaced by cable channels. Most important is the rise of the Internet, which has sped up the fashion life cycle by letting kids everywhere find out about even the most obscure trends as they emerge. It's the Generation Y medium of choice, just as network TV was for Boomers.

Marketers who don't learn the interests and obsessions of Generation Y will meet a wall of cynicism and distrust. To break through this, marketers are making their **campaigns** more subtle and more local. A growing number, including Universal Studios, Coca-Cola, and McDonald's are using 'street teams'. Made up of young people, the teams hang out in clubs, parks and malls talking to teens about everything from fashion to finance. Will the brands that grew up with Baby Boomers re-invent themselves for Generation Y, or will the new brands of the Millennium bear names that most of us have not yet heard of?

Business Week

Target markets 1

LANGUAGE FOR
giving opinions

1 **(12)** Three people are discussing an advertisement showing children doing dangerous activities. Listen to their conversation and decide who you agree with.

2 **(12)** Listen again and fill in the gaps.

MARTIN: So ¹_____ this kids' commercial, then?
CAROL: I think it's ²_____. It's a lot of fuss about nothing.
MARTIN: Yeah, I ³_____. ⁴_____, advertising is just a bit of fun.
CAROL: Yes, ⁵_____ we should be more worried about the TV programmes themselves.
MARTIN: ⁶_____, Megan?
MEGAN: Well, I suppose so, ⁷_____. I mean, ⁸_____, but don't you think advertisers should be more careful? Kids can be very influenced by advertisements.
MARTIN: ⁹_____! Even children don't believe everything they see on TV.

3 Which expressions are used to:
- introduce opinions?
- invite other people's opinions?
- agree?
- disagree?
- acknowledge what someone has said?

4 What other phrases for giving opinions do you know of?

SPEAKING

1. What advertising controls exist in your country?

2. Adbusters is an anti-consumerism organization based in Canada. It campaigns against big brand advertising and the over-consumption of developed countries. Look at this Adbusters 'un-commercial' which is trying to encourage people to turn their TVs off for a week. What other meaning of 'turn off' is used in the commercial?

   1. Do you agree with Adbusters that the child will have watched 350,000 commercials by the time she graduates from high school?
   2. How easy do you think it is to influence children with advertising?
   3. Can TV advertising be a force for good?

'By the time this child graduates from high school, her brain will have absorbed 350,000 television commercials, 100,000 alcohol ads and a daily barrage of sex and violence. If that doesn't turn you off, nothing will.'

http://adbusters.org/camp

3. Look at this second 'un-commercial' from Adbusters. What do you think it is trying to say?

"The living room is the factory, the product being manufactured is you."
http://adbusters.org/camp

4. Work in two groups. Group A, think of arguments in support of the advertisement. Group B, think of arguments against it. When you are ready, find a partner from the other group and give each other your opinions. Try to use words and phrases from the Language for section on page 10.

Target markets 1

Tip

The Boston Matrix

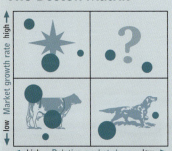

Arrows and position show the direction the product is moving in. Size shows the relative importance of the product.

Stars
New products with a large market share. The need to keep spending on promotion and development means that profits remain low. Stars appear in a growing market.

Cash cows
Mature products with a large market share of a low-growth market. Highly profitable.

Question marks
Low market share in high-growth market. Could become stars or cash cows!

Dogs
Products with low market share and little / no growth. Products near end of life cycle or unsuccessful products.

CASE STUDY

1 Nearly all products follow a typical life cycle. Study the graph below.

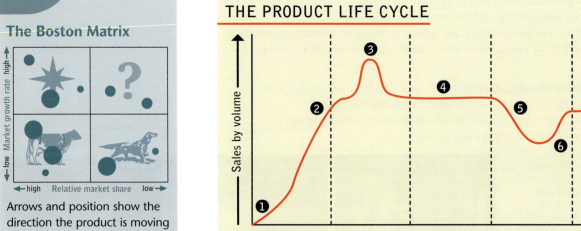

1 Decide where the stages in the box belong.

| decline | launch | peak | final decline and death |
| relaunch | growth | maturity | |

2 How do companies relaunch products?

2 The *Boston Matrix* is a way of classifying a company's product range.

1 Read about the four categories the Boston Matrix uses. How do the categories relate to the product life cycle?
2 Think of a well-established business in your country. Think where its products might fit on the product life cycle and the Boston Matrix.

3 Stevens is a British manufacturer of boxed board games.

1 Read the notes about four of its key products.

 Gangstaz A game based on criminals and the police.

 **Wordsters** A word-based game.

 **Sherlock** A murder mystery board game.

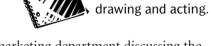 **Sketchit** A game based on drawing and acting.

2 🔊 13 Listen to members of Stevens's marketing department discussing the games. Decide where each one belongs on the Boston Matrix.

3 🔊 13 Listen again. Which game …
- has won a large share of the market in its first year? ....
- has been a big disappointment? ....
- should have a special edition? ....
- finds itself in a saturated market? ....

4 Look at the boxes in the picture and read the information about three further games which the company produces. Who would the games appeal to?

a Empire: Players rule the world by throwing dice and defeating the other players' armies.
b Who's there?: A logic-based game where two players guess the identity of a character.
c Bidders: An auction game based on works of art and antiques.

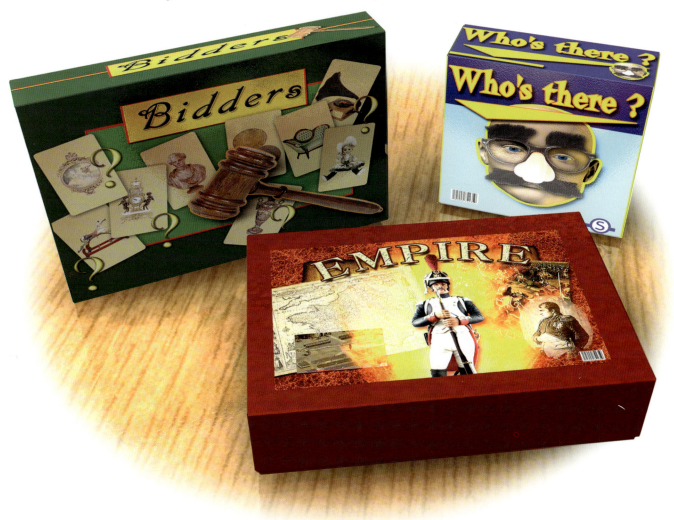

5 Work in groups of three (A, B, and C) and have a board meeting about the performance and future of these three games. You have $1,000,000 to invest. Decide:

- where to invest the money
- whether to discontinue any of the games
- whether to repackage any of the games.

Student A turn to File 1 on page 126. Student B turn to File 11 on page 129. Student C turn to File 24 on page 132. Study your notes and role-play your meeting.

6 Brainstorm ideas for other games you could produce.

Target markets 1

WRITING

Tip

AIDA

Advertisers often follow an AIDA model in their advertisements and sales literature. AIDA stands for:
A – getting the reader's **attention**
I – developing the reader's **interest**
D – encouraging the reader to make a **decision**
A – the reader **acts** on his / her decision.

1 Using the AIDA principle from the business tip, rearrange the advertisement below in the correct order.

Three words you thought you'd never hear:

Cool helmet, Mum!

a What's more, with thirty funky designs to choose from, your kids will be proud to wear them.

b Could it be that they're such a hassle to put on, or that they're just not cool?

c So don't delay: for a full-colour brochure and your nearest stockist, call the free phone number or visit our website on www.koolcasque.com.

d At Koolcasque, we've taken ten years to develop our Super-clip system, which means our feather-light helmets can be put on or taken off in seconds.

e As parents we know that even a simple fall from a bike can cause a serious head injury.

f So why is it a constant battle to get our kids to wear a helmet?

2 BMW has introduced a City Scooter. Read the information and identify its Unique Selling Points (USPs).

Features of the C1

- stylish and different – a new concept
- all-weather protection
- 125 cc engine: cheap to tax and insure
- low fuel consumption and environmentally clean
- as safe as a small car: aluminium frame and seat belts
- provides pleasure of two-wheeled transport without the dangers

www.bmw.co.uk

3 Work in three groups. Following the AIDA principles, write advertising copy for:

Group A – a business magazine for young urban professionals. (Turn to File 3 on page 126)

Group B – the motoring section of a Sunday newspaper. (Turn to File 15 on page 129)

Group C – a magazine for students. (Turn to File 25 on page 132)

1 Target markets 15

VIDEO CD-ROM INTERVIEW

1 **PAUSE FOR THOUGHT:** You are going to hear Matthew talking about advertising. Before you watch, complete the sentences below, according to your own opinion.

  1 The ...... to ...... age group is the hardest to reach through advertising.
  2 The most memorable advertising campaigns are ones that
     ....

2 Now watch **1 Target markets, INTERVIEW**. Compare your answers in **1** with what Matthew says.

3 Read the questions below, then watch **1 Target markets, INTERVIEW**, again, and answer the questions.

  1 What is the most difficult thing to get right in advertising?
  2 What mistake do people tend to make when trying to do this?
  3 What product does Matthew give as an example?
     product: .... features: .... benefit: ....
  4 Matthew talks about one particular age group. Why don't they watch TV?
  5 What examples of media does Matthew say you could use instead?
  6 What other difficulty does this age group present?
  7 What three key elements of a successful advertising campaign does Matthew mention?
  8 According to Matthew, what type of advertising should have limits placed on it?

Matthew Le Fevre
Managing Director, marketing agency

LANGUAGE REVIEW

1 Watch **1 Target markets, LANGUAGE: The present**, and answer the questions below.

  1 Has Matthew finished his advertising brief and his preparations for the meeting?
     yes / no / we don't know
  2 Has Jon finished getting ready for the exhibitions and seminars?
     yes / no / we don't know
  3 When is Jon speaking?
     in summer / before summer / either is possible
  4 What completed projects will Lucy's current work be part of?

2 Write a sentence about your day. Include a finished activity, and one that is ongoing.
   Today, I have ....

WORDBANK

1 Complete the collocations from the interview in the Vocabulary notebook opposite. Then write a definition in English for each collocation, as in the example.

2 Complete the sentences below with a preposition from the box.

   | across | into | down |

  1 Let's focus on translating this list of features .... benefits.
  2 A billboard must put a message .... in a very simple way.
  3 He agreed to have a meeting next week, but it's difficult to pin him .... to a particular time.

Vocabulary notebook

compelling message
= exciting content that
   attracts attention
memorable c............
= ....
  ....

peer g............
= ....
  ....

social r............
= ....
  ....

Click on WORDBANK.
Practise the words in
1 Target markets.

Triumph and disaster

TALKING BUSINESS

1 Match the comments with the cartoons below.

1 'I don't mind getting overdrawn. If I need the money, I just take it out of the bank.'
2 'I never think twice before I buy something.'
3 'It's better to enjoy yourself while you are young even if it means being broke when you're older.'
4 'It's too easy to borrow money from banks and stores.'
5 'People who don't pay their debts must expect an unwelcome visitor.'
6 'Our parents' generation had a different attitude to managing money than our generation.'

2 Which of the statements 1–6 above do you most / least agree with?

2 Triumph and disaster

LISTENING

1 🔊21 You are going to listen to interviews with two people who advise on debt. There are many special terms used to discuss debt. Listen to a university lecturer explaining these terms. Then match the words 1–10 with the definitions a–j.

1	hire purchase	a	one of a series of payments used to pay for an expensive product
2	mortgage	b	the movement of money coming into and out of a company
3	instalment	c	not being able to trade because you cannot meet your financial obligations
4	cash flow	d	a long-term loan which is used to buy a home
5	outgoings	e	the fixed costs such as electricity and salaries, which a business has to support
6	overheads	f	the money going out of a company
7	bankrupt	g	to close a company
8	to be insolvent	h	buying a product by paying off money over months or years. You only own the product when the payments are complete
9	to wind up a company	i	to satisfy your financial responsibilities
10	to meet your liabilities	j	not having enough money to pay debts

YOUR TURN!

1 You are going to discuss two situations involving debt counselling. First look at the situation below. Then work in pairs to find a solution.

Peter Forbes
Peter was unemployed for six months and built up large debts. He has a new job which pays the same salary as before. A year ago he bought a TV, washing machine, and furniture for his new flat on hire purchase. He has fallen behind with the payments and has received threatening letters from the finance company which made him the loan. He uses public transport to go to work. He has a car he uses at weekends.
He owes £3,000 on credit and store cards. He spends a lot on designer clothes because he claims that he needs to look smart for work. He is a member at a private gym which costs £50 per month.

2 Work in pairs again. Turn to File 4 on page 126.

2 You are going to listen to two interviews. The first is with an accountant who specializes in businesses which go bankrupt. The second is with a debt counsellor, a professional who helps individuals who get into debt.
  1 How similar do you think the problems are which individuals and businesses suffer?
  2 🔊22 Listen to the interview with the accountant and answer the following questions.
   a Are companies' debt problems the result of poor business plans?
   b What is the danger point for a small business?
   c What example of a failed business does the accountant give?

3 🔊23 Now listen to the interview with the debt counsellor and answer the following questions.
  1 What is the most common cause of individuals getting into debt?
  2 How does the debt counsellor help his clients?
  3 What example of an individual in money trouble does the debt counsellor give?

4 How far should businesspeople be responsible for their business debts?

Triumph and disaster   2

READING

1 Jonathan Elvidge is a successful businessman who has built a retail chain. Before you read the text, discuss questions 1 and 2.

1. Look at the pictures of objects he sells. What kind of shop is it?
2. Why do you think he chose this type of market?
3. Quickly read the text and check if your guesses were correct.

Jonathan Elvidge was ordinary once. He came from a humble background, left school and worked as a salesman for nine years. Then, aged 27, he founded The Gadget Shop, which – now in its tenth year – has 46 stores and sales of £40m.

For most of us, making millions is just a dream. Only a few will ever manage it and Elvidge didn't think he would be one of them. 'I always thought that rich and successful people were different. I imagined that they had special genes,' he says.

But Elvidge was fascinated by the business elite and wanted to learn from them. He went to a book shop and started reading. 'I devoured every book on the best salesmen of all time,' he says. 'When I had finished I started on the next-door section which had biographies on successful people in general.' He tried to identify 10 points that had ensured each person's success. 'Despite the variations of circumstance and business I started to notice a pattern in the stories, it was quite easy to draw parallels in the different experiences. Then it dawned on me that these were ordinary people and that ordinary people could achieve extraordinary things.'

Inspired by the phrase adopted by Andrew Carnegie – 'Conceive, believe and achieve' – Elvidge decided to build his own business. One year he had left his Christmas shopping too late and was trying to find a retailer that stocked a large range of innovative presents.

Unable to find one, Elvidge realised that he had come across a gap in the market. He explored every angle from financing to shop sites and he went to every trade fair in search of gadgets for the shop.

One tip Elvidge picked up was the importance of visualising his business. He even built up a model of the shop. All this time he had been working for another company, but it became clear that Elvidge couldn't set up the new business and keep his job. In deciding to quit, he lost the only income he had. He also had a bank loan that would swallow £30,000 a year. Elvidge then faced disaster. His shop was not ready and he had to delay opening by four months, which meant missing out on the crucial Christmas sales. As a result, the bank withdrew his loan.

'I could have given up but I remembered from my reading that Sophie Mirman had got funding from a government initiative when she set up The Sock Shop and luckily I managed to get some help too. You have to be prepared to break conventions and be able to see a way out when all seems lost.' When The Gadget Shop eventually opened it was an instant success and it is still growing. As Elvidge discovered, entrepreneurs don't possess a magic formula. 'The prospect of making a fortune is a strong motivator to start a business but, to succeed, entrepreneurs also need to have a lot of energy. Passion and belief are key to finding a way to achieve your goals. The fortune will follow afterwards.'

Sunday Times

YOUR TURN!

Work in pairs. Imagine you are starting up a business together. What lessons could you learn from Jonathan Elvidge's experience?

2 Read the article again carefully and answer the questions below.

1. According to Jonathan Elvidge, are entrepreneurs different from other people?
2. What qualities do entrepreneurs need to succeed?
3. What risks did he take in developing his business?
4. How big was the difference between success and failure for Jonathan Elvidge?

2 Triumph and disaster

GRAMMAR
The past

1 Identify the verb tenses in *italics* in sentences 1–4.

1 He *came* from a humble background, *left* school and *worked* as a salesman for nine years.
2 One year *he had left* his Christmas shopping too late…
3 and [he] *was trying* to find a retailer that stocked a large range of innovative presents.
4 All this time he *had been working* for another company.

See page 141 of the grammar guide.

YOUR TURN!
Work in pairs to create the story of another entrepreneur. Student A turn to File 5 on page 127. Student B turn to File 26 on page 133.

2 Which tense in **1** is used to describe:

a an action happening before a later past action?
b an action which was in progress at a point in the past?
c a sequence of completed past actions?
d an action that began and was still in progress before a later past action?

3 Complete the text by changing the verbs in brackets into a suitable past form.

Even as a child Jane Cavanagh was more at home with the circuit boards from her father's electronics business than dolls' houses. At the age of seventeen, she ¹ _____ (demonstrate) her entrepreneurial capabilities by buying two cars at an auction. She ² _____ (spend) half the summer renovating them, and afterwards she ³ _____ (sell) them at a profit. Some years later while she ⁴ _____ (work) for Telecom-Soft, a division of BT, she was given the task of developing its computer games brands. She ⁵ _____ (travel) to Japan and ⁶ _____ (build up) a portfolio of products for BT to sell. At this time, games consoles ⁷ _____ (become) increasingly popular and she ⁸ _____ (realize) the sector's enormous potential. She ⁹ _____ (still work) for BT when she ¹⁰ _____ (approach) by FIL, a division of the French conglomerate Thomson. For some time, FIL ¹¹ _____ (look for) someone with good contacts in Japan to expand their games development. FIL ¹² _____ (offer) her the job of negotiating the rights of arcade games which could be converted into computer games. However, it ¹³ _____ (always be) at the back of Cavanagh's mind to start her own business. She ¹⁴ _____ (start) SCI and was in profit from day one.

Sunday Times

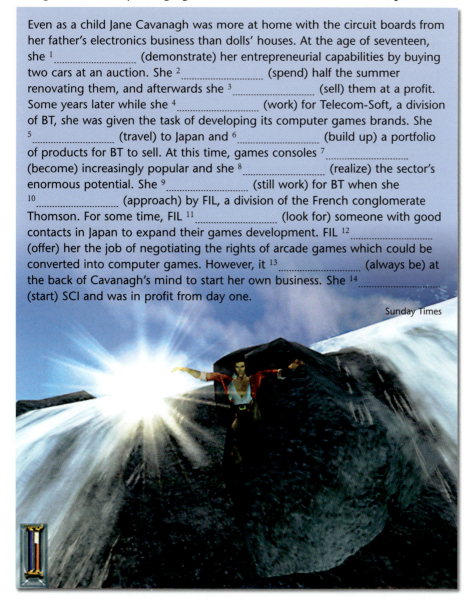

Triumph and disaster

LANGUAGE FOR
apologies, criticism, and deductions

1 When things go wrong, how easy do you find it to say sorry?

2 Read sentences 1–8 and say which are:
- apologies
- criticisms
- deductions.

1 She must have been really embarrassed.
2 I am so sorry for the misunderstanding.
3 He can't have been very pleased.
4 Oh dear, you really shouldn't have said that.
5 I do hope you'll forgive me for the other evening.
6 I would like to apologize for what happened.
7 We ought to have briefed them better.
8 Why weren't you there?

3 Which responses a–g below are used to:
- continue a complaint or criticism?
- politely refuse responsibility?
- accept an apology?

a It shouldn't have happened in the first place.
b I didn't realize I was supposed to do that.
c Don't worry about it. It couldn't be helped.
d Never mind, these things happen.
e I appreciate you're upset, but it's nothing to do with me.
f It was unacceptable!
g Don't blame me – it's not my fault.

4 In pairs, create mini-dialogues around 1–3 below based on the forms and expressions in **2** and **3**.

1 A colleague has badly damaged the photocopier by trying to photocopy onto a sheet of plastic which has melted inside the machine.
2 A colleague tells you that they have just been speaking to someone who was sent the wrong order not just once, but three times!
3 You asked a junior colleague to complete some important documents for you. Unfortunately he or she has made a mess of it and is very upset. You realize that it was really your fault because you didn't tell them what to do.

SPEAKING

1 Read the situation. Who do you think was responsible for what happened? Rank these people 1 (most responsible) to 5 (least responsible).

...... the group leader
...... the group of visitors
...... the driver of the fork-lift truck
...... the manager who authorized the visit
...... the employee who was acting as a guide

Sexton's shoe factory often conducts tours. Normally such visits are without incident, but last week a group was walking through a storage area where an accident with a fork-lift truck occurred. Some dangerous chemicals were spilt resulting in the evacuation of much of the factory. No one was hurt but the fire brigade had to be called to clear up the mess and there was some bad publicity for Sexton's in the local news.

2 Work in pairs to discuss your ranking.

3 Work in groups of three. Sexton's is having a meeting to discuss the accident. Each member of the group takes one of the roles below, either the manager, the guide, or the fork-lift truck driver. Read your information carefully and then role-play the meeting between the three people. Decide who is responsible for the accident and who should apologize. Try to use words and phrases from the Language for section on page 20.

The manager

There was a mix-up over the time of the visit. You asked an inexperienced member of staff to accompany the visitors. However, you didn't imagine that she would take the group into one of the most dangerous parts of the factory. The fork-lift truck driver has been involved in a number of other accidents. The level of damage suggests he was driving it too fast.

The guide

The manager asked you to conduct the visit even though you'd never done this before. You didn't know that the warehouse was 'off-limits'. You found the group difficult to control, particularly when their leader left to make a telephone call. You are very upset by what happened.

The fork-lift truck driver

There is a strict one-way system in the factory. You lost control of the fork-lift truck when a group of people unexpectedly walked across your path. You crashed into the drums of chemicals. You don't want to be made a scapegoat for what happened.

Triumph and disaster

CASE STUDY

Work in pairs. You are both students at art college. For the last two winters you have had holiday jobs as skiing instructors. Two seasons ago you started to sell distinctive items of jewellery made to your own design. They were very popular and you have earned £3,000. You are now deciding what you should do.

You are going to make a series of business decisions which will lead to triumph or disaster, or a mixed triumph. Work together and make your first decision. Go to point ten or fifteen depending on your choice and follow the instructions there. Points 1–23 are below. Points 24–35 are on page 134.

1 If you stop now you will miss a once-in-a-lifetime business opportunity. You should give up your art course and concentrate on the jewellery business. **Go to 10.**

You should carry on with your art course and graduate in two years' time. Afterwards you can always go back to the jewellery business. It will still be there. **Go to 15.**

2 The department store says it will carry on buying your jewellery on condition that they sell it under *its* name. (You will have to remove any details of your company from boxes and packaging.)

You like the idea of a guaranteed income which will help your company grow. You accept their offer. **Go to 13.**

You insist on your independence and look for other customers. You turn down the offer. **Go to 21.**

3 Your fragrances and clothes are a complete flop and damage your reputation. You are lucky enough to have another offer from the Luxury Label. However, the offer is greatly reduced. You still have enough to pay off your debts and walk away with enough money to start again.
MIXED TRIUMPH

4 The department store buyers like your designs but think they need more work. However, you have spent most of your bank loan and need to raise some more money.

You go back to the bank and ask for a new loan. **Go to 28.**

You abandon your ambitious plans and sell the car. You invest the last of your money on a new workshop and perfecting your designs. **Go to 17.**

5 Your shop in le Marais becomes very successful. You are still quite ambitious for further success.

You open shops in St Petersburg and Palm Beach. **Go to 30.**

You decide to stretch your brand and produce accessories such as belts and leather goods carrying your logo and jewellery. **Go to 25.**

6 The franchise is a limited success but takes all your energy and creativity. You haven't become rich but at least you are comfortably off.
MIXED TRIUMPH

7 Your customer accepts the new deal you offer them. They recognize that your goods offer quality and good value for money. The business grows and you develop a wider customer base. You now aim to establish your jewellery as a recognizable brand.

You spend a large amount of money on advertising in fashion magazines. **Go to 27.**

You convince well-known celebrities to wear your jewellery and focus on product placement on TV programmes. **Go to 17.**

8 You meet a small but successful firm of jewellery makers at the fair. They are very excited by your designs and the quality of your work. They invite you to go into partnership in the States. This will mean sharing the secret of your techniques.

You decide to trust them and take up their offer. **Go to 14.**

You are flattered by their offer but think the risk is too great. **Go to 19.**

9 The department store's offer guarantees you an income for the next two years. On the strength of this you become a limited company. You can now plan your next step.

You continue to design and develop your range. You employ more people. **Go to 2.**

You focus on finding new customers for your existing designs. **Go to 21.**

10 You realize that you need more money than your £3,000 to expand your business.

You go to the bank and ask them for a loan. **Go to 18.**

You approach family and friends to see if they are willing to finance you. **Go to 23.**

2 Triumph and disaster

11 Congratulations! The bank has accepted your business plan. You now have enough money to invest in your company's future.

You invest in a new workshop and equipment and work on perfecting your designs and a characteristic new logo. **Go to 17.**

You buy a Smart Car, invest in brochures, and entertain buyers in department stores. **Go to 4.**

12 There is no snow this winter in the resorts where the chain has its shops. They return all their goods to you and you cannot meet your liabilities. You go bankrupt and lose everything.
DISASTER

13 The department store can now dictate terms to you: they demand to pay for all orders in instalments, among other things. However, they promise continued business.

You stay with the store's exclusive contract and plan for the future. **Go to 35.**

You decide to leave the rat race and explore other options. **Go to 27.**

14 Well done for trusting your judgement. Your acquaintances become dynamic business partners. You become an overnight success. You open a chain of jewellery shops and become rich, successful, and happy.
TRIUMPH

15 The moment has passed and you never get organized. You spend the next twenty years wondering what would have happened.
DISASTER

16 With the business angel's money you expand rapidly. You can improve on your designs and invest in marketing. A top department store is interested in stocking your jewellery. However, it insists on exclusivity for the first two years.

You decide to take the store's offer and do not look for other opportunities. **Go to 9.**

You decide that you do not want to be tied to an exclusive contract. **Go to 21.**

17 A fashion magazine writes an article about you and you are approached by small shops and private buyers and jewellery collectors. You have to decide whether to expand or consolidate.

You decide to raise awareness of your name by investing money in advertising on local radio. **Go to 27.**

You decide to keep your business small and produce expensive upmarket items. **Go to 20.**

THE NEXT BEST THING!

18 The bank says you can't have a loan without a business plan which includes a budget, sales, and cash-flow forecasts.

You produce a business plan you think the bank will accept. **Go to 11.**

You decide to approach your family and friends. **Go to 23.**

19 By turning down this opportunity you have had your last chance. You simply run out of money and have to get a job with another jewellery firm.
DISASTER

20 Your work is becoming better-known and you sell some expensive items to celebrities and film stars. You want to broaden your customer base.

You consolidate and open a tiny shop in le Marais, an exclusive area of Paris. **Go to 5.**

You invest heavily in a website and selling over the net. **Go to 24.**

21 You have found two large potential customers. You only have the resources to supply one. Customer A insists on double discount but will pay in thirty days. Customer B is a chain of gift shops in mountain resorts. They offer to stock your jewellery on a sale or return basis. This means they will pay if they sell the goods or else they will return them to you. However, they promise to sell your jewellery at the full recommended price.

You choose customer A. **Go to 26.**

You choose customer B. **Go to 12.**

22 Even though the factory's samples were good, its real production was of low quality. About 20% of the production is sub-standard.

You send the goods anyway and offer a substantial discount. **Go to 33.**

You send a part-shipment and promise to send the rest when it is ready. **Go to 34.**

23 Unfortunately no one in your family is prepared to risk their money!

However, an uncle introduces you to a business 'angel' who is prepared to invest money in your business for a 25% share.

You accept the 'angel's' offer and sign a legal agreement. **Go to 16.**

You decide to approach the bank again with a plan you think the bank will accept. **Go to 11.**

24–35 on page 134

WRITING

1 Abbreviations are generally not used in formal letters. However, there are a few which are commonly used conventions. Complete the list and then match 1–6 with the definitions of use a–f below.

1	c.c.:	a	to add something at the end of a letter, after the signature ......
2	enc.	b	to show a letter was signed on behalf of another person ......
3	FAO:	c	to introduce the topic of the letter ......
4	re:	d	to say who the letter is for ......
5	p.s.	e	to say who else receives a copy of the letter ......
6	p.p.	f	to say something is included with the letter ......

2 When using fast methods of communication such as emails and memos, abbreviations and acronyms may also be used in order to save time. This is most often done in emails sent to people working in the same company or department. Look at the abbreviations in the email below. What do they mean?

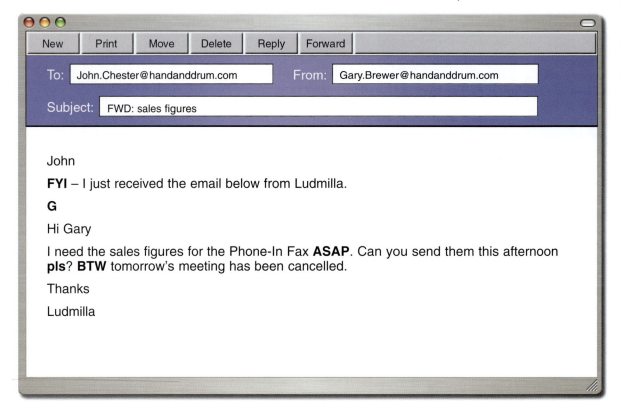

3 Now write an email using your own name. You are a manager asking your PA, Grazia, for an address list of all your main customers. You need this list immediately. Your PA needs to know that you are leaving ten minutes early today for a dentist appointment. She needs to contact the sales manager, Sergio Albero, to send him the agenda for next week's meeting: you have enclosed a copy of the agenda in your email.

2 Triumph and disaster

VIDEO CD-ROM INTERVIEW

1 **PAUSE FOR THOUGHT:** You are going to hear Tony talking about the history of his company. Before you watch, think about what kind of business decisions you would find it difficult to make.

2 Now watch **2 Triumph and disaster, INTERVIEW**. Compare your answer in **1** with what Tony says.

3 Watch **2 Triumph and disaster, INTERVIEW**, again. Make notes on what Tony says, under the headings below.

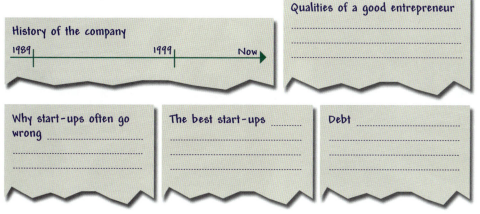

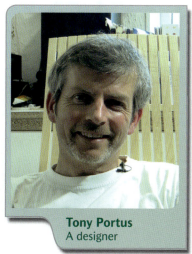

Tony Portus
A designer

LANGUAGE REVIEW

1 Listen to the first three extracts in **2 Triumph and disaster, LANGUAGE: The past**. Add to the time lines to represent what Tony and Robert say, as in the example:

```
                                     started company
                                            ▼
TONY:  ──────────────────────────┬──────────┬──────────►
                                 │ managing │        Now
                                 │ large store │

ROBERT: ─────────────────────────────────────┬─────────►
                                                     Now
```

2 Now watch Martin's and Tony's stories in **2 Triumph and disaster, LANGUAGE: The past**. Write a summary of what they say, using the phrases in the boxes below.

MARTIN:

| first business | mistake | contract | joke |
| interview | Wall Street | share/stock price | American company |

TONY:

| not paid | successful | difficult | project |

WORDBANK

1 Write definitions of the collocations from the interview, in the Vocabulary notebook opposite.

2 Complete the sentences below with a preposition.

   1 The factory is to close ...... , with the loss of 120 jobs.
   2 Pottery used to be his hobby, but now he makes a living ...... it.
   3 She doesn't see the merit ...... using consultants.
   4 It's a very impressive invention, but I don't see a market ...... it.

Vocabulary notebook

DEBT:
create debt
= ....

fall into debt
= ....

service a debt
= ....

Click on WORDBANK.
Practise the words in
2 Triumph and disaster.

Prioritizing

TALKING BUSINESS

1 Fifty years ago, experts predicted that in the future people would work less, and have more free time for themselves and their families.

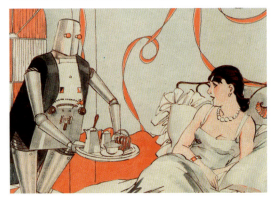

   1 How true has this become?
   2 How likely is this to change in the future?

2 In some companies workers choose their own hours.

   1 Do you think this is a good idea?
   2 How would this affect managers?

3 If you could choose your perfect working week, how would you do it? Think about:

| working hours | free time | days off | flexitime |
| the weekend | meetings | holidays | lunchtime |

LISTENING

1 **31** Franco Ardovini works for a Swiss civil-engineering firm which works on international projects. He is discussing scheduling and prioritizing in large-scale projects. Listen to part A and answer the questions below.

   1 What type of engineering projects does Franco's company perform?
   2 What does his company insist on before starting a large project?
   3 What problems can companies make for themselves?
   4 What can happen if a company fails to meet its targets?
   5 What kind of project is Franco working on at the moment?

2 **31** Now listen to part B and answer the questions.

   1 Franco discusses some of the difficulties his firm can face. Listen to part B and tick (✓) the ones he mentions.

   archaeological problems ......   legal problems ......
   environmental problems ......   crime ......
   technical problems ......   strikes ......
   political difficulties ......   the weather ......

   2 What happened in each of the cases you ticked?

GRAMMAR
The future

1 The sentences 1–6 below come from listening script 3.1. Match the verb tenses in 1–6 with the future meanings in a–f below.

1. Hold on, I*'ll show* you the schedule for our latest project. (*will*)
2. The project *ends* on 17th November next year. (present simple)
3. By January we*'ll have finished* the control tower. (future perfect)
4. In March *we'll be laying* the runways. (future continuous)
5. Tomorrow we*'re starting* to build a tunnel. (present continuous)
6. There are rumours that the electricians' union *is going to go* on strike. (*going to* future)

a an event based on a timetable
b a future prediction based on evidence
c an action in progress at a stated future time
d a specific arrangement
e an action finished before a stated future time
f a decision made at the moment of speaking

2 Now choose the best future form in the sentences below.

1. Just look at this traffic! We *will be / are going to be* late.
2. A: Shall I phone for a taxi?
   B: Don't bother, I *am going to give / will give* you a lift.
3. She *will meet / is meeting* her new boss tomorrow at three o'clock.
4. What time *will / does* the next flight leave?
5. By this time next year he *will have left / is going to leave* the company.
6. This time next week we *will be working / are working* round the clock.

See page 138 of the grammar guide.

3 Certain adjectives can convey a future meaning.

1. Replace the words in **bold** with *certain*, *quite possible*, or *arranged*.
   a The presentation is **due** to begin at eleven o'clock.
   b It's **likely** that we won't get the components in time.
   c They are **bound** to blame us for their delivery problems.
2. Turn to listening script 3.1 on page 148 and find one more example of *bound*, *due*, and *likely*.

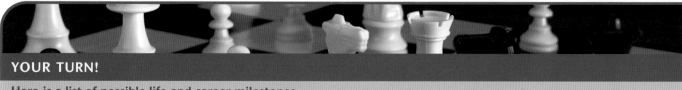

YOUR TURN!

Here is a list of possible life and career milestones.

1 Choose five out of the eight and add any others you wish. Now arrange these into lists of things you expect to have achieved in one, five, and ten years from now.

- finish higher education
- go into politics
- have a baby
- start a completely new career
- set up my own business
- become famous
- have a company car
- write a book

2 Work with a partner. Use an appropriate form of the future to discuss your answers to 1. Express things that:
- will be in progress
- you expect to happen
- you will have already achieved / done.

READING

1 How good are you at managing your time? Do you complete tasks before they are due, or leave everything to the last minute?

2 You are going to read an article by an expert on time management. Read the first paragraph and find out:

1. what problems poor time management can cause.
2. who is usually responsible for wasting our time.

3 Now read the whole article. What practical suggestions does the writer give each of the types of people: 'tomorrows', 'disorganized types', 'poor delegators'?

TIME MANAGEMENT

Time, like money, is a limited resource. However, although it is possible to make more money, unfortunately you can't create more time; there are only twenty-four hours in a day. The inability to manage time effectively is often a big source of stress. Although frequently we may blame others for wasting our time, the most guilty party is usually ourselves.

Tomorrows

Tomorrows prefer to think about work rather than doing it. They **postpone** decisions so that tomorrow becomes the busiest day of the week. Here are some tips for this type.

Break huge tasks down into smaller jobs. Set a **deadline** for the entire task. Don't put it off, instead do a little every day.

Draw up a to-do list for the short term (i.e. within the next week); medium term (the next month); and the long term. Each day list the things you need to do today.

Make a work **schedule** which balances routine tasks with more enjoyable ones.

Handle each piece of paper once only: read it, act on it, file it or throw it away.

Disorganized types

You can recognize these people by the piles of paper on their desks. They're always late for meetings and **waste time** hunting for lost files, and messages written on small pieces of paper. They are always trying to make up lost time. Typically they believe that creative minds are rarely tidy! Here are some tips for them:

Use colour coding to **prioritize** your work. Invest in a year planner chart.

Stick to one task and make sure you finish it. If you fall behind, do what you can to catch up.

Record messages, notes and phone calls in one place.

Group less important or routine tasks, and treat them as a single task.

Poor delegators

They waste time doing tasks which could be done by someone else. They lack trust in others and the ability to say 'no' so they take on too much. Some of the following might help:

If a deadline is unrealistic, re-negotiate it or delegate the task.

Remember that delegation isn't the same as abdication. Take time to explain what is required and check if the person **anticipates any problems**.

If you **delegate** a job, leave the person to get on with it.

Learn to say no politely and assertively.

Sunday Times

4 Which of the three stereotypes is speaking in 1–6?

1. If you want a job done well, do it yourself. ......
2. Now, where's that address? I wrote it on a bus ticket. ......
3. I don't feel like doing the accounts. We'll have time next week. ......
4. It's such a big job. I don't know where to start. ......
5. I must have a quick look at my email – it'll only take a minute. ......
6. Well, I am really busy, but if you think nobody else can do the job … ......

5 Which personality type best describes you? Which tips would help you manage your own time better?

6 Match the definitions below to the words in **bold** in the text.

1. the very last date by which a task must be completed ......
2. give some of your own responsibilities to someone else ......
3. select the most important or urgent things to do first ......
4. delay an event until a later date ......
5. a timetable ......
6. expect that an unplanned event will happen ......
7. use time unproductively ......

7 Complete the sentences below by using an appropriate form of the phrasal verbs in the box.

| fall behind | catch up | get on with | put off |
| take on | draw up | break down | make up |

1. We have .... far too much work lately. I just don't know how we are going to manage.
2. The bad weather means that we have .... schedule on the building contract.
3. It's time we let them know about the delays. It's embarrassing, but we can't .... it .... any longer.
4. If everyone works night shifts, we should be able to ....
5. Is it OK if I leave early today, Judith? I'll .... the time on Monday.
6. I have .... a list of things we need to do.
7. We've analysed the problem and have .... it .... into five different areas.
8. You should spend less time gossiping and .... your work.

8 Work in pairs. Take turns reading and responding to 1–8 in the previous exercise, for example:

We have taken on far too much work lately. I just don't know how we are going to manage.

Why don't we recruit new staff?

9 You have to lead a seminar on time management for a group of colleagues. Which points from the article on page 28 will you tell them about? What other useful tips would you add?

Prioritizing

LANGUAGE FOR
requests and offers

I'd like you to leave the company. Do you think you could clear your desk on the way out?

1 Complete the sentences with expressions from the box. Which phrases can be used in more than one sentence?

| Can you ring … | I'd like you to … | I was wondering … |
| So if you'd like to … | Do you think you could … | Would you mind … |

1 .... if you could spare me two minutes.
2 .... help me sort out these invoices?
3 .... Richard to organize coffee and biscuits for the conference?
4 .... organizing the collection for Melissa Bevan?
5 .... deal with this straightaway.
6 .... organize your own flight and we will reimburse you.

2 🔊 32 Listen and check your answers.

3 Which request could you agree to by answering 'Of course not'?

4 The following orders a–f are not very polite. Express each one as a polite request using the prompts in *italics*.

a Post these letters! *think*
b File these documents! *mind*
c Tidy up the office! *I'd like*
d Answer this fax! *could*
e Book your own taxi! *if you'd*
f Take me to the airport! *wondering*

5 Look at these replies. Which requests in **1** above do they answer?

1 I **am** rather busy. Could we meet later?
2 I **could**, but he doesn't like taking orders from me.
3 Actually, I **would** mind. I hate asking people for money.
4 I **will**, just as soon as I've finished this.

6 🔊 33 Listen.

1 How are the words in **bold** in **5** pronounced?
2 Why do you think the words in **bold** are stressed?

7 In pairs, read the following questions and answers, paying attention to the words which change their pronunciation according to their stress.

1 A: Do you think we'll reach a decision today?
   B: Yes, I do. We have all the information we need now.
2 A: I'll have your report by the end of the day, won't I?
   B: Yes, you will. I'm finishing it off now.
3 A: I don't think he was there. I didn't see him.
   B: He was. He arrived late and sat at the back.
4 A: Can you show me how the fax machine works, please? I haven't used this type before.
   B: Yes, of course I can. You press this button …

SPEAKING

1 It is Monday morning. Jude James is the PA to the Managing Director of a London-based company. Study her diary and the notes on her desk. Then prioritize the tasks and compile a 'to do' list.

Memo

To: Jude **From:** Managing Director
Date: 19th June **Subject:** Thefts

There have been quite a few thefts recently by outsiders coming into the building. Please do a letter to all staff warning them about valuables: bags, coats, etc.

Thanks. TJ

Hi Jude,

How are my flights coming along? I can finally confirm my sales trip to Brazil and Argentina next month. Can you confirm flight details **ASAP** with Argos Travel?

Thanks,

Astrid.

2 Work in pairs. Try to use words and phrases from the Language for section on page 30.

Student A: You are the office manager. Jude is ill and won't be back for the rest of the week. You need to give instructions to a temporary secretary who has come from an employment agency to help out while Jude is away. Tell him / her what to do and what the priorities are. Decide which tasks he / she can do and which ones you will have to delegate to another member of staff.

Student B: You are a temporary secretary from an employment agency. You have been called in to help out at an office. You are going to ask Student A to help you decide what your priorities are. It's 9.30 on Monday morning. Sound enthusiastic and ready to take charge of what needs to be done.

Ask for brochures for new office photocopiers.

Order samples for new carpet for reception area.

Send out questionnaire for this year's Christmas party.

March

3 Monday
Visitors from Brussels. Richard to meet Eurostar at 14.15.
Book restaurant for dinner. 7-8 people - Beppe's?
Talk to Stuart Leman about job ad.

4 Tuesday
Get card signed for Catherine Moore. Buy present. (add £50 from petty cash).
Brochure to printers - final deadline.
Confirm flights for Astrid Winter's South American sales trip.

5 Wednesday
Deadline for job ad. Check details with Stuart Leman?

March

Thursday 6

Friday 7
Presentation in conference room pm.

Catherine Moore's leaving party.

Saturday 8

Sunday 9

Prioritizing

Tip

Critical Path Analysis

This is a way of planning a project so that it can be carried out in the shortest possible time.

It involves:
- making a schedule covering all activities in the project
- deciding how long each activity will take
- setting realizable deadlines for each activity
- deciding how activities relate to each other.

CASE STUDY

1 Read the tip on critical path analysis.

2 Read the situation. What could go wrong?

> You specialize in organizing conferences. The World Computer Games Confederation wants you to organize next year's award ceremony ('the Oscars of computer games'). The WCGC has asked you to find a suitable venue (e.g. hotel, famous building) to arrange entertainment and a charity dinner on the night of the ceremony. Tickets cost $2,000 each and about 800 guests are expected. The event will be hosted by the famous comedian Sammy Webb.

3 Work in groups and study the 'to do' list. After each item in brackets is an estimate of the time which it will take. Produce a schedule which shows how the event can be organized in the most efficient way.

'to do' list

1 send out requests for prize nominations (two weeks)

2 deadline for nominations (six weeks after requests sent out)

3 print invitations (two weeks)

4 make a shortlist of venues (two weeks)

5 make final selection of venue with sponsor (one week)

6 book venue (eight months' notice usually required)

7 approach caterers to tender for charity dinner (two months before the event)

8 decide menu and check with sponsors (two weeks)

9 produce and print tickets and programmes (three weeks)

10 invite celebrities to present the different awards (six months before the event)

11 send out tickets and programmes (eight weeks before the event)

12 decorate and arrange venue (one week)

13 contact TV chains about filming awards (as soon as the date and venue are known)

14 visit venues and ask for quotations (six weeks)

15 advertise event in trade magazines (five months before the event)

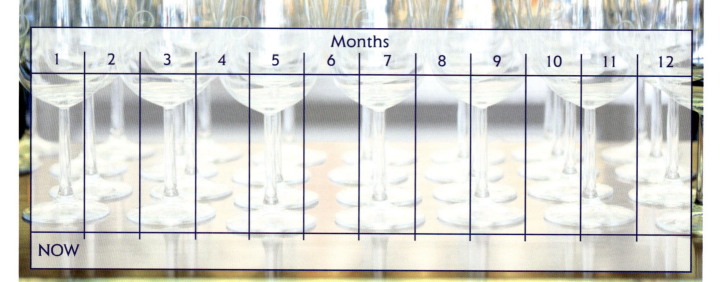

| NOW | 1 | 2 | 3 | 4 | 5 | Months 6 | 7 | 8 | 9 | 10 | 11 | 12 |

4 When will you need to start in order to keep the preparation period as short as possible?

5 Present your critical path analysis to another group.

6 'Murphy's law' means 'anything that can go wrong, will go wrong'. Do you have a similar saying in your country?

7 🔊 **3.4** Listen to four problems which have come up with the organization of the ceremony.

1 Summarize each in your own words.

Timing	Problem
four months before	1
two months before	2
six weeks before	3
one week before	4

2 You don't want to postpone the event and your deadline is definite. What could you do to minimize or deal with the problems from listening script 3.4?

Prioritizing 3

WRITING

1. What is the difference between a *debtor* and a *creditor*? Which would you rather be?

2. What reasons can you think of for not paying a bill on time?

3. Read the letter below. Is it aggressive or supportive?

> I am writing to you concerning our invoice JAC/638 for building supplies. According to our records, the invoice, which *fell due* two weeks ago, is still *outstanding*. We feel sure that this is *a simple oversight*: however, if you are experiencing difficulty in paying this account please contact me so that we may discuss alternative ways of settling it.
>
> As you will remember, we offered a 10% discount *on condition that* payment was received within thirty days. Unless we *are in receipt of* payment within five working days we shall *be obliged to* issue a new invoice for the full amount.
>
> If, in the meantime, you have already *settled* the original invoice, please *disregard* this letter.

4. Find the words and expressions in *italics* which mean the following:

   a became payable ....
   b a mistake made by forgetting to do something ....
   c take no notice of ....
   d as long as ....
   e not paid, late ....
   f receive ....
   g have to ....
   h paid. ....

5. Why do you think the invoice has remained unpaid? How could the supplier have protected itself?

6. Use the information below to write a letter demanding payment. Use the language in **3** to help you:

> You supplied 200,000 blank CDs to Skunkx records. It was an emergency order, so you supplied them straightaway on the promise that your invoice would be paid within ten working days. You have been working with the studio for the past three years and there has never been a problem. However, the invoice is now seriously overdue. You suspect that the company may be in financial difficulty. However, you supplied the goods in good faith and want your invoice to be paid. Otherwise you may have to take legal action to recover the debt.

3 Prioritizing 35

VIDEO CD-ROM INTERVIEW

1 **PAUSE FOR THOUGHT:** You are going to hear Lucy talking about project management. Before you watch, guess which options in the sentences below will best reflect what Lucy says.

   1 Model-making requires a lot of *creativity / concentration / patience*.
   2 Lucy *does not have to / often has to* work evenings and weekends.
   3 For Lucy, *everything always goes to plan / there are often last-minute changes*.

2 Now watch **3 Prioritizing, INTERVIEW**. Were your guesses in **1** right?

3 Read the questions below, then watch **3 Prioritizing, INTERVIEW**, again, and answer the questions.

   1 How many breaks do Lucy's model-makers have in a day?
   2 How does Lucy plan her day?
   3 What does she do when scheduling a meeting?
   4 Why does Lucy 'leave a little space' when she is prioritizing jobs?
   5 What different people might typically be involved in a big project?
   6 What two things does Lucy schedule dates for?
   7 During a project, what usually happens every couple of weeks?
   8 Why did one of Lucy's model-makers have to go to Scotland recently?

Lucy Wells-Fraser
A project manager, model-making

LANGUAGE REVIEW

1 Watch **3 Prioritizing, LANGUAGE: The future**, and complete the table below, as in the example.

Speaker	Ongoing activity	Specific arrangement	Plan	Action finished before a stated future time
1 Lucy			put in a café, ...	
2 Tim	work on job positions			
3 Jon				
4 Lucy				

WORDBANK

1 The idioms below are from the interview. Match them to their definitions in the Vocabulary notebook opposite.

   be everything to somebody   put a hundred per cent into something
   move something to one side   think nothing of

2 To help you remember the idioms in **1**, complete the sentences below for yourself.

   1 I put a hundred per cent into ....
   2 I move everything to one side when ....
   3 .... is everything to me.
   4 I think nothing of ....

3 Complete the sentences below with a preposition.

   1 Let's schedule ...... a couple of progress meetings next month.
   2 When scheduling a project, you have to allow for people having time ....
   3 Once a client gives final approval to a piece of work, we sign it ....

Vocabulary notebook

= do something using all your effort

= do something as if it is normal, and not unusual or too hard

= be the most important thing in somebody's life

= stop something to make time for something else

Click on WORDBANK.
Practise the words in
3 Prioritizing.

Globalization

A

'It creates jobs; it causes economic growth, and it creates local wealth. It shares ideas around the world.'

TALKING BUSINESS

1 Compare opinions A and B on globalization. Which opinion do you agree with?

B

'It exploits people in poor countries: they work long hours for peanuts. The only countries who benefit are the rich western ones. They even use children as workers in their factories!'

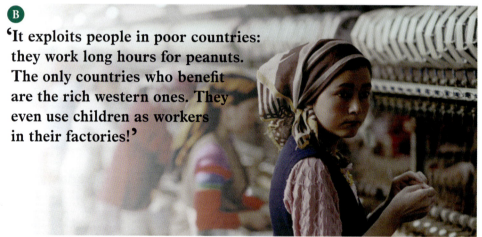

YOUR TURN!

1 Has globalization affected your country? Think about changes in recent years in:
- job opportunities
- culture
- fashion
- ideas.
2 Do you think your country needs to be protected from the effects of globalization?

LISTENING

1 Indira Prabhu, an economist from India, is being interviewed about globalization. Work in pairs. Before you listen, brainstorm what you think Indira's views on the following topics will be:

1 globalization as colonialism
2 social justice
3 the relationship between commodity-producing countries and multinationals.

2 ((41)) Now listen to part A and see if you were right.

3 ((41)) In part B Indira discusses the impact globalization has had on developed countries. Listen and answer the questions.

1 According to Indira, who has most to fear from globalization?
2 What does the interviewer say is a main worry for the West?
3 What, according to Indira, is the main reason for job losses in the USA?

4 ((41)) Listen to part C and answer questions 1–3 below:

1 What problems are created when countries export knowledge?
2 How does Indira feel about the move into the service sector?
3 How can developed countries maintain their world position?

5 How far do you agree with what Indira said? Were you surprised by any of her views?

GRAMMAR
Routines and habits

1 Look at the sentences 1–7 from listening script 4.1. What do the words in *italics* mean?

1 People talk about the benefits of globalization, but they *hardly ever* consider its downside.
2 *As a rule*, poorer countries benefit when they open up to foreign trade.
3 *Most of the time*, western firms dictate prices and take advantage of producing countries.
4 The producers *rarely* see the larger part of the value added.
5 The reason for job losses in the US, for example, is *generally* labour-saving efficiencies.
6 But a driving force for economic growth like that powered by the IT boom only *seldom* appears.
7 Interviewer: But companies do move abroad.
   Indira: *From time to time*, but it doesn't happen as often as people think.

See page 143 of the grammar guide.

2 Complete the chart on the right with these words and phrases in order of frequency.

| hardly ever | seldom | rarely | generally |
| from time to time | most of the time | as a rule | now and again |

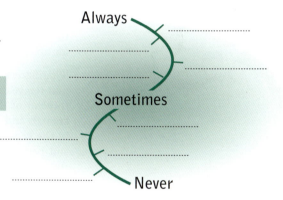

3 *Always* has a number of uses. Which sentence a–b below:

1 describes an annoying habit or action?
2 introduces an option or alternative?

a You could always recruit a new salesperson.
b People are always repeating this same nonsense.

4 Forms of *used to* can be used to express habits and routines.

1 Match examples of *used to* in sentences a–c to their meanings in the box below.

> become familiar
> a past habit or state that no longer happens
> be familiar with something

a Think of the social conditions which *used to exist* in early US and UK factories.
b People in the West have all *got used to working* less and earning more.
c At the moment people *are used to buying* consumer products from the East at low prices.

2 What form of the verb follows each example of *used to*?
3 Rewrite the sentences using a form of *used to*.
   a In the old days, everyone wore jackets and ties to work.
   b When Markus first lived in the UK, he found driving on the left difficult.
   c I don't have much experience of dealing with computers.
   d I found it hard to adapt to the new computer system.
   e Isn't that the house where you once lived?

4 Describe how the way of life in your country has changed between your grandparents' generation and your generation.

Globalization

READING

1 What does 'globalization' mean?

2 Scan the text and answer the questions.

1 Which western multinational companies does it mention?
2 What is the significance of these numbers?

| 600 | $995 bn | £2.7 bn | 50 miles | 365 m | 235 | 80 m | 200 |

L'Oréal

L'Oréal, the French cosmetics giant, is hoping to take advantage of one of the world's most fertile emerging markets. On the twentieth floor of its China HQ in Shanghai is a bathroom where L'Oréal researchers have watched more than 600 women taking a shower. The study's purpose is to discover how Chinese consumers, unfamiliar until recently with western grooming, use the make-up, hair- and skin-care products which the organization is introducing to a nation that has traditionally had little use for luxury.

'Pharmacies here have changed a lot over the past ten years,' says Paolo Gasparini, Managing Director of L'Oréal China. 'It used to be dried animals and plants, but it's moving very fast.' In the People's Republic, the use of deodorant and perfume is very unusual and pale skin is the beauty ideal women strive for. 'The people and culture are so different here that we have to be very prudent,' says Gasparini. But the company – with brands that include L'Oréal Paris, Giorgio Armani fragrances, Maybelline New York and Lancôme make-up – is determined to be at the forefront of China's latest cultural revolution. Unlike other aspirational western brands such as Coca-Cola and McDonald's, which offer a single cultural icon, L'Oréal can offer Asian consumers French chic, New York attitude and Italian elegance. Already about 80% of L'Oréal's £7.5 bn turnover is generated outside France and 40% outside Europe. L'Oréal, like many other businesses expanding into China, believes the market has outstanding potential.

The government's more open economic outlook, combined with a growing urban population which currently stands at 365 m, and a GDP put at $995 bn, have combined to produce a consumer base with disposable income and a taste for modern, western goods. Other western multinational corporations have been expanding throughout China too. Beijing has the distinction of being the site of the largest Kentucky Fried Chicken restaurant in the world. McDonald's, the rival fast-food chain, operates more than 235 outlets in 41 Chinese cities and earlier this year hospitality group Hyatt opened the third tallest hotel in the world in Shanghai.

Last year, the Chinese cosmetics market was worth £2.7 bn and Gasparini estimates that in the People's Republic there are 80 m purchasers of L'Oréal products. At the same time, the company, together with other European businesses including Glaxo Wellcome and Siemens, has taken advantage of the new economic development zone 50 miles outside Shanghai, to build a production facility. The factory is the culmination of a push into China that began in 1993, when L'Oréal put together a small team in Hong Kong to test the Chinese market. The company had been evaluating the market for years, but until the early 1990s it considered average incomes too low, and distribution channels too poor, to merit a launch.

In the following two years the company tested about 200 products and has recently launched a joint venture with the medical college in Suzhou. The research revealed some surprising results. For example, Asian hair is more porous than the European variety, so dye products need a different formulation. An extensive programme of research and development encouraged L'Oréal to launch both its international brands and more technical products throughout China. Maybelline is positioned as a mass-market name available in supermarkets and department stores. L'Oréal Paris is on offer in department stores only, while Lancôme is sold in just the most exclusive outlets.

Despite its success, L'Oréal, like other western investors, is facing commercial and cultural hurdles in China. 'This country is not familiar with marketing so it is a huge job to train and keep clever young people,' says Gasparini. 'My priority is to take care of our staff; the battle will be won by the company with the best people.'

Sunday Times

4 Globalization

3 Read the text again and answer the questions.

1. What does L'Oréal's 'bathroom' research hope to achieve?
2. Why do you think Paolo Gasparini talks about Chinese pharmacies?
3. Why is China such an attractive market for foreign businesses?
4. What has China done to encourage foreign businesses to set up near Shanghai?
5. Why didn't L'Oréal enter the Chinese market earlier?
6. How did L'Oréal plan its entry into the Chinese market?
7. How useful has L'Oréal's joint venture with the Suzhou medical college been?
8. Maybelline, L'Oréal Paris, and Lancôme are all brands of L'Oréal, but they are sold in China through different sales outlets. Why do you think this happens?
9. According to Paolo Gasparini, what is the difficulty and importance of recruiting good local staff?

4 Match a word from box A with one from box B to form collocations from the text.

A	B
outstanding	facility
economic	outlook
production	base
distribution	income
development	venture
consumer	potential
joint	channel
disposable	zone

5 Complete sentences 1–8 with an appropriate collocation from 4.

1. The government has created a _____ _____ to attract foreign investors to the region.
2. We really need to attract more customers. Our _____ _____ is simply too narrow.
3. We need to build another _____ _____ to cope with the increased demand.
4. The _____ _____ is poor. There is high inflation and fear of a recession.
5. After paying for food and rent, low-income earners have very little _____ _____ for luxuries.
6. We should consider a _____ _____ with a local partner as a way of entering the market.
7. The _____ _____ is far too complicated. We should consider appointing a wholesaler.
8. This market shows _____ _____. It's an opportunity we can't miss!

YOUR TURN!

Read the quotation below.
'Global companies must forget the idiosyncratic differences between countries and cultures and instead concentrate on satisfying universal drives.'
Theodore Levitt, marketing expert.

1. What do you think *idiosyncratic differences* and *universal drive* mean?
2. How far does what you have read about L'Oréal prove or disagree with what he says?
3. What universal drives do companies like L'Oréal, McDonald's, and Coca-Cola satisfy?

Globalization

LANGUAGE FOR
speaking with conviction

1 How have email and the Internet changed the way we work and do business? Have these changes always been for the better?

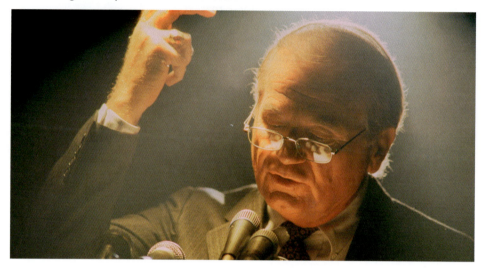

2 (42) Andrew Vine is taking part in a debate about the Internet in business: '*Is the Internet a blessing or a curse?*' He has just one minute to put his views across. Listen and decide which side of the debate Andrew is on.

1 According to Andrew, what effect has the Internet had?
2 What are his views on the Internet as a way of conducting business with the outside world?
3 How does Andrew feel about the amount of information on the Internet?

3 (42) Listen again and complete the sentences from the recording.

1 So _____ really mean for our everyday working lives? _____ hours wasted by junk email, the _____ human contact, and drowning in a sea of information.
2 I _____ that most natural business relationships are _____, not _____.
3 _____ the only way to measure and judge any future partner.
4 _____ there are millions of impressive websites which provide useful information, but _____ behind them?
5 The Web is _____ piracy and plagiarism.
6 Providing personal details is risky if they _____.
7 And finally, if we ask _____ the question, 'What does _____ produce?', the answer is 'nothing'.
8 It's only a source of information, like a _____, but much less reliable.

4 Rhetoric is using language to influence people's opinions. Look at the tip on rhetoric. Now look at sentences 1–8 in **3** again and find examples of rhetoric.

Tip

Rhetoric

Speakers often use a range of rhetorical devices:
- lists of three: 'Government of the people, by the people, for the people' Abraham Lincoln
- rhetorical questions (the speaker asking himself / herself a question)
- contrasting pair of ideas: 'Man is born free and everywhere is in chains' Jean-Jacques Rousseau
- use of metaphor / simile: 'The office was a beehive of activity'.

SPEAKING

1 You have to give a one-minute reply to Andrew Vine in which you present the advantages of the Internet. Using the notes to help you, brainstorm further arguments that you can use to put your case.

- stay in contact more easily
- do business more quickly
- faster than the post, more convenient than faxes, instant response
- online discussions cut down the need for face-to-face meetings
- paper-free offices
- allows people to work from home
- good for customers and encourages competition
- cannot be 'un-invented', so just needs to be used more wisely

2 Now work in pairs and write a one-minute reply to Andrew. Try to use at least one example of rhetoric, as explained in the Language for section on page 40.

3 In a debate, members of the audience usually have the opportunity to say what they think, or ask the speakers for clarification. Look at listening script 4.2 on page 150. Use the phrases below to make questions about the arguments presented there.

I take Andrew's point, but …
Don't you think that …
The thing that I don't agree with is …
The point I'd like to make is …
It's simply not true / the case that …
We mustn't forget that …
I'd just like to say that …

4 Work in groups of four to have a debate. Choose two topics from the list below and discuss them for five minutes each. Try to choose topics that you disagree on, and try to reach a consensus.

- Multinational companies have far too much power in today's world.
- Free trade guarantees world peace.
- Developed countries should pay producers in less-developed countries a fair price for their tea and coffee.
- Anti-globalization demonstrators are naïve and unrealistic.
- In the long-term, globalization will benefit everyone.
- We worry too much about the environment and not enough about business.
- It is the responsibility of government to control the activities of business.
- Workers should be able to move freely between countries with no restriction.

Globalization

CASE STUDY

1. Read the information about Greenglade and study the advertisement for its current UK advertising campaign.

> Greenglade is a British-based soft-drinks manufacturer. Its fleet of distinctive lorries delivers to hotels, supermarkets, and its distributor network. Greenglade's most popular drink is Three Feathers, a bitter-sweet fizzy drink produced and packaged at its factory. Apples from English orchards are used to make the drink.

2. Work in groups. Look at the advertisement above. Brainstorm reasons why Greenglade has chosen to advertise Three Feathers in this way.

Globalization

3 Greenglade has identified Caronesia, a group of islands in the Pacific Ocean, as a new market. Read the market intelligence and decide how Greenglade should enter the Caronesian market. Use the tip on the Marketing Mix to help you. What will be a correct marketing mix for the Caronesian market? Points to consider:

- What changes, if any, will Greenglade need to make to its product?
- Where should it be sold and how should it be priced?
- How can shopkeepers be encouraged to adopt the product?
- How should it be promoted?
- How can Greenglade test the market before making an important financial commitment?

> **Tip**
>
> **The Marketing Mix**
> The four Ps:
> - Product. What are its characteristics: its brand name, packaging?
> - Price.
> - Place. Where and how will it be sold?
> - Promotion. How is the customer going to know about this product?

Background information on Caronesia

Population: 50 million spread over 200 islands.
Climate: Hot and humid
Language: Caronesian and English (ex-British colony)
Political situation: Stable. Governments encourage foreign investment by setting up local economic development zones
Economy: Stable. Main source of GDP is agriculture. Major exporter of tropical fruit. Some manufacturing: assembly of electronic goods, textiles, footwear, and furniture. There has been a history of manufacturing if the company wants to set up a production facility. Main service industry is tourism – beautiful coastal resorts and luxury hotels. Most tourists come from the UK, Australia, and the Republic of Ireland. The economic outlook is good and Greenglade believes the market has outstanding potential.

Consumer behaviour
- Most shopping is done at cash-and-carry warehouses. Men do the shopping.
- Small local shops have refrigerators for drinks which are often supplied by a major US soft drinks manufacturer.
- People have money to spend on soft drinks but Caronesia is a price-sensitive market.
- Consumers prefer bottles to cans.
- Main distribution channel of food/drink products is by boat and small van.
- Consumers do not have a lot of disposable income.
- 65% of the population is under 30, a very young consumer base.

Cultural information
1. Number three is considered unlucky. Four and seven are lucky.
2. Dogs are considered unclean. Parrots and small monkeys are popular pets.
3. People wear blue when someone dies. Orange is a lucky colour. Green is associated with sickness.
4. 'Thirst' sounds like a common Caronesian name.
5. Caronesians admire all things modern. Their ambition is to live in a new air-conditioned home.
6. The older generation prefers sweeter, less fizzy drinks.
7. The thumbs-up sign is obscene.
8. Winston Caruna is a national hero who led his country to independence from the British.

WRITING

1 Sometimes it is necessary to present information without giving a personal opinion. An employee may have to summarize two or more sides of an argument so that someone else can make a final decision. Look at the email below which introduces a report into whether the German paint manufacturer Konstanz Farben should expand into the South African market.

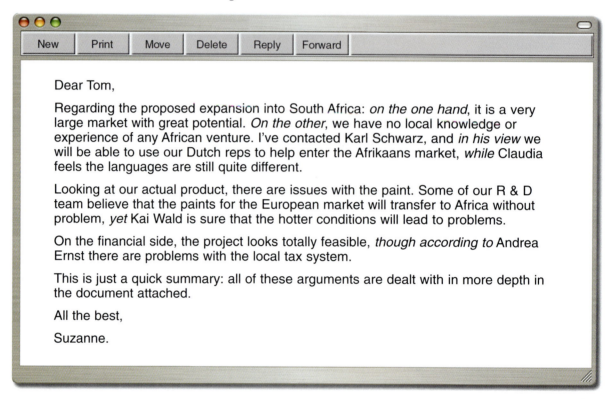

Dear Tom,

Regarding the proposed expansion into South Africa: *on the one hand*, it is a very large market with great potential. *On the other*, we have no local knowledge or experience of any African venture. I've contacted Karl Schwarz, and *in his view* we will be able to use our Dutch reps to help enter the Afrikaans market, *while* Claudia feels the languages are still quite different.

Looking at our actual product, there are issues with the paint. Some of our R & D team believe that the paints for the European market will transfer to Africa without problem, *yet* Kai Wald is sure that the hotter conditions will lead to problems.

On the financial side, the project looks totally feasible, *though according to* Andrea Ernst there are problems with the local tax system.

This is just a quick summary: all of these arguments are dealt with in more depth in the document attached.

All the best,

Suzanne.

2 Look at the words and phrases in *italics*.

1 Which words are conjunctions (words like *and*, *but*, etc.)?
2 What phrases are used to introduce someone else's opinion?
3 Is it correct to say 'on the one side' instead of 'on the one hand'?
4 Is it correct to say 'according to me' as well as 'according to Andrea Ernst'?

3 Now write the email below using all the phrases from the email in **1**. Do not give your own opinion!

> You must report to Cristiano Bahia, the sales manager of Ben Snacks, a crisp and nut manufacturer based in Portugal which exports throughout Europe. The meeting was to decide if a new brand of cashew nuts should be developed for sale in cocktail bars.
>
> The results to summarize are:
>
> The French office feel there is no need for a new cashew snack: the company makes three already. The British office feel there is a market.
>
> Marco Costinha wants the snack to appeal to wealthy customers 30+. George Freehouse thinks the snack should be marketed at the 18-25 age group.
>
> The packaging could be foil or paper. Paper is cheap. Paper is not popular in certain markets (UK, Republic of Ireland).
>
> Cashews are cheap to buy from suppliers in South America. They sell at a high price in Europe.
>
> Sales of existing nut products are falling. Existing nut products do have good brand awareness. The Danish office want to promote the existing products and not develop a new cashew range.

4 Globalization

VIDEO CD-ROM INTERVIEW

1 **PAUSE FOR THOUGHT:** You are going to hear Andrew talking about his clothing business. Before you watch, think about fashions in your country. Are they the same everywhere, or do they vary from city to city?

2 Now watch **4 Globalization, INTERVIEW**. According to your answer in **1**, is your country more like Germany or the UK?

3 Watch **4 Globalization, INTERVIEW**, again. Tick (✓) each part of the spidergram as Andrew mentions it. Then listen again, and make notes to complete the diagram.

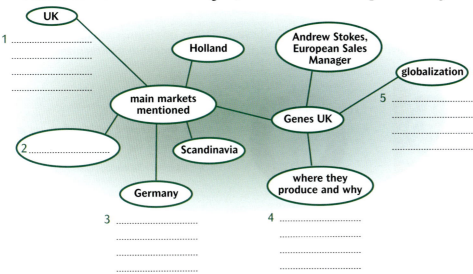

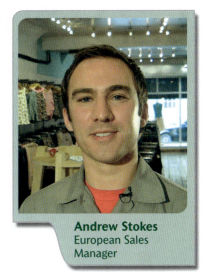

Andrew Stokes
European Sales Manager

LANGUAGE REVIEW

1 Watch **4 Globalization, LANGUAGE: Routines and habits**, and answer the questions below.
   1 What adverbs of frequency do the three speakers use? Make a list as you listen.
   2 What two verb forms do the speakers mainly use to describe their routines and habits?

2 Write about how you spend the first hour in your day. Include some of the adverbs of frequency that you listed in **1**, and use both verb forms that the speakers used.

WORDBANK

1 Read the extracts from the interview below, then write a definition of the idioms in *italics* in the Vocabulary notebook opposite.

> ... H&M and GAP ... *have got more money behind them*
>
> ... that's the big danger of globalization – that ultimately, it does exploit *the smaller people*
>
> ... the effects of these big companies on us as *a small fish in a big sea*
>
> ... we don't really change much – *we stick to what we are doing*

2 Write the stress patterns of the adverbs below, as in the example.

obviously	Oooo	particularly	....
predominantly	....	actually	....
ultimately	....		

Vocabulary notebook

have money behind you
= ....

the smaller people
= ....

a small fish in a big sea
= ....

stick to what you are doing
= ....

Click on WORDBANK. Practise the words in 4 Globalization.

Company culture

TALKING BUSINESS

1 Most organizations and companies have a mission, or vision, statement which states its business or goals. Match each mission statement to its organization's logo or emblem:

International Red Cross and Red Crescent Movement
www.redcross.int/en

www.intel.com

www.bmw.com

www.greenpeace.org

- to prevent and alleviate human suffering wherever it may be found, to protect life and health and to ensure respect for the human being
- to promote brand values and customer service above all else
- do a great job for our customers, employees and stockholders by being the preeminent building block supplier to the worldwide digital economy
- to further public understanding in world ecology and the natural environment.

2 Is it important for an organization to have a mission statement?

3 The WWF (Worldwide Fund for Nature) licenses its logo to a few carefully chosen businesses such as Canon. How does this benefit the WWF and the licensing company?

LISTENING

1 Intercultural management experts Fons Trompenaars and Charles Hampden-Turner have identified four distinct organizational cultures. Read the descriptions below and decide:

1 in which culture(s) personal relationships are very important.
2 which culture has the least formal organization.
3 which culture has the strictest hierarchy.
4 which culture regularly sets employees different goals and objectives.

> **The family culture**
> Highly personal with close face-to-face relationships, but also hierarchical. The leader is the caring father.
>
> **The Eiffel Tower culture**
> Has a steep hierarchy, broad at the base and narrow at the top. Impersonal. Authority comes from a person's role and position in the hierarchy.
>
> **The guided missile culture**
> Egalitarian and oriented to tasks typically undertaken by teams or project groups. Impersonal.
>
> **The incubator culture**
> The organization serves as an incubator for self-expression and self-fulfilment. Personal and egalitarian with almost no structure at all. Often a strong emotional commitment to the work.
>
> *Riding the Waves of Culture* by Fons Trompenaars and Charles Hampden-Turner

2 🔊 51 Four people (A–D) speak about the organization in which they work.

1 Listen and decide which culture from **1** is being described.
   A .... C ....
   B .... D ....
2 Turn to listening script 5.1 on page 150 and underline the key words and phrases that gave you the answer in 2.1.

3 Match 1–6 to a–f to form complete sentences.

1 This firm is extremely *hierarchical* – … ......
2 We're very *familiar* and *informal* here – … ......
3 He pretends to be *egalitarian*, … ......
4 They're rather *conservative* and *paternalistic*, … ......
5 Relationships were so *impersonal* and *unfriendly* … ......
6 My old boss was very *authoritarian* – … ......

a … but they do take good care of their staff.
b … he expected complete obedience from his staff.
c … that I felt I didn't exist as a human being.
d … each level has its specific powers and responsibilities.
e … everybody uses first names.
f … but in the end it's him who makes the decisions.

4 Decide which adjectives in *italics* in **3** belong to which organizational culture.

> **YOUR TURN!**
>
> 1 Look again at the organizational cultures in the listening. Which of these is most common in your country?
> 2 Which organizational culture would you feel most comfortable in? Why?
> 3 Is it more stressful to be responsible for your own work or to have a lot of superiors?

Company culture

READING

1 Read the text below. Do you think this is a common feeling? What is *a sabbatical*?

> Many company employees wonder whether they should do something more with their life. Should they give up their career, bonus, and company car to work in a charity and do something to help society? Or perhaps they would like to return to a path they left when they started work. They think back to things they could do when they had more free time: art, writing, playing music. They wonder whether they could make a living out of these interests from the past.
>
> Would these employees have the courage to say to their boss: 'Would it be possible for me to go on a sabbatical for a year?'

2 Other people gain their motivation from their work. Study the picture of a bronze statue which stands in the headquarters of the American pharmaceutical company Merck.

1. What does the statue show?
2. Why do you think it is called 'The Gift of Sight'?
3. Why is Merck proud to display it?

The Gift of Sight

Imagine the discovery of a medicine that could – with just one annual dose – treat one of the worst diseases imaginable and prevent blindness.
Imagine more than 40 million people lining up each year to receive the medicine for free.
Imagine defeating a disease that has blinded so many for centuries. There is such a story.

www.merck.com

3 Read the first paragraph in the text on the right.

1. How did the drug's development begin?
2. What does this tell us about the importance of research for pharmaceutical companies?

Merck & Co., Inc.

In 1975 Merck & Co., Inc. researchers, while evaluating microbes from soil samples for possible therapeutic value, began research on a molecule that proved to be extremely effective against parasites in many animals. It was later realized that this molecule (ivermectin) could be adapted to treat river blindness, a terrible human disease, affecting 18 million people in the developing world with a further 126 million at risk. Merck eventually succeeded in developing an effective medicine called Mectizan. The drug underwent many clinical trials and finally received clinical approval in 1987.

During the late 1980s, as clinical trials were proving the breakthrough nature of Mectizan, a debate was taking place at Merck.

What price – if any – should the company charge for Mectizan? The company's dilemma was that the people who could benefit from this medicine were also the least able to pay for it.

If the company donated the medicine, would it create an expectation that future medicines for diseases in the developing world would be donated? Would this philanthropic act prove, in the long run, to be a disincentive for research against tropical diseases?

In addition to manufacturing and administrative costs, what risks would Merck face if Mectizan caused unexpected adverse reactions?

In vain Merck investigated third party payment options such as the World Health Organization and the US Agency for International Development. But in the face of limited health budgets and competing health priorities no legislation was passed. Meanwhile people continued to suffer from river blindness.

In the end the company's decision would be based on one simple yet profound belief expressed by George W. Merck, the company's president from 1925–1950, who said, 'Medicine is for the people. It is not for the profits. The profits follow, and if we have remembered that, they have never failed to appear'. In the same speech Mr Merck said, 'How can we bring the best of medicine to each and every person? We cannot rest until the way has been found with our help to bring our finest achievements to everyone'. Today, these words form the foundation of Merck's values. They define what the company does and why it does it. In 1987 Roy Vagelos, then Merck's chairman and CEO, made the historic announcement in Washington DC, that the company would donate Mectizan for the treatment of river blindness to all who need it for as long as needed.

© 1995–2004 Merck & Co., Inc., Whitehouse Station, NJ, USA. All rights reserved. Adopted and used with permission of Merck & Co., Inc.

4 Read the rest of the text which explains how Merck proceeded.

1 Why wasn't Mectizan a commercially viable product?
2 What dilemmas did Merck face?
3 How could the launch of the drug affect the pharmaceutical industry in the longer term?
4 Why do you think it failed to find 'third party' funding?
5 How did the company's philosophy guide it towards a final decision?
6 Why was their decision 'historic'?

GRAMMAR
Modals

1 *Could, would,* and *should* are three of the most commonly used modal auxiliary verbs. Their meaning changes according to the context of the sentence. Which sentence 1–3 below using *could*:

a describes a general ability in the past?
b is a request for permission?
c expresses a theoretical possibility?

1 Could I leave ten minutes early today?
2 They think back to things they could do when they had more free time.
3 We could send it by courier, I suppose.

2 Which sentence using *would*:

a indicates the future in the past?
b describes a habitual activity in the past?
c is a polite request?

1 Would it be possible for me to go on a sabbatical for a year?
2 We decided we would submit our revised proposals as soon as possible.
3 In the past, they would work from dawn to dusk.

3 Which sentence using *should*:

a expresses the best course of action?
b says that something is morally correct?
c says that something is expected to happen in the normal course of events?

1 Your delivery is on its way. It should arrive just after lunch.
2 Many company employees wonder whether they should do something more with their life.
3 Multinational companies should pay producers a fair price for their coffee.

See page 139 of the grammar guide.

4 Complete the sentences by choosing between the forms in *italics*.

1 Fifty years ago people *would / should* use traditional cures and remedies.
2 I really think you *should / would* reconsider our offer.
3 *Would / Should* it be possible for you to do the report?
4 As long as we keep up the hard work, we *should / would* be on schedule for the end of the month.
5 We *could / would* organize a meeting with managers from our overseas branches, but it may be difficult to find a suitable date.
6 I'm sorry, we had no idea that it *could / would* cause such a scandal.
7 *Would / Could* I borrow your notebook this weekend?

YOUR TURN!

Read the quotation below and discuss the questions.
'There is one and only one social responsibility of business – to use its resources and engage in activities designed to increase its profits.'
Milton Friedman, economist.

1 Do you agree with Friedman?
2 How reasonable is it to expect the pharmaceutical industry to behave differently from any other business?

Company culture

LANGUAGE FOR
obligation and necessity

1 🔊 5.2 Gavin Wilson is starting a new job. A colleague, Judith Parker, is showing him around his new workplace. Listen to their conversation and make notes about the rules for the following:

- dress _____
- name tags _____
- the R & D section _____
- smoking _____
- telephoning. _____

2 Decide which forms in sentences a–f below are used to:

1 express a strong prohibition.
2 describe general duties or obligations.
3 describe an important requirement or obligation.
4 say something is unnecessary.
5 talk about a regulation that is not always respected.
6 say someone didn't do something because it wasn't necessary.

a I *had to* wear a jacket and tie in my last job.
b You *needn't* do that here.
c You*'ve really got to* wear your ID tag.
d I *didn't need to* do that in my old job.
e You*'re supposed to* use the pay phones.
f You *mustn't ever* bring anyone in without senior management approval.

3 Turn to listening script 5.2 on page 150. Find another expression which means:

- don't have to
- mustn't.

4 🔊 5.3 Listen to situations 1–6 and respond accordingly using the forms in **2**.

SPEAKING

1 Many companies have special rules for their employees which they make available on company intranet rulebooks. Look at the page below from a company intranet site.

1. Why do you think the company created these rules?
2. Do you think the rules are fair?
3. Would you like to work for a company like this?

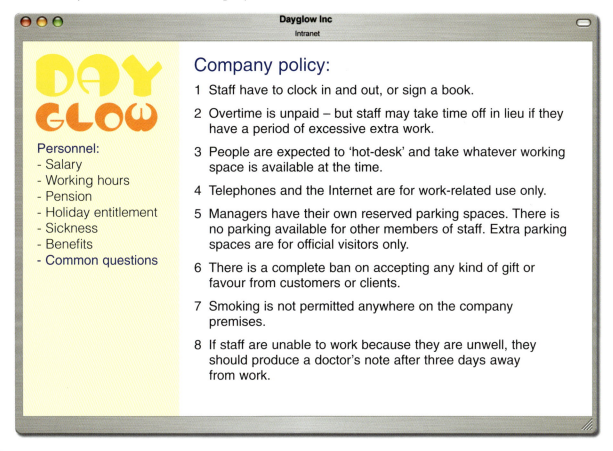

Dayglow Inc
Intranet

Personnel:
- Salary
- Working hours
- Pension
- Holiday entitlement
- Sickness
- Benefits
- Common questions

Company policy:

1. Staff have to clock in and out, or sign a book.
2. Overtime is unpaid – but staff may take time off in lieu if they have a period of excessive extra work.
3. People are expected to 'hot-desk' and take whatever working space is available at the time.
4. Telephones and the Internet are for work-related use only.
5. Managers have their own reserved parking spaces. There is no parking available for other members of staff. Extra parking spaces are for official visitors only.
6. There is a complete ban on accepting any kind of gift or favour from customers or clients.
7. Smoking is not permitted anywhere on the company premises.
8. If staff are unable to work because they are unwell, they should produce a doctor's note after three days away from work.

2 Now work in groups. Design a set of rules for:

a a typical company in your country / countries
b a small company with young employees.

Think about rules for:

- forms of address
- working space
- dress codes
- timekeeping
- overtime
- telephones and the Internet
- parking
- gifts
- sickness
- any other areas.

Try to use words and phrases from the Language for section on page 50.

Company culture

CASE STUDY

Background.
Frost's Offices specializes in space-saving home offices. The firm has no showrooms and generates business through advertisements in newspapers and magazines. People who respond to the ads are visited by a salesperson who designs the office and closes the sale. Previously the company was quite egalitarian, although Malcolm Frost, the company's founder, had a very paternalistic management style. Last year he went into semi-retirement and appointed Trudy Thorne as the new Managing Director. Before he left he made some important changes.

1 Study the changes shown in the table below. What effect do you think they have had since they were introduced?

OLD SYSTEM	NEW SYSTEM	MALCOLM FROST'S REASONS FOR CHANGE
Pay. Salespeople basic salary + commission.	Commission only.	'I lost too many good salespeople to the competition. Now my top people can earn a lot more.'
Sales team worked in teams of five around a large table.	Salespeople 'hot-desk', i.e. find a different workstation every day.	'Salespeople should be out selling, not drinking coffee in the office.'
Salespeople made own appointments with customers who replied to ads.	Tele-sales specialists make the appointments.	'I want my salespeople closing sales, not wasting time on the phone. Good sales leads were lost because we took too long to answer calls and respond to requests.'
Each team of five had an administrator who handled the paperwork.	Salespeople do own paperwork and invoicing.	'Cut costs.'

FROST's — feel at home in your home office

Company culture

2 🔊 54 Members of Frost's have reacted differently to the changes. Listen to what five employees have to say about their present working lives. Summarize their opinions.

1. Frank aged 31 – three years with the firm.
2. Helen aged 25 – eighteen months with the firm.
3. Trudy Thorne – twelve years with the firm. One year as Managing Director.
4. Ralph aged 43 – ten years with the firm.
5. Melanie aged 40 – eight years with the firm. Sales Manager.

3 Staff morale is now extremely poor. Sales staff are leaving or actively looking for other jobs. Malcolm Frost has called an emergency meeting to discuss what can be done to rescue the situation. In groups, study the agenda and make proposals which will allow Frost's to restore staff morale without damaging its competitiveness.

The reward system

What are the advantages and disadvantages of the new system?
Possibilities:

- Keep commission-only system.
- Return to old system (basic salary + lower commission).
- Another system, e.g. pay-scale with bonuses.

Staff morale

Identify any problem people.

What can be done to motivate staff again, e.g.

- team-building weekends
- sales seminars from sales 'guru'
- social activities for staff and families?

Administration

- Administration and paperwork.
- Office layout and staff morale.
- Support staff (tele-sales team, administrators).
- Individual desks? Hot-desking? Other ideas?

Company culture

WRITING

1 In your country how common is it for people to smoke at work? Is smoking allowed in restaurants, theatres, cinemas, and on public transport?

2 🔊 55 Simon Jones and Andrea Fox are discussing smoking in the company where they both work. Listen and answer the following questions.

1. What is the background to the smoking ban?
2. How many staff agreed with it?
3. Who do they suspect is breaking the rules?
4. What solution do they come up with?
5. What will happen to staff who continue to break the rules?

3 Expressions a–f all appear in the listening passage. Match them to their written equivalents in the box below.

> It has recently come to our notice that …
> I am writing to express my concern about …
> … state that smoking is not permitted.
> There are a number of employees smoking on the premises despite the no-smoking policy.
> Failure to comply with the new regulation will lead to serious action.
> This has implications for our insurance.

a I'm really fed up, …
b We've got this no-smoking policy but nobody seems to respect it.
c The other day I noticed that ….
d People who don't respect the new rules will really have to go!
e It will affect our insurance.
f … make our no-smoking rules clear.

4 You are the manager of a company with strict visitor rules. Visitors must wear a guest ID on company premises, must be accompanied at all times, sign in and sign out on arrival and departure, and sign an agreement not to reveal any confidential information they learn. You have recently learnt these rules are not being followed. Write an email to all staff. Try to use some of the written expressions from **3**.

Company culture

VIDEO CD-ROM INTERVIEW

1 **PAUSE FOR THOUGHT**: You are going to hear Jon talking about his company's culture. Before you watch, think of four adjectives to describe your ideal working conditions and environment.

....

2 Now watch **5 Company culture, INTERVIEW**. Compare your answers in **1** with the adjectives Jon uses to describe his working environment.

3 Read the questions below, then watch **5 Company culture, INTERVIEW**, again, and answer the questions.

1. What kind of institutions does Jon's company provide a service for?
2. Draw a simple diagram of the hierarchy in Jon's company.
3. In the hierarchy of Jon's company, how do groups at the top differ from groups at the bottom?
4. What informal contact do employees have with one another?
5. Would Jon's boss call him 'Jon', 'Mr Gower', or 'Gower'?
6. What is the company's attitude to employees' use of the Internet, telephones, and company credit cards?
7. What kind of clothes do employees have to wear in Jon's company?
8. What is staff turnover like, and why?

Jon Gower
A webmaster

LANGUAGE REVIEW

1 Before you watch, write down the rules or guidelines that exist in your place of work / organization, in the categories below.

1. working hours
2. food
3. make-up
4. company credit cards

2 Now watch **5 Company culture, LANGUAGE: Obligation and necessity**, and compare your answers in **1** with what Jon and Katja say about their organizations.

3 In your opinion, is Tim stating a rule, or a strong piece of advice?

WORDBANK

1 Write words from the interview next to their definitions in the Vocabulary notebook opposite.

2 Complete the sentences below with a preposition.

1. Older members of staff feel they don't fit ..... with this new informal culture.
2. There are few rules, so it's down ..... individuals to behave responsibly.
3. It's ..... the interests of all employees to respect the rules.
4. Employees who interface ..... customers have to dress smartly.

Vocabulary notebook

a_____e rules
= ignore rules or use them in an unfair way

a_____e
= the feeling or mood that a place has

d_____ c_____
= rules about what clothes you should wear

e_____t
= the place and conditions that you work in

Click on WORDBANK.
Practise the words in
5 Company culture.

Supply and demand

TALKING BUSINESS

1 **How far do you think everything has a fair price? Decide how you would react in the following situations. Work in pairs to compare your answers.**

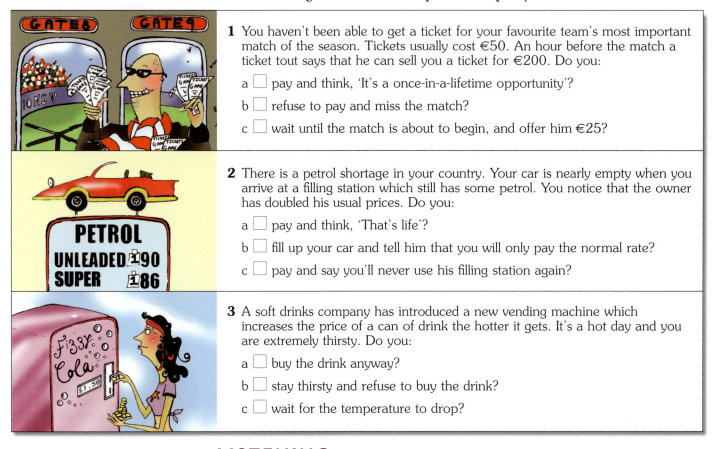

1 You haven't been able to get a ticket for your favourite team's most important match of the season. Tickets usually cost €50. An hour before the match a ticket tout says that he can sell you a ticket for €200. Do you:
   a ☐ pay and think, 'It's a once-in-a-lifetime opportunity'?
   b ☐ refuse to pay and miss the match?
   c ☐ wait until the match is about to begin, and offer him €25?

2 There is a petrol shortage in your country. Your car is nearly empty when you arrive at a filling station which still has some petrol. You notice that the owner has doubled his usual prices. Do you:
   a ☐ pay and think, 'That's life'?
   b ☐ fill up your car and tell him that you will only pay the normal rate?
   c ☐ pay and say you'll never use his filling station again?

3 A soft drinks company has introduced a new vending machine which increases the price of a can of drink the hotter it gets. It's a hot day and you are extremely thirsty. Do you:
   a ☐ buy the drink anyway?
   b ☐ stay thirsty and refuse to buy the drink?
   c ☐ wait for the temperature to drop?

LISTENING

1 Read the tip about elasticity of demand. What goods can you think of which are particularly elastic, or inelastic?

2 《6 1》 Tara Williamson is an economist who is being interviewed by Jay Thomas about setting prices. Listen to part A and answer the questions.
   1 How did she feel about the actions of the petrol station owner from the point of view of:
      ■ an ordinary citizen?
      ■ an economist?
   2 Which economic principles does she claim her story illustrates?
   3 What were the short-term benefits, and long-term consequences of the owner's actions?

Tip

Elasticity of Demand
Price elasticity describes how sensitive the demand for a product is to a change in its price. If a small change in price causes a large change in demand, then we can say that demand is highly elastic.

3 🔊 **61** **In part B Tara talks about pricing policy. Listen and find out:**
1 what unhappy experience Jay had recently
2 how Tara explains what happened to Jay
3 what is the second stage of the pricing strategy used by many companies.

4 🔊 **61** **In the final part of the interview, Tara and Jay discuss the price-fixing powers of manufacturers and retailers. Listen to part C and decide if statements 1–6 are true (*T*) or false (*F*).**

1 Big brands often leave prices to the discretion of retailers. ......
2 Discounted prices can hurt some brands. ......
3 Supermarkets buy luxury brands on the black market. ......
4 Supermarkets will resell luxury brands at a loss. ......
5 Loss leaders attract customers to stores. ......
6 Brands simply accept the supermarkets' action. ......

5 Many verbs are used with the noun *price* to form collocations. Replace the words in *italics* with one of the verbs from the box below.

set	fix	fetch	match	charge	raise	dictate

1 That shop's really expensive – they are always *increasing* the prices.
2 He *asked me to pay* a high price to repair my car.
3 She said she would *equal* the price if I could find it cheaper elsewhere.
4 If you *put* your prices too high, then people simply won't be interested.
5 He knows everybody will buy his goods, so he is able to *control* the prices.
6 The clock *got* a surprisingly good price at the auction.
7 It is considered unfair for competing shopkeepers to *secretly agree on* their prices.

6 Match definitions 1–5 with expressions from the box below.

price range	price war	asking price	retail price	cut price

1 greatly reduced price ....
2 in a negotiation, the price the seller wants ....
3 a battle between retailers who reduce the price ....
4 spread of prices ....
5 the standard agreed price suggested by the producer ....

YOUR TURN!

Work in pairs. Discuss how you would explain concepts 1–5 to someone with little understanding of business. Think of clear and concrete examples to illustrate each concept.
1 the grey market
2 skimming the market
3 elasticity of demand
4 a loss leader
5 predatory pricing

READING

1 What essential commodities can you think of?

2 Read the text about commodities and commodity prices, and answer the questions.

1. Why was *The Lord of the Rings* published in three volumes?
2. How is the price of agricultural products determined by the law of supply and demand?
3. What competing forces caused the crisis of the 1970s?
4. What is powering current growth in commodity prices?

Commodities

It is hard to imagine what connection could possibly exist between **commodity** prices and the publication of J.R.R. Tolkien's *The Lord of the Rings*. In spite of the author's original wish to publish his work as a single book, his publishers refused because at that time, paper was so expensive that they felt it had to be spread out as a three-volume series. Since then, paper, in common with other commodities, has experienced highs and lows. When a commodity is in short supply its price soars; when there is a glut or drop in demand it falls. If something is scarce, the more it is worth.

The nightmare of any producer of a commodity or raw material is that a cheaper source becomes available elsewhere, or, worst of all, that a substitute is found. For instance, Brazilian rubber producers lost their **monopoly** in the 1880s when British growers transported precious rubber plants to Malaysia. Worse was to come with the invention of synthetic rubber based on oil in the first half of the twentieth century. All this shows that a commodity's price results from the relationship between demand, stocks, and production.

Furthermore, there is the relative power-relationship existing between suppliers and buyers. Even though we might think that it is the producer who holds all the cards, the reverse is often true – prices can be dictated by powerful multinationals. This has always been the case for tea and coffee producers, who are often small farmers with a low output, at the mercy of the big companies which process their crop and add most of its value.

A classic example of this is oil. For many decades the price of petroleum was more or less dictated by 'the seven sisters' – massive petroleum multinationals who controlled the extraction, refining, and the transport and distribution of this most precious of commodities. However, one way that commodity producers have of winning a bigger slice of the pie is to band together and to form a **cartel**. OPEC was founded by a group of oil-producing nations in 1960 as a way of controlling oil output within their countries. The decision to limit output saw oil prices leap fourfold in the oil shock of 1974. The vastly increased price was fed into the cost of other manufactured goods and fuelled a jump in **inflation**. As prices rose, demand for manufactured goods fell, which triggered a global **recession**. Despite the oil shock and economic slowdown, the world economy gradually recovered. Thirty years on, while OPEC is far less powerful than it once was, the availability of plentiful crude oil at a reasonable price is still crucial for the world economy.

However, the price of crude oil and other commodities is likely to be forced higher and higher with the continuing growth of the Chinese economy, which needs raw materials to sustain it. China now accounts for a fifth of global crude oil and aluminium and over a quarter of the world's iron ore consumption. Daily consumption leapt from 4 million barrels per day in 2000 to 6 million in 2004. Nevertheless, North America remains by far the world's biggest consumer.

3 List the words and expressions in the text which refer to a lot or a little of something.

A LOT	A LITTLE

4 Write definitions for the following words from the text. Try to get the meaning from the context.

commodity: ....
cartel: ....
recession: ....
monopoly: ....
inflation: ....

YOUR TURN!

Work in groups and discuss these questions.
1 How fair is it for producing countries to control the supply of an essential commodity to the rest of the world?
2 In what circumstances should governments interfere with the prices which are charged by private companies?
3 What monopolies, if any, exist in your country (e.g. tobacco, electricity)?

GRAMMAR
Conjunctions

1 Find extracts a–d in the text on page 58.

a Daily consumption leapt from 4 million barrels per day in 2000 to 6 million in 2004. *Nevertheless*, North America remains by far the world's biggest consumer.
b *In spite of* the author's original wish to publish his work as a single book, his publishers refused.
c For many decades the price of petroleum was more or less dictated by 'the seven sisters' … *However*, one way that commodity producers have of winning a bigger slice of the pie is to band together and to form a cartel.
d *Even though* we might think that it is the producer who holds all the cards, the reverse is often true.

2 Which of the words / phrases in italics:

■ show a contrast between two ideas in the two parts of the sentence?
■ modify something that has just been stated?

3 What form of the verb follows *although* and *despite / in spite of*?

See page 144 of the grammar guide.

4 Rewrite these sentences using the words listed.

1 Plastic is not a commodity in the usual sense but people have started to treat it as one.
   a Nevertheless
   b Although
2 There are oil reserves in the North Sea. It is too expensive to drill for them.
   a Although
   b Despite
   c However
3 Anyone is able to speculate on commodity prices but we should leave this to the experts.
   a Even though
   b Despite
   c Nevertheless

Supply and demand

LANGUAGE FOR
participating in meetings

1 6.2 Listen to part of a meeting in a company. What problem is being discussed?

2 Match the headings 1–7 to the expressions a–g.

1 asking for clarification
2 contributing / asking to interrupt
3 asking for contributions
4 summarizing
5 dealing with / resuming after interruptions
6 keeping the meeting on track
7 clarifying

a It's an interesting point but I'm not sure how relevant it is to our discussion.
b Does anyone have anything further to add?
c I'd just like to say that we have very little time.
d What does 'a negative outcome' mean exactly?
e What I meant is we should wait and see what happens.
f Can I just finish off what I was saying?
g So, to recap, we all feel that these costs have risen too high.

3 Group these other expressions under the right heading in the table below.

I'm sorry, let me run through it again	The point I'm trying to make is …
Can I just say that …	I'd like to come in here
Sorry, I don't quite follow what you're saying	If I understand correctly …

MAKING A CONTRIBUTION	ASKING FOR CLARIFICATION	CLARIFYING

4 What would you say in the following situations?

1 You have just listened to a complicated explanation. Ask the other person to repeat what they said.
2 You want to end a discussion about the cost of distribution in Canada.
3 You don't want the group to make a decision now about moving offices because of rising rent: the situation might change.

SPEAKING

1 Sometimes candidates for jobs are rejected because they are not 'team players'. What exactly do you think this means? How important do you think it is to be a 'team player'?

2 The following key roles have been identified for effective teams. Which role would suit your character best?

> **Key roles within teams**
>
> **Team leader:** Finds new team members and develops the team-working spirit.
>
> **Critic:** Guardian and analyst of the team's long-term effectiveness.
>
> **Implementer:** Ensures the momentum and smooth-running of the team's actions.
>
> **External contact:** Looks after the team's external relationships.
>
> **Coordinator:** Pulls together the work of the team as a whole into a cohesive plan.
>
> **Ideas person:** Sustains and encourages the team's innovative vitality and energy.
>
> **Inspector:** Ensures that high standards are sought and maintained.

3 Work with a partner. Read the extract below from the *Essential Manager's Manual* and then discuss the questions.

1. To what extent should you adapt when you take up a new post in a company?
2. Is it easy to find a job which suits your individual character?
3. Which roles from the list above do you think share similar characteristics?

> Try to match roles to personality rather than attempting to shoehorn the personality into the role. It is not necessary for each person to perform only one function. If the team has only a small number of members, doubling or trebling up the roles is fine – as long as all the needs of the team are truly covered and the members feel comfortable with their roles.
>
> *Essential Manager's Manual* by Robert Heller and Tim Hindle

4 Work in groups of four. You are members of the quality control team at Harper's Cameras. You are going to hold a meeting to discuss a problem with breakages and losses. Decide who will take on each of the roles below and turn to the information for your role. When you are ready, hold your meeting. You can invent and improvise as much as you wish. Try to use words and phrases from the Language for section on page 60.

- the team leader / external contact, turn to File 6 on page 127
- the critic / inspector, turn to File 14 on page 129
- the coordinator / implementer, turn to File 19 on page 131
- the ideas person, turn to File 27 on page 133

Supply and demand

CASE STUDY

1 Read the text below about the Caxton Reader.
   1 Who do you think would be the market for the Caxton Reader?
   2 What problems might it face?

Virfen's Caxton Reader

Background
Virfen is a Cambridge-based company which has built a strong reputation with its personal organizers. It has recently developed the Caxton Reader, an electronic book used to view books, newspapers, and magazines downloaded quickly from the Internet using its powerful modem. Unlike its rivals, the Reader's tough, flexible screen folds in two, just like a real book. Virfen has spent $2 million developing the Reader and creating a production line capable of producing 500 units a day. Each Reader costs $50 to produce in materials, labour, and shipping. Virfen now has to finalize its marketing strategy for the next three years. The company would like to recover its development costs quickly.

Competitors

The Lector
First reader in the market. Heavier and less strong than Reader. Rigid screen. Price $250. Three years old.

The Paston Voyager
Same weight as Reader. Accepts book cards: users can buy books in the form of plastic cards which they can insert into the Paston Voyager. Rigid screen. Slow download time. Price $200. Eighteen months old.

Other manufacturers are developing similar products.

2 Now read all the information below and on page 63.

3 Work in groups and role-play the meeting in the agenda on page 63. Discuss as much of the information as possible.

Tip

Costs

Fixed costs
Business costs which do not vary with the amount of work produced, e.g. rent.

Variable costs
Production costs which vary according to the quantity of goods produced, e.g. raw materials, labour.

Break-even point
The number of units a business has to sell to cover its costs. A project starts to become profitable after it has passed its break-even point.

Economies of scale
Savings which result from producing goods in large numbers.

Target customer groups
Virfen has researched four potential markets.

Group 1 High-level managers who travel a lot and need non-fiction information quickly. Also academics whose books tend to be larger and heavier to carry. These would be early adopters, and ready to pay $300.

Group 2 Middle-level office workers who read while commuting to work. Also university and high school students. Virfen would have to price the Reader at $150 to penetrate this market.

Group 3 Mass market. General public. Consumers ready to pay a retail price of between $75 and $100.

Group 4 Poorer export markets (e.g. Southland) $60.

Projected first year's sales, domestic and overseas, according to price	
Price ($)	Projected sales
300	10,000
200	15,000
150	30,000
100	75,000
75	120,000
60	200,000

Southland

Virfen is considering whether to sell the Reader in Southland, a non-EU market with a weak currency. Consumers in Southland could only pay $60.

Agenda:

Caxton Reader Marketing Strategy

1 Which markets should we target?

How should we price it?
- 1st year
- 2nd and 3rd year

Should we adopt a skimming policy?

2 Southland

Should we sell to Southland?

If we sell to Southland at a cut price, will sales outlets in richer countries exploit a grey market situation?

Should we adopt variable pricing in different markets?

3 Promotion

How will we promote it? USPs.

What problems will the competition give us?

Would predatory pricing erupt into a price war?

Do we want a mass-market product? Do we want a luxury product that will sell at a high price?

Supply and demand

WRITING

1 🔊63 Listen to a presentation describing the graph below.

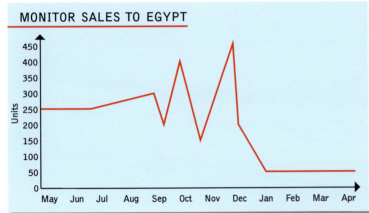

This chart represents sales of monitors to Egypt over the last financial year, including both our fourteen- and fifteen-inch screens.

At the outset of the year, sales ¹_____ until June. Then they ²_____ for two months until in September sales began ³_____ for three months. They proceeded to ⁴_____ by a hundred units in September but then ⁵_____ in November, ⁶_____ 450 in December – to an unprecedented level. However, sales then ⁷_____ to fifty units in January! There are various reasons for this but the big worry is that they ⁸_____ at that low level.

1 Now complete the description of the graph using the words in the box below.

peak	remain steady
plummet	level off
soar	creep up
fluctuate	slump

2 Which words mean:
  a to rise?
  b to fall?
  c to stay the same?

3 What is the past tense of *creep*?
4 Which of these verbs can also be used as nouns?

2 Which of the adjectives in the box suggest a small change and which suggest a large change?

| dramatic | slight | steady | sharp | steep |

3 What differences do you notice between the following sentences? What forms are the words in *italics*?

1 There was a *dramatic rise* in the price of crude oil.
2 The price of crude oil *rose dramatically*.

4 In each of the sentences 1–4, continue the second sentence so that it means the same as the first sentence, as in the example.

1 The cost of crude oil rose slightly.
   There was a slight *rise in the cost of crude oil*.

2 There was a dramatic collapse of the property market last year.
   The property market _____.

3 Fuel prices have climbed steeply over the past six months.
   There has been a _____.

4 There has been a steady increase in charges since the introduction of the euro.
   Charges _____.

5 Write a paragraph. Turn to File 7 on page 127.

6 Supply and demand

VIDEO CD-ROM INTERVIEW

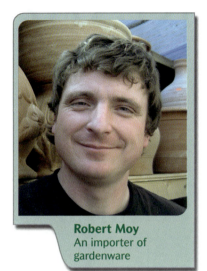

Robert Moy
An importer of gardenware

1 **PAUSE FOR THOUGHT:** You are going to hear Robert talking about importing. Before you watch, guess what two factors Robert takes into account when pricing his plant pots.

2 Now watch **6 Supply and demand, INTERVIEW**. Compare your answers in **1** to what Robert says.

3 Watch **6 Supply and demand, INTERVIEW**, again. Complete the sentences below, to summarize what Robert says.
   1 Robert feels good about his business because ....
   2 The pots Robert sells the most of in England are .... because ....
   3 Robert's customers are mainly ....
   4 Five years ago, the fashion was .... but now his customers prefer products from ....
   5 Robert keeps his prices competitive by ....

LANGUAGE REVIEW

1 Watch **6 Supply and demand, LANGUAGE: Describing trends**, and note down the phrases used, as in the example.

Robert	Martin	Ray
1 unusual plants *have risen dramatically (↑)*	4 property prices	6 interest rates
2 interest rates	5 inflation and interest rates	7 salaries and property prices *not going up quite in line with (property prices ↑ salaries ↗)*
3 fuel costs, the dollar, the euro		

2 Now write an arrow ↓, ↑, or → next to your answers in **1**, to indicate the direction of the trend.

WORDBANK

1 Write a definition or an example of the collocations from the interview in the Vocabulary notebook opposite.

2 Complete the table below with forms of the words given. Then write down their stress pattern, as in the example.

NOUN	NOUN (AGENT)	ADJECTIVE	VERB
	competitor oOoo		
fluctuation ooOo	-	-	
production oOo			

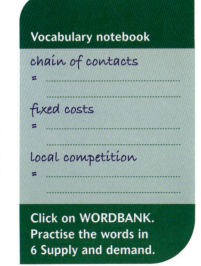

Vocabulary notebook

chain of contacts
= ....
....

fixed costs
= ....
....

local competition
= ....
....

Click on WORDBANK.
Practise the words in
6 Supply and demand.

Negotiations

TALKING BUSINESS

1 Read the situation and decide how Barry and Martha should act.

Barry Meadows and Martha Windsor are the CEO and Chief Accountant of a large US company. They have both been arrested on suspicion of the lesser crime of insider trading and the greater crime of fraud. The authorities have enough evidence to convict both of insider trading but need a confession from one of them to get a conviction for fraud. They are being interviewed in separate cells and are not allowed to speak to each other. The authorities have offered the following deal to both suspects:
– you confess but your partner in crime doesn't. You give evidence against your partner and go free. Your partner gets ten years in prison.
– you both confess and you each get five years.
– neither of you confesses. You each get two years for the lesser crime.

adapted from *The Economist Book Pocket Negotiator*
by Gavin Kennedy

LISTENING

1  Eric Perrot is an area sales manager of a Belgian company which sells chips and other potato-based products. Eric negotiates supply contracts with many of the biggest food retailers in Europe. Listen to part A of the interview in which Eric talks about the key to a successful negotiation and summarize what he says about:

- being prepared
- winning or losing a negotiation
- companies' policy towards their buyers.

7 Negotiations

2 🔊 **Listen to part B and answer the questions.**

1 According to Eric, what qualities should a good negotiator have?
2 How important is the ability to be persuasive?
3 Who are the most difficult customers for Eric? How does he deal with them?
4 How controlled does he stay in negotiations?

3 🔊 **In part C, Eric gives an example of two deals he made. Listen to part C and answer the questions.**

1 What concession did the buyer in the first deal want? What was Eric's reaction?
2 Why does Eric believe that you should never give something for nothing?
3 What went wrong in the second deal and what did he do?

4 Look at the words in the box below.

| negotiable | persuasive | concession |
| compromise | proposal | confrontation |

1 Find the words in the box in the listening script on page 153.
2 Then complete the gaps in each sentence a–f below with one of the words from the box.

  a He will do anything to avoid a ....
  b I found his reasons extremely ....
  c The union has made an important .... on overtime pay.
  d Management says that the issue is not ....
  e We can reach a .... if both sides are prepared to give and take.
  f We are ready to listen to your revised ....

5 Complete the sentences below by choosing between the words in *italics*. All of the words appeared in listening script 7.1.

1 After hours of discussion we finally managed to *overcome / come over* our differences.
2 I managed to beat them *up / down* from $60 a tonne to $55.
3 You can't expect to get *out of / through to* the contract as easily as that.
4 It was a tough negotiation but we *reached / decided* a compromise.
5 When he heard how high the price we agreed was, he *found / lost* his temper.
6 I had to *take / start* the initiative because their representatives were so quiet.
7 We were satisfied with the *outcome / income* of the negotiations.
8 She managed to talk her boss *into / out of* the contract even though he wanted to sign it.

YOUR TURN!

Read the quotation below.
'Any business arrangement that is not profitable to the other fellow will in the end prove unprofitable for you.'
B. C. Forbes, publisher
1 Do you agree?
2 Think of an occasion when you agreed to an unfavourable business or personal arrangement. How did you feel about the other person in the arrangement? Was the final result good for everyone?

READING

1 How possible do you think it is for both sides in a negotiation to feel happy with the outcome? How can a good range of negotiating techniques help?

2 You are going to read two stories about different negotiations. Work in two groups. Half the class should read article A and complete column A of the table on page 69. The other half should read article B in File 10 on page 128 and complete column B of the table on page 69.

A Swiss entrepreneur once asked me to help set up a golf game outside Paris with a top French government official. My Swiss friend had sold merchandise to the government, but was deadlocked on some major issues. He thought that if he could get the official outside his official environment, the negotiations might improve. So he enlisted my help. I brought along a golf client whom the official admired, which made the outing special.

It was an interesting round of golf, largely because both the French official and my Swiss friend played abysmally. As the day wore on, their poor play seemed to bond them. 'Transaction golf' has a special protocol. If you bring up business at all, you have to be very subtle. It's understood, not spoken. But by the tenth hole, the two men were having such a bad day that they were ready to talk about anything but golf. My Swiss friend handled this beautifully, assembling his argument with a sound bite or two on every remaining hole. By the time we reached the clubhouse, the two men had ironed out all their differences and scribbled their agreement on a cocktail napkin.

I'll never know if it was the beauty of the day that made them so agreeable or their poor play that brought them together. But I do know that getting people out of the usual business setting and placing them in a congenial environment for four or five hours will improve almost any negotiation.

If you press the issue, you'll find that most people don't want to spend their time haggling with the other side. It's not that they don't like negotiating. They like the friendly competition, the manoeuvring, the development of a strategy and its execution. But more than anything, they like reaching an agreement.

I'm sure that's what's going on when people brag about the deals they've negotiated over casual drinks or a meal or a round of golf. When they come back to the office brandishing the cocktail napkin on which the deal terms are scribbled, I often think they're more pleased about how they negotiated an agreement than what the terms actually are. The cocktail napkin is a testament to their negotiating skill. Actually, it's a testament to negotiating in a quasi-social setting. It's proof of the wisdom of getting away from the 'negotiating table'.

Mark H McCormack on Negotiating

Negotiations

	A	B
People involved		
Object of negotiation		
Obstacle		
Formal / informal		
Level of experience of negotiators		
Techniques used		
Direct / indirect style of negotiation		
How an agreement was reached		
Winner / loser of the negotiation		

YOUR TURN!
1 Have you ever negotiated a cheaper price for something? How were you successful?
2 Do you think the other person in your negotiation was happy with the result?

3 Work in pairs with a partner from the other group. Exchange information to complete the second column of the table.
  1 What piece of wisdom did the narrator learn about the negotiation in each case?
  2 How important was the setting?

GRAMMAR
Conditionals

1 Match the conditional sentences a–e with the definitions of their use 1–5.
  a If you press the issue, you'll find that most people don't want to spend their time haggling with the other side.
  b If you bring up business at all, you have to be very subtle.
  c If you paid cash, I could work out a discount.
  d If I'd been her, I'd have paid the money.
  e If I'd had the same determination, I'd be as rich and famous today.

  1 a unreal situation entirely in the past ......
  2 an unreal past situation with a result in the present ......
  3 a present action with a predictable future result ......
  4 a polite and diplomatic proposal ......
  5 a general truth or fact ......

2 Decide which sentence in **1** is an example of the following conditional forms:
  1 zero ......
  2 first ......
  3 second ......
  4 third ......
  5 mixed ......

See page 136 of the grammar guide.

3 Complete these sentences by changing the verbs in brackets into an appropriate conditional form.
  1 How much .... (pay), Martin, if you .... (be) at yesterday's meeting?
  2 If we .... (sign) now, she .... (give) us a 25% discount. Let's do it before she changes her mind.
  3 What .... (say) if I .... (pay) you some buyer's commission as an incentive?
  4 Unless they .... (agree) to an extra thirty days' credit, I .... (not go ahead) with the order.
  5 If you .... (pay) by credit card, you .... (have to) spend more than £5.
  6 I .... (accept the delivery) as long as you .... (replace) the damaged goods.
  7 We have lost a good customer. They .... (renew) the contract if we .... (not be) so greedy.
  8 If you .... (not agree) to their ridiculous conditions, we .... (not be) in this awful situation now.

Negotiations 7

LANGUAGE FOR
dealing with customer complaints

1 The following complaints are part of a customer complaint on the telephone. Put them in the correct order. What question do you think is being answered in each case?

a   Yes, please. It's about a waterproof jacket I bought last year.
b   Thank you for your help.
c   Could you put me through to Customer Services, please?
d   I washed it according to the instructions on the label and now it's leaking.
e   I bought it in your branch but I don't live in the area. Can I return it to my local branch?
f   I realize it's no longer under guarantee but I don't think a quality item should wear out so quickly.

2 🔊 7.2 Listen and check your answers.

3 What different structures does the speaker use to make polite requests?

4 Answering calls from angry customers requires very diplomatic language.

1   Match the beginnings of sentences 1–6 to their endings a–f to form complete sentences.

1   I can fully appreciate …
2   Do you happen …
3   I'm just …
4   If you'd like …
5   I'll …
6   I do apologize …

a   … accessing your details on my screen.
b   … enter your details straightaway.
c   … your frustration, Mr Miller.
d   … for any inconvenience you've suffered, Mr Miller.
e   … to bear with me a moment.
f   … to have a reference number?

2   🔊 7.3 Listen and check your answers.
3   Now match the sentences to their functions a–f.
   a   promising action
   b   saying what you're doing
   c   asking for information
   d   saying sorry
   e   giving a polite order
   f   sympathizing

SPEAKING

1 Read the tip on how to deal with difficult customers.

    1 How realistic do you think they are?
    2 How possible is it to follow them at all times?

2 Work in pairs. Act out role-play 1 below. You need to negotiate a settlement. One of you should be the call handler, the other the customer. Try to use words and phrases from the Language for section on page 70. Use the flow chart below to help you.

> **Role-play 1**
>
> **Customer:** You went on a flight to Moscow for a business trip. The plane was four hours delayed, your luggage was lost, and there was no food available on the flight. You feel the company should refund you the price of the ticket and apologize for their poor service. You are in no mood to compromise.
>
> **Call handler:** You want to be friendly and helpful. You can give the customer a free upgrade to business class on their next flight but you cannot offer any refund. Your company does not want to apologize because the lost baggage was the airport's fault, not your company's. Try to be as persuasive as possible.

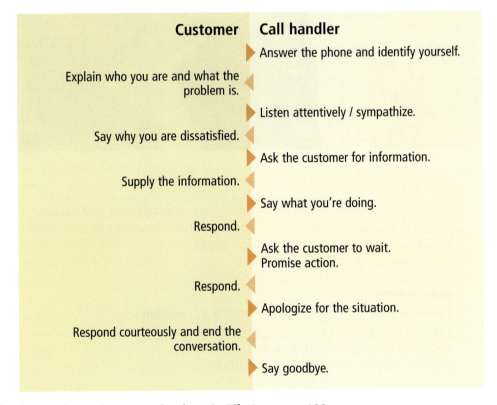

Customer	Call handler
	Answer the phone and identify yourself.
Explain who you are and what the problem is.	
	Listen attentively / sympathize.
Say why you are dissatisfied.	
	Ask the customer for information.
Supply the information.	
	Say what you're doing.
Respond.	
	Ask the customer to wait. Promise action.
Respond.	
	Apologize for the situation.
Respond courteously and end the conversation.	
	Say goodbye.

3 Swap roles and act out role-play 2 in File 9 on page 128.

Tip

Dealing with customers and their complaints

1. Allow angry customers to express their feelings without interrupting them.
2. Try not to take their complaints and criticisms personally.
3. Never argue with a customer.
4. Look or sound concerned. Show that you are listening.
5. Sympathize without accepting liability.
6. Never show your irritation or lose your temper.

CASE STUDY

1 Read about the negotiating styles of red and blue stylists.

Red stylists
- see each negotiation as a separate contest with a winner and a loser
- believe you win by dominating your opponent, beating him / her down
- enjoy using manipulative tricks and bluffs
- want something for nothing.

Blue stylists
- believe both sides can win by reaching a compromise
- regard negotiations in the longer term
- recognize each party's interests
- will only trade something for something.

2 Discuss which colour stylist would be more likely to make statements 1–5.

1. I'm giving you this proposition once only. Take it or leave it.
2. We're happy to discuss a discount if we can work something out.
3. I want you to show your good faith by agreeing to this proposal now.
4. I can understand that you don't want to leave yourself vulnerable to price rises.
5. How do you think we can overcome our differences in the future?

3   Background: Last year Wakely's – a British engineering company – was taken over by an American conglomerate, Stonebridge Inc. Changes in management style have caused tension at the plant. The union is ready for confrontation and an argument took place on the shop floor yesterday when some of the older blue-collar workers lost their temper at the extra work they were being asked to do. Read the grievances and identify the cause in each case.

Grievance 1
Language training. As part of its export drive Stonebridge is investing heavily in language tuition for sales and marketing staff. Courses take place during work time. Language tuition is available for blue-collar staff but in their own time.

Grievance 2
Sam Walker, Stonebridge's vice-president, has reduced the subsidy paid to the factory's rugby and football team and club. The Managing Director, who does not drink alcohol, says the subsidy encourages drunkenness. Golfing weekends at expensive hotels, and foreign travel are offered to senior executives.

Grievance 3
A female American manager has accused male assembly-line workers of negative behaviour and sexism. She claims they are resistant to new techniques and equipment. They say she does not respect their skill and is young and aggressive.

4   A meeting has been arranged to try to find a solution to the problems. Work in groups of four. Student A, you are a senior member of management: turn to File 2 on page 126. Student B, you are also a member of senior management: turn to File 12 on page 129. Student C, you are a union representative: turn to File 20 on page 131. Student D, you are also a union representative: turn to File 22 on page 132.

5   Work in groups. Once you have studied and prepared your case, role-play the meeting. Decide if you will be a red or blue stylist!

Negotiations

WRITING

1 Lori Greene, the customer services manager of *Scandipine*, has received a letter of complaint from Ms Davina Manners, a disabled customer. Read the reply. What do you think was the cause of Ms Manners' complaint?

2 Work in pairs to discuss these questions.

1 Does the letter contain an unconditional apology?
2 What phrases does the writer of the letter use to show she cares about her customer's feelings?

Dear Ms Manners

I was extremely concerned to receive your letter and have **looked into the matter very closely**. I fully share your displeasure and dissatisfaction with the treatment you received. **I hope you will accept my sincerest apologies on behalf of** Scandipine. I have discussed this matter with the individuals concerned. While this is no excuse, the young woman who greeted you so discourteously was a trainee who would normally not have been working alone. Saturday is our busiest day of the week and we were understaffed on that day. **I would like to assure you that** we take customer care very seriously and ensure that our staff are fully trained.

We regularly receive disabled customers and do our very best to **assist** them. However, to be absolutely certain of avoiding any future difficulty at the store I have enclosed my personal card. Do not hesitate to ring me the next time you are planning a visit to our store so that I can **ensure** that there will be someone available to accompany you.

I hope you will accept as a token of our goodwill the enclosed voucher for £100 which can be exchanged against goods at any of our stores. Once again, I hope you will accept my most sincere apologies for this unfortunate incident.

I look forward to meeting you in person the next time you visit us.

With very best wishes

Yours sincerely

Lori Greene

Lori Greene
Customer Services Manager

---

3 We use different phrases in formal written English and speaking. Look at the phrases in **bold** in the letter. What language would you use in spoken English?

4 Some people say that a complaint is 'an opportunity in disguise'. How does this letter turn the original complaint into an opportunity?

5 Turn to File 8 on page 128. Work in pairs to write the letter described there.

VIDEO CD-ROM INTERVIEW

1 PAUSE FOR THOUGHT: You are going to hear Tim talking about negotiation. Before you watch, answer the questions below.

1 In your opinion, what is the ideal outcome in a negotiation?
2 How would you go about reaching such an outcome?

2 Now watch **7 Negotiations, INTERVIEW.** Compare your answers in **1** with what Tim says.

3 Watch **7 Negotiations, INTERVIEW**, again. Make notes on what Tim says, under the headings below.

A good negotiator	How Tim negotiates ....
Negotiating styles	Do's ....
Tim's preferred negotiating style	Don'ts ....

Tim Dare
A headhunter

LANGUAGE REVIEW

1 Before you watch, complete the sentences below for yourself.

1 If somebody speaks to me rudely, I ....
2 If something goes wrong at work, I ....
3 If I hadn't chosen this career, I ....
4 If I went bankrupt, I ....
5 When I retire, I ....

2 Now watch **7 Negotiations, LANGUAGE: Conditionals**, and compare your answers in **1** with what the speakers say.

WORDBANK

1 Complete the collocations from the interview in the Vocabulary notebook opposite.

2 Match the definitions below to the collocations in the Vocabulary notebook.
- the ability to communicate well with people
- build up a good relationship with somebody over time
- find you immediately have a friendly relationship with somebody

3 Complete the sentences below with prepositions.

1 We eventually came ...... a solution after four hours of negotiation.
2 If you are aggressive, you will end .... an outcome that doesn't suit anybody.
3 If negotiators get ...... well ...... each other, it is easier to reach an agreement.

Vocabulary notebook

g.................... rapport
= ....

i.................... skills
= ....

s.................... a rapport
= ....

**Click on WORDBANK.
Practise the words in
7 Negotiations.**

Staying competitive

TALKING BUSINESS

1 A *killer application* is a new invention, or a new use / feature of an invention. A killer application becomes an essential part of people's lives and improves on all existing products. For example, the word processor and the PC killed the typewriter. Decide if the following inventions are killer applications:

- photo-messaging
- the digital camera
- the palm pilot
- replacing paper money / coins with a money card
- email.

2 What new inventions have appeared in your lifetime? Which was the most important?

LISTENING

1 What do you understand by the term *management consultant*? Discuss the following questions in pairs.

1 Why do you think companies might call in management consultants to advise them?
2 What experience and personal qualities do you think people might need to be successful consultants?

2 ((81)) Before he retired, Bill Watts used to work for top management consultants McKinsey.

1 Listen to part A and note down the reasons he gives for firms calling in a consultant.
2 How closely do they match the ones you gave in **1**?
3 According to Bill, what kind of advice might management consultants give in order to help companies deal with change?

3 ((81)) Listen to part B and find answers to these questions.

1 How did he feel when he went into a new company?
2 How old was Bill when he started as a consultant for McKinsey?
3 How was he regarded by the staff of the organization he visited?
4 Why did he feel confident about his abilities?
5 How involved were clients in the consultation process?

4 ((81)) In part C, Bill discusses the company's 'up-or-out' policy for its staff. What do you think this means?

1 Listen and check your answer.
2 Listen again and answer the questions below.

a What are the long-term prospects for consultants at McKinsey?
b Why is management consultancy a high-pressured job?
c What are some of its compensations?

8   **Staying competitive**   77

5   How tempted would you be by a career as a management consultant?

6   Complete the sentences below by changing the word in *italics* into an appropriate form, as in the example. Then turn to listening script 8.1 on page 154 to compare your answers with the words in context.

1. We work in a high-pressure environment and so we demand total <u>commitment</u> from our staff. *commit*
2. They tried to improve their _____ by calling in a firm of management consultants. *compete*
3. Departmental _____ between Marketing and Production have damaged the firm's reputation. *rival*
4. I've always admired her high level of _____. *profession*
5. The CEO should focus on _____ issues, not day-to-day management. *strategy*
6. The firm changed its _____ policy to hire people from ethnic minorities. *recruit*
7. I thought some of their _____ were totally unrealistic. *recommend*
8. We managed to uncover some important market _____. *intelligent*

> **YOUR TURN!**
>
> Read the quotation below.
> 'If you want to make enemies, try to change something.' Woodrow Wilson, American president (1913–21)
> 1. Can you think of a situation when this happened to you?
> 2. Are you the sort of person who welcomes change or do you prefer to keep things as they are?

GRAMMAR
Verb patterns

1   **Study the example sentence. Which verb is followed by the infinitive? Which verb is followed by the gerund?**

When a consultancy tries to introduce change, it means working closely with the people involved.

2   **Now look at the verbs in the box below.**

avoid	plan	suggest	manage
finish	look forward to	hope	refuse
agree	enjoy	be interested in	tend

1. Which are followed by a verb in the infinitive? Which are followed by the gerund?
2. Create five sentences about yourself using a selection of these verbs.

3   **Some verbs can take the gerund or the infinitive. How does the meaning change according to the form used in 1–5?**

1. a   Before you do anything, stop to think about our overall strategy.
   b   Stop thinking about strategy and find some new customers!
2. a   Oh, no! I didn't remember to bring the report. Can you make me a copy?
   b   I don't remember bringing the report to that meeting.
3. a   I tried to speak to the boss but he wasn't interested in listening to me.
   b   I tried speaking to the boss and phoning our suppliers but nothing worked.
4. a   We meant to inform her but we completely forgot.
   b   The damage meant spending £30,000 on repairs.
5. a   She started as a PA and went on to become the Group Manager.
   b   She went on working for the company even after they refused her a pay rise.

4   **Turn to listening script 8.1 on page 154. Identify the gerund and infinitive forms and say why they are used.**

See page 138 of the grammar guide.

Staying competitive

READING

1 What are the biggest drinks manufacturers in your country? How competitive is their promotion of their products?

2 Read the text on page 79 about the rivalry between the world's two biggest beer companies and answer questions 1–3.

1 Why can Anheuser-Busch claim to be the world's most important brewer?
2 How did the Belgian beer company Interbrew grow to become the world's biggest brewer?
3 Complete the table below comparing the two rivals.

	ANHEUSER-BUSCH	INTERBREWAMBEV
Brands		
Strengths		
Weaknesses		
Geographical influence		

3 Which firm is in the strongest position to contest domination of the world beer market?

4 Match words from the text in the beginnings of sentences 1–5 with their endings a–e.

1 We are currently *bidding* to … ……
2 The *merger* between the two rival companies … ……
3 They bought enough shares to *gain a controlling interest*, … ……
4 The *acquisition* of our main supplier … ……
5 This *joint venture* with a Mexican telecommunications company… ……

a … will mean that we can direct their production to our needs.
b … should be in the mutual interest of both.
c … take over our main competitor.
d … means we can gain their local knowledge while they gain our expertise.
e … so they were able to force their own appointee to be chairman of the board.

5 Look at the text below on types of merger. Which kind of merger is described in the text on page 79? Can you think of other examples of horizontal or vertical mergers?

> **Types of Merger**
>
> **Horizontal**
> Two companies making the same product combine
>
> **Vertical**
> A company merges with another company in an immediately related stage of production / distribution

YOUR TURN!

1 What is the difference between a joint venture and a merger?
2 How many reasons can you think of to explain why a company should take over another one?
3 Which of the two great rival companies in the reading would you invest in?
4 How much control do you think governments should have over mergers and acquisitions?

Anheuser-Busch
Budweiser®   Tsingtao beer®

InterbrewAmBev
Beck's®   Brahma®   Stella Artois®

Anheuser-Busch makes Budweiser, the world's biggest-selling beer. The company's beers account for 48% of the US market and 11% of world beer consumption. Thanks to its dominance in the lucrative US market, it makes 25% of global brewing revenues. It had risen to become the world's biggest brewer. That is until Belgian brewer Interbrew, the company behind Stella Artois and Beck's, paid around €9.2 bn for a 57% controlling interest in Brazil's AmBev, the makers of Brahma. AmBev is Latin America's largest brewer, selling a third of the region's beer. InterbrewAmBev will overtake Anheuser-Busch to become the world's largest brewer by volume. Interbrew chief executive John Brock was bullish about the merger. 'Putting these companies together is a match made in heaven,' he said.

Anheuser-Busch itself had been considering a move on AmBev and has seemed unsure how to react. Its reliance on Budweiser, while the reason for the company's success, may be at the root of its future problems. Its major competitors are global brewers with revenue sources distributed around the world. By contrast the brewer of Budweiser derives 80% of its income from the US. It is thus caught in homeland honey-trap, a position made more difficult by stagnant beer consumption. Its overseas ventures have lacked conviction. In 1993 it bought 50.2% of Mexico's Grupo Modelo, but lacks operational control of what is basically a Mexican-oriented brewer. Anheuser-Busch has also invested noisily, but modestly (9.9%) in China's Tsingtao brewery. Although its products sell in 80 markets, its presence outside the US is weak.

Whereas Anheuser-Busch has largely built its reputation on the Budweiser brand, Interbrew has done it differently, growing through a series of acquisitions. In the 1980s it concentrated on purchases in Belgium and the Netherlands, but since 1991 its growth has been more dramatic and global, buying or launching joint ventures in Canada, the UK and Germany. Interbrew's acquisition of AmBev will give the company more leverage in Latin America just as demand stalls in Europe and the US. 'Brewing is a business where if you want to make a profit you have to be global,' said Johan Van Geeteruyen of Petercam in Brussels.

Even so, while Interbrew may have taken the initiative away from the American giant, Anheuser-Busch has many assets in the coming fight for the world's beer market: a strong balance sheet, clear lines of management and a brand with global potential. It is inevitable that the company will be bidding for other companies around the world. For Interbrew there is the danger of growing too far, too fast. Interbrew will have to prove that it is as good at running and managing businesses as buying them. At the time of his appointment Brock said there were 'terrible tales of acquisitions that went bad, largely because they didn't get integrated properly.' Interbrew shareholders will hope that he listens to his own advice.

The Business

LANGUAGE FOR
making presentations

1 Max Wilkes is a management consultant. Read his introduction to a presentation and find out how he:

- states his aims
- tells his audience about the different stages of the presentation
- thanks the audience for their cooperation.

'Good morning everybody. As you know I'm here today to present the findings and share our suggestions with you. First of all, I'll outline the firm's current position and talk you through the evidence. Next, I will propose some immediate steps it should take. Finally, we shall put forward some recommendations for the longer term and discuss the alternatives. However, before I begin, on behalf of the entire team I'd like to thank you all for your openness and cooperation. We all appreciate how difficult it is to be under the microscope.'

2 Match introductory phrases 1–10 to endings a–j.

1 Let's take a look at … ……
2 If you'd like to … ……
3 As you can see, … ……
4 I'd like to draw your attention … ……
5 Right, I'm going to begin by … ……
6 So what can we … ……
7 I'd like to hand you over … ……
8 Sylvie will be talking you … ……
9 This brings me to the other key issue, … ……
10 Finally, I shall attempt to outline … ……

a … this pie chart reveals two other worrying features.
b … running through our main findings.
c … the evidence, shall we?
d … through our short-term recommendations.
e … a longer-term strategy for growth.
f … namely, the company's image.
g … learn from all of this?
h … to the following market intelligence.
i … open the report on page four.
j … to my colleague, Sylvie Grey.

3 🔊 8 2 Listen and check your answers.

SPEAKING

1 **Electrical appliances such as coffee makers are popular consumer goods.**

   1 How has their range and design changed over the last fifteen to twenty years?
   2 What has happened to their price and quality?

2 **Caetano has produced high quality coffee makers since its foundation in 1963. However, in recent years sales have fallen dramatically. You are management consultants who have carried out a study for Caetano.**

   1 You are going to make a presentation based on the notes and graphs below. Work in groups of three or four. Study the notes and label the graphs and diagrams.
   2 What abbreviations are used in the notes? What do they mean?

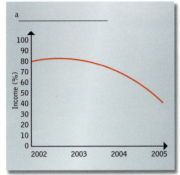

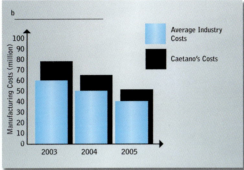

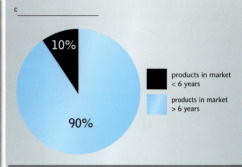

background:
- old management teams resigned / you invited by chairman to conduct in-depth research.
- research findings: discuss data from graphs
- market position – research:
- Many existing users middle-aged couples.
- Young couples, 75% women 25–40 think Caetano is old-fashioned and v. expensive.
- Design and quality as impt. as cost, quality.

Conclusions
- No reason for decline to stop w/ market conditions not changing. Immediate action essential.
- Must renew image and appeal to new generations of consumers.

Options
- Your own ideas for how to save the company.

3 Use the notes to prepare a presentation to Caetano's senior management. Decide who will give the different sections of the presentation, including the introduction. Try to use words and phrases from the Language for section on page 80.

Staying competitive

> **Tip**
>
> The management expert and writer Michael Porter has broken down the rules of competitive forces:
> - the entry of new competitors
> - the threat of substitutes
> - the bargaining power of buyers
> - the bargaining power of suppliers
> - the existing rivalry between competitors.

CASE STUDY

1 **Read the background information on Bibliofile and discuss answers to the questions.**

   1 What strategic mistakes has Bibliofile made in recent years?
   2 Compare Bibliofile's case with the tip box. Does Bibliofile's case match Michael Porter's theory on competition?

Bibliofile

Bibliofile is a magazine publisher and mail-order book company founded in 1982 by Rona Kenton. The company's business mainly comes through The Bibliofile Quarterly. This is a magazine containing reviews and interviews with authors. Readers pay a £20 annual subscription and can use the magazine to order from Bibliofile's catalogue. For twenty-five years it was a lifeline for British people who live abroad. However, in the past four years subscriptions have fallen from a peak of 110,000 to 37,000.

One problem is that recently price protection on UK-published books has disappeared. UK bookshops are able to offer books at discount rates like any supermarket. Bibliofile has always followed a no-discount policy.

The company has also been worried by online competition. Kenton understood the threat posed by the Internet but wanted to see what her competitors would do before making a heavy investment in online selling. Three years ago £185,000 was invested on a website and online version of the magazine. This has been the responsibility of Keating's daughter-in-law, Marina. Another £80,000 is planned for this year. However, the online ordering system is unreliable and often crashes.

2 Study the comments made by employees at Bibliofile. How optimistic do you feel about the firm's future?

'Our biggest mistake was not reacting early enough. It's Rona Kenton's fault. We told her things were changing but she just stuck her head in the sand. We'll never catch our rivals up now.'

'The biggest mistake was when Kenton asked her daughter-in-law to design the website. I say we should call in the professionals! We need to make our website different. We need to have book experts available online and add a forum where customers can chat with writers and other book lovers.'

'I feel certain that our customers appreciate the Bibliofile magazine, and will continue to order books from us. There's still a place for mail-order booksellers, even in the days of the Internet.'

'Bibliofile needs to stop being a generalist company and concentrate on a niche market such as cookery or gardening, and establish a brand that stands for better and personalized service.'

'The days of mail-order book selling from printed catalogues are dead. We either need to go for e-commerce in a big way or close down before we lose any more money.'

'We've just been pouring money down the drain on this website. Either we need to invest a fortune or not bother at all. But Marina, Rona Kenton's daughter-in-law, is just a useless amateur and our livelihoods depend on her.'

'I'm sure we can get subscribers back if we make our magazine more attractive. We offer a fantastic service, and people love our reviews. Book lovers do not buy just on price.'

3 Work in groups and create a strategy which will ensure Bibliofile's short- and longer-term survival.

WRITING

1 Writing a report requires formal language. Sentences a–h below come from a formal report. Match them to the part of the report in the box below.

> options
> recommendations and conclusions
> background
> results

a Clearly, immediate action must be taken to guarantee short-term survival.

b One possibility is to design a completely new product range.

c Design and style are as important as quality and durability in determining choice.

d Caetano should immediately hire a world-class designer to produce a new range of products and give a kick-start to our search for competitiveness.

e One possibility is to find a buyer for the Caetano name and trademark, or a company to manufacture under licence.

f Following the resignation of the old management team, we were invited to evaluate the company's position vis-à-vis management-level recruitment.

g The company should consider locating production abroad whilst maintaining our current level of professionalism.

h We conducted research among consumers of a wide age range. Some had purchased Caetano products. Others had purchased a coffee-maker within the past year.

2 Read about the language of reports in the tip.

3 In sentences a–h in **1** find one example of:

- an adverbial phrase
- the infinitive used to introduce new options
- the passive voice.

4 In sentences a–h in **1** find more formal words which mean:

asked	bought	think about
make sure	give a job to	do (research)

5 Think of a company you know which is in danger of going out of business, or which needs improvement. It could be a company, a shop, or a service (such as a hairdressing salon). Write a report explaining how this company could develop its business to stay competitive.

Tip

Reports

- often use the passive voice instead of the active
- introduce options using the infinitive
- may begin sentences with an adverbial phrase, e.g. *As a result, the decision to introduce variable pricing was taken.*
- use more formal vocabulary, e.g. *undertake* (rather than *agree*), *retail outlet* (rather than *shop*).

8 Staying competitive

VIDEO CD-ROM INTERVIEW

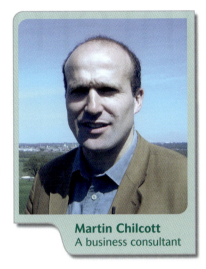

Martin Chilcott
A business consultant

1 **PAUSE FOR THOUGHT:** You are going to hear Martin talking about his job. Before you watch, decide which of the characteristics below you think a business consultant should have, and add two more of your own.

a good listener ......   tough ....
diplomatic ......   experienced ....

2 Now watch **8 Staying competitive, INTERVIEW**. Compare your answers in **1** with what Martin says.

3 Watch **8 Staying competitive, INTERVIEW**, again. As you listen, look at the spidergram below, and tick each part as Martin mentions it. Then watch again, and add to the diagram yourself.

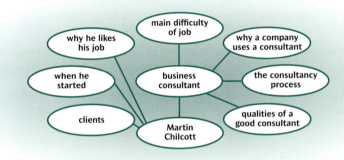

LANGUAGE REVIEW

1 Before you watch, complete the sentences below for yourself.

  1 I intended .... , but ....
  2 I (try / solve) .... a problem by ....
  3 I (like / relax) .... by ....

2 Now watch **8 Staying competitive, LANGUAGE: Verb patterns**. Compare your answers in **1** with what the speakers say. Check the verb patterns you used.

WORDBANK

1 Complete the collocations from the interview in the Vocabulary notebook opposite.

2 Complete the sentences below with prepositions.

  1 We'll call ...... a consultant to help us deal with the problem.
  2 When you're involved with a project, it can be hard to step ...... and be objective.
  3 I'd like to just talk you ...... some of these ideas.
  4 I don't know this system, so it will take me some time to get .... speed.

Vocabulary notebook

a........................... a company
= buy a business

c........................... direction
= take a new route

f........................... up to problems
= deal with something that is difficult

w........................... business
= gain new clients

**Click on WORDBANK.
Practise the words in
8 Staying competitive.**

International business

TALKING BUSINESS

1 Nowadays, people are more mobile than at any other time in history. Read the information below. Should the New Zealand government be worried?

> One million New Zealanders, about one in five of the population, live abroad. Half a million live in Australia, and a further 200,000 in England. There are even 3,000 New Zealanders in the US state of Utah. Many of these expatriates are highly educated and are at the cutting edge of new technologies and academic research. They are attracted by better salaries and opportunities on offer elsewhere.

2 When a country loses a large number of talented people through emigration, it is called a 'brain drain'. Has your country suffered or benefited from a brain drain?

3 What personal experience do you, or your family, have of working and living abroad?

LISTENING

YOUR TURN!

A businessman you know has decided to start selling to overseas markets. Study what he says.
Do you agree with his thoughts?
'I don't want to bother with lots of paperwork. I want to make life as simple as possible'.
'I trust my customers and I never ask for payment until after my goods have arrived in their market'.

1 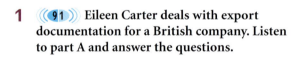 Eileen Carter deals with export documentation for a British company. Listen to part A and answer the questions.

1 What is the main concern for an exporter?
2 What is the main concern for an importer?
3 What solution is there to the problem?

2 Listen to part B and answer the questions.

1 What is the purpose of a letter of credit?
2 What is the purpose of a bill of lading?

3 Listen to part B again and put stages a–f in the correct order 1–6.

a Buyer's and seller's banks confirm details. ......
b Buyer's bank authorizes payment. ......
c Buyer and seller agree a deal. ......
d Buyer shows proof of payment and collects goods. ......
e Consignment arrives at destination. ......
f A letter of credit is set up by the buyer. ......

GRAMMAR
Passives

1 **Read sentences 1–3 below and decide which definition of use a–c best describes each sentence. Note: the *agent* = the person / thing doing the action.**

 1 The documents were taken from my desk while I was out at lunch! ......
 2 The Managing Director has been arrested for fraud. ......
 3 Wow! Michael has been given a promotion. ......

 a the agent is assumed
 b the agent is not known
 c we are more interested in what happens to someone than the agent

2 **Now study these further examples of different uses of the passive from listening script 9.1. Decide why the passive form is used in each case.**

 1 Both sides *are made to* think carefully.
 2 This promises that the exporter *will be paid*.
 3 In these cases a letter of credit *is often used*.

3 **Turn to listening script 9.1 on page 155 and find other examples of the passive.**

 See page 140 of the grammar guide.

4 **Look at sentences 1–7. Rewrite the sentence in a passive form, so that it is similar in meaning to the first sentence, as in the example.**

 1 Someone had deleted the file.
 The file had been deleted.
 2 We are doing everything to speed up your order.
 3 We have processed your request for a letter of credit.
 4 Someone stole the goods while they were in transit.
 5 I use a freight forwarder to deal with my exports.
 6 They lifted the cargo from the hold with a crane.
 7 Someone should find a way of making it more efficient.

5 **Complete the sentences by choosing between the prepositions in *italics*.**

 1 These forms have to be filled in *by / with* hand.
 2 Our products are made out *of / from* the finest ingredients.
 3 Pencil won't do. It has to be signed *in / by* ink.
 4 The goods were unloaded *by / with* a crane.
 5 Fragile goods should be transported *by / with* extreme care.
 6 Some of these carpets were woven *with / by* expert craftsmen.
 7 You could see that her shoes were made out *of / by* Italian leather.

International business

READING

1 What do you think are the benefits / risks of shipping goods by road, ship, or air?

2 You are about to read a text about container shipping. Scan the text on page 89 quickly and find out the significance of these numbers:

8th	8–10	40
100,000,000,000	3	7,000
1960s	10	2,500

3 Answer questions 1–8 below based on the article.

1. Why has container shipping been called the eighth wonder of the world?
2. When did the container revolution begin?
3. How has the Internet contributed to the container revolution?
4. How quickly has containerization grown?
5. What was wrong with the old method of loading and unloading cargo?
6. How can container ships be unloaded so quickly?
7. Have transportation costs continued to rise?
8. How has containerization contributed to international trade?

4 Complete the sentences with a word from the box below. All the words appeared in the text opposite.

cargo	cranes	freight	docks
consignment	vessel	paperwork	

1. No ships arrive at the city _____ any more. The area has been converted into a new business centre.
2. Powerful _____ load and unload the ships.
3. There are a lot of documents and other _____ to deal with.
4. We sent a _____ of components by sea three months ago but it still hasn't arrived.
5. In the old days, a ship's _____ could easily be damaged in bad weather.
6. There was a terrible accident when two _____ trains ran into each other. One was carrying bricks, the other coal.
7. A _____ is simply another word for a ship or large boat.

5 Words in context. Study the article and find words and expressions which mean:

1. made smaller
2. energetic
3. a measurement of speed at sea
4. to follow the movements of something
5. growing / expanding very quickly
6. to achieve a price.

YOUR TURN!

What for you are the wonders of the modern and business world?

A simple box which changed the world

How could a simple box become the eighth wonder of the world? The answer is before our eyes every day – the container. 'Container shipping has shrunk the planet and brought about a revolution because the cost of shipping boxes is so cheap,' says Martin Stopford of Clarksons, the shipping broker. 'People talk about the contribution of Microsoft, but container shipping has got to be among the ten most influential industries over the past thirty years.'

The simple standardized box that transformed seaborne freight in the sixties has taken on a vibrant 21st century life and the Internet may add a knot or two to the speed. With the Internet, operators have been allowed to cut paperwork and reduce reliance on middlemen. It also lets customers track their consignments more easily.

The shipping industry is booming, underpinned by solid economic growth. In the thirty years the boxes have been around, the amount of goods shipped in them has expanded at 8 to 10 per cent a year, and the industry is now worth an annual $100bn. The expansion of container shipping far outstrips growth in the world economy, historically about 3 per cent a year, and even growth in world trade, which runs up by 5 per cent a year.

Before container shipping, seaborne trade was slow and unreliable. In the early sixties, at Liverpool docks for example, ships were made to spend weeks, even months in port while they were being unloaded. And during that time a substantial proportion of the goods would be stolen, or get damaged by the weather. Today the goods are protected in a container during passage and in port. With cranes specially built to lift the containers, a ship can be in and out of a port in 10 hours, saving thousands in port charges and speeding up trade.

The world's container shipping fleet trebled in the nineties and it now accounts, by value, for more than half all cargo shipped. Ships can carry 7,000 standard containers compared with 2,000 in 1990. In 1980, to ship a 40ft container from North America to Europe would have cost $2,500. Today that cost is $2,200. With vessels getting bigger, each new one adds to capacity.

Seaborne transport is so cheap it makes sense for Nike to have its trainers made in South East Asia. And companies in remote parts of the world can snatch business from under the nose of a local producer. In fact, if moving goods by container were not so inexpensive, trading many of the products shipped around the world today would not be worthwhile. Second-hand motorcycles are shipped from America to be sold in Europe where they fetch twice the price.

The Independent

90 International business

LANGUAGE FOR
welcoming visitors

1 A group of businesspeople is visiting a textile factory which produces silk goods. Complete the guide's introduction by joining the beginnings of sentences 1–8 with endings a–h.

1 Good morning everybody, may I …
2 On behalf of Xu Silks …
3 My name is Mei and …
4 As you can see …
5 Now before we begin our tour …
6 At this point I'd also like to remind you …
7 So do be very careful and …
8 Anyway, if you'd like to gather round the display…

a … we're standing in the information centre.
b … I'd like to tell you about the production of silk.
c … have your attention, please.
d … I'd like to welcome you to our factory.
e … I'm going to be your guide today.
f … that this is a working factory.
g … I'll tell you about the silkworms which produce it.
h … please keep well back from the machinery.

2 🔊 92 Listen to the introduction and check your answers.

3 Mei describes how finished silk is produced. Using the pictures to help you, rearrange sentences a–h to put the process in the correct order.

a Only perfect cocoons are chosen, which means each one is carefully examined.
b After a month, the worms are large enough to make a cocoon.
c Each cocoon is carefully undone, which creates a fine thread.
d Several of these fine threads are twisted together to form a thicker thread that is then coloured or made into cloth.
e First of all, silk moths produce hundreds of thousands of eggs which later hatch into silkworms.
f After that the cocoons are brought to a smoking chamber where the sleeping moths are painlessly destroyed.
g Afterwards they are washed to remove the glue that holds them together.
h Once they have made their cocoons, the silkworms go to sleep.

4 Look at the sentences below. What does *which* refer to in each sentence: a single word or a complete clause?

First of all, silk moths produce hundreds of thousands of eggs which later hatch into silkworms.
Each cocoon is carefully undone, which creates a fine thread.

5 Now look again at sentences a–h in **3**. Find the relative pronouns (*which, where,* etc.). Do these relative pronouns refer to a single word or a complete clause?

9 International business

SPEAKING

1 Work in pairs. You are going to describe a process and provide a guided tour for a visitor. Using the notes and diagrams to help you, describe the process which has been outlined. Try to use words and phrases from the Language for section on page 90.

1 cocoa beans / fruit of cacao tree

2 beans / fermented / dried

3 beans cleaned / roasted / shell removed

4 cocoa beans processed → makes cocoa butter and cocoa mass

5 milk + sugar cooked together = thick liquid

6 cocoa butter / mass from 4 added to milk and sugar = creamy chocolate

7 evaporated = basic milk chocolate

8 basic milk chocolate broken up and extra cocoa butter added → final chocolate

International business

CASE STUDY

1 Work in groups. Study the background information and documents and decide:
- if Kasada should build a small or large factory
- where the factory should be built.

2 Consider the kinds of risk the plant could face in each of the proposed countries.

Background

Kasada is a computer company based in Montreal. Components manufactured abroad are imported to Canada where they are assembled. In the past three years it has been having problems with its suppliers of components, so it is going to construct its own production facility abroad. It has selected three possible locations for the factory. For the first few years members of management and core staff are likely to be expatriate Canadians.

Analysts believe that there is a 60% chance of a growing market in the next three years, and a 40% chance of a downturn.

Three potential sites for the new plant have been shortlisted. Because management do not want preconceptions to prejudice the negotiations, they are only being named as A – Asia, B – Latin America, C – Europe.

A – Asia

Financial: Wages in A are much lower than the Canadian or European average. There have been rumours of child labour. Land is also cheaper and building costs would be lower. Initial costs of a small facility would be $5 million and a large facility $7 million. The government would waive tax for the first five years to encourage investment.

Political: Although there have been no recent problems, A does have a history of warfare with two of its neighbours. There was a war in 1999 that lasted a week.

Geographic: There are only two main ports in A and both are in a bad state. Technology such as cranes and cargo shipping facilities are poor. There is a good railway system with a developed freight-carrying service, but goods still need to reach Canada by sea.

Other: English is widely spoken and there is an excellent, educated workforce that is computer-literate. Other Canadian companies have set up business in the country.

B – Latin America

Financial: Wages and construction costs are low. There is a problem with inflation which currently runs at 20%. In the last ten years inflation reached a high of 200%. Initial costs of a small facility would be $10 million and a large facility $20 million.

Political: The president is under pressure and there have been demonstrations in the streets of the capital. Nevertheless there has been no revolution in the last century and the government is a stable coalition.

Geographic: The transport infrastructure is excellent: goods could be transported by land, sea, or air. It would be in easy reach of head office in Montreal. The country is situated on a major fault line, so there is an earthquake risk.

Other: There is a high standard of education, so management and production staff would be easy to employ. A key problem has been a brain drain of talented IT staff to the USA – and these are Kasada's main recruitment need.

C – Europe

Financial: Expensive. Wages, construction, and other costs will be high. Initial costs of a small facility would be $24 million and a large facility $36 million.

Political: The country is a member of the European Union and has a very stable government. The government is keen to encourage investment in the country and has promised to waive tax for the first five years of the project. But there is a general election next year and the government could change.

Geographic: Shipping and air costs would be expensive but the transport links are good. There is a lot of paperwork connected to exporting into and out of the EU from this country.

Other: A well-educated and dynamic workforce. A key problem would be paying high enough wages to hire and keep staff. There is plenty of work in the country and employees are keen to move to further their career. Public service unions are very strong, while strict employment laws tend to favour employees over employers.

WRITING

1 Poster presentations are a common way of presenting information at conferences. Study the poster below.

1. What is the point of this poster presentation?
2. What methods can the authorities use to combat money laundering?

The battle against money laundering

Money laundering: transforming dirty money gained through criminal activity into money which looks legitimate. One way of doing this used by criminals is the purchase of large value items (boats, etc.) in cash. Mainly though, the banking sector is used.

Criminal activity is a big part of international commerce.

Why should banks worry?

Because they are legally responsible: if found guilty of facilitating money laundering, they risk prosecution, closure, and even prison for staff.

Pre-wash

The Criminals:
- deposit large sums in small amounts over a length of time, or find a friendly bank, offshore with weak regulatory control. It is very difficult to manoeuvre large amounts of cash: a pile of one million dollar bills is ten feet high!

The Banks Can:
- check ID of all people making deposits, especially with foreign exchange
- place a ceiling on cash deposits above which strict checks will be made
- demand stricter international banking laws / constant audit of staff and their activities

Soap

The Criminals:
- spin a web of deception by creating a complex trail of electronic transactions

The Banks Can:
- ensure that the money trail remains traceable: look out for warning signals like suspect financial institutions being involved in transactions

Spin-dry

The Criminals:
- put clean money back into circulation by investing in legitimate businesses
- buy shares and bonds
- transfer money into normal, law-abiding banks

The Banks Must:
- know the customer: ask for details of the client's business: documents like invoices, tax returns, etc.

2 Almost everyone in the developed world uses the Internet today, but how many of us really understand how it works? Read the article in File 16 on page 130.

3 Work in groups and decide how you will transform this information from the text in File 16 into an eye-catching poster presentation. Consider:

- the poster's layout
- what diagrams you could use to bring the presentation to life, and make the operation of the Internet clear to your audience
- how you could make it easier for a non-technical person to visualize the process
- how many stages you will include in your explanation of the process.

9 International business

VIDEO CD-ROM INTERVIEW

1 **PAUSE FOR THOUGHT:** You are going to hear Katja talking about relocating to another country for work. Before you watch, what would be the advantages and difficulties of moving to a foreign country:

   1 at work?   2 in your private life?

2 Now watch **9 International business, INTERVIEW**. Compare your answers in **1** with what Katja says.

3 Watch **9 International business, INTERVIEW**, again. Make notes on what Katja says about the places below, and the people from them.

- Germany
- France
- England / UK
- Oxford
- Developing countries and Asia
- America

Dr Katja Simon
A research scientist

LANGUAGE REVIEW

1 Watch **9 International business, LANGUAGE: Passives,** and complete the diagrams of processes described by Katja and Luke.

   1 Katja – Medical research & development

   2 Luke – Producing a record

2 Write a summary of the publishing process Catherine describes, using the diagram to help you.

WORDBANK

1 The words below are from the interview. Match them to their syllable count in the Vocabulary notebook opposite. Then write their stress patterns next to them, as in the example.

~~ambitious~~	experience	dynamic	insecure
relocation	collaboration	collaborator	

2 Complete the sentences below with two prepositions.

   1 As a research scientist, you have the opportunity to move ...... from country ...... country.
   2 If you settle .... a family, you may not want to relocate for your work any more.
   3 You come ...... a point ...... your life when you want to make a home for yourself.

Vocabulary notebook

3 SYLLABLES:
ambitious   oOo
....
....

4 SYLLABLES:
....
....
....

5 SYLLABLES:
....
....

Click on WORDBANK. Practise the words in 9 International business.

Human resources

TALKING BUSINESS

1 **Read the text about CV fraud and then answer questions 1–3 below.**

1 According to Steven Sayers, why is CV fraud so common?
2 Why do you think Experian's service has become so popular with businesses?
3 How dishonest is it for candidates to exaggerate on a CV?

> Experian, a company specializing in checking CVs, completes between five and six hundred checks a week. Steven Sayers of Experian claims that 75% of CVs carry embellishments while 25% contain complete lies. 'The job market has become increasingly competitive,' said Mr Sayers. 'People will do anything to ensure that they get on shortlists. They think the CV is just a tool to get them inside – into an interview'. For about €80 Experian constructs a highly detailed picture of each applicant, investigating everything from date of birth and school records to specific projects undertaken at previous jobs.
>
> Independent on Sunday

2 **How far would you go to get the job of your dreams?**

10 Human resources

LISTENING

1 Look at this list of ways of finding a job or getting an interview. Do you have personal experience of any of them?

1. careers and placement services
2. family contacts
3. networking and professional contacts
4. responding to advertisements
5. speculative applications made by approaching organizations directly
6. being headhunted

2 10.1 Listen to six people describing how they got their current job.

1. Match the methods from **1** to person a–f in the table below.
2. Listen again. Each person describes how they feel about their jobs and how they are rewarded. Complete the second and third columns in the table.

Person	Method	How he / she feels about job	How he / she is rewarded
a			
b			
c			
d			
e			
f			

3. Look at the ways of finding a job in the table above. Are any of these methods used in your country?

3 What is the difference between the following words?

1. a *demanding* job and a *challenging* job
2. a job which is *worthwhile* and one which is *rewarding*
3. a person who is *skilled* and one who is *talented*
4. a *dead-end job* and one *with prospects*
5. the next *rung on a ladder* and *a stepping stone*
6. to *pull strings for* someone and *to headhunt* them
7. a good *aptitude* and a bad *attitude*
8. a *golden hello* and *golden handcuffs*

YOUR TURN!

1 Read about the elevator test. How difficult do you think it is?

You have been called to the final interview for the job of your dreams. For years you have planned and prepared yourself for this moment. You are about to talk to the Managing Director, who will make the final decision, when suddenly the phone rings. There is a crisis and she has to leave immediately, but she asks you to take the lift with her. As the doors close she says, 'OK, I'm listening. Tell me why I should hire you.' The journey down takes just 60 seconds.

2 Work in groups. Take it in turns to listen or say why you should be hired. Who would get the job in your group?

Human resources

> Nicholas Ross, a helicopter pilot, has donated a kidney to save the life of his boss, billionaire businessman Kerry Packer. Mr Ross has worked for the tycoon for thirty years. He is so devoted to him he even calls him 'father'.
>
> *Evening Standard*

Tip

The City
Used in British English for the financial district in London (note capital 'C')

READING

1 Read the first text and find out the connection between the two men. How common is such loyalty?

2 You are going to read an article about how some companies try to encourage their employees to stay loyal. Before you read, discuss the questions.

1. Which sectors of the economy suffer most from staff and skills shortages?
2. What sort of organizations and businesses have a high turnover of staff?
3. What methods and incentives could companies use to prevent staff from leaving?

3 Read the article carefully and answer the questions below.

1. What is the reason for Arthur Andersen's gift to new recruits?
2. Why does Nick Page feel that it is no longer appropriate to give employees universal benefits?
3. How far do you think people can be customers as well as employees?
4. What does Microsoft do to keep its workforce happy? How successful has its policy been?
5. How do other companies try to make their employees feel at home?
6. According to Nick Page, what price does the employee pay for all these benefits?
7. How does the writer feel about attempts to make the workplace like a home or village?

So you think you **get on with** your boss? Enough for them to remember you in their will? A wealthy couple recently left money to fifteen members of staff. Whereas most employers might not go this far, there is evidence that an increasing number of firms are keen to **build up** a similar pattern of paternalistic culture of loyalty in order to attract or retain staff. Management consultants Arthur Andersen recently announced £10,000 golden hellos to graduate trainees to help them **pay off** their student debts.

Elsewhere, particularly in the City, companies are so desperate to **hold onto** staff that they will do almost anything. Increasingly companies are trying to remind stressed-out workers that the boss really cares. According to personnel expert Nick Page, the days of the wise boss **handing out** universal benefits are dead. 'Now bosses are having to wake up to the fact that their staff are both individuals and customers. Companies are having to address the diversity of lifestyles among their workforce.' In a creative business with a young staff, it's not appropriate only to offer childcare and pension plans. By contrast, many people in those types of firm **go for** pet insurance. Other companies offer grocery shopping and laundry services while one firm has even **come up with** providing fresh underwear and free toothbrushes to staff when they **stay on** late.

'If you want to keep staff then you have to **look after** them,' says Hilda Barrett, group human resources manager at Microsoft. 'That's why we try and create a campus atmosphere in our office.' At their headquarters there is an area called the 'anarchy zone' where stressed-out workers can play pool, watch TV, play video games and read the latest magazines. Despite the fact that a writer recently called the firm's employees Microserfs, the staff turnover is only 8%. 'We must be doing something right' says Barrett.

But even though forward-looking firms are **sorting out** your shopping or laundry, Nick Page believes you may **end up** working longer hours with no overtime. Many employers are attempting to restore the work-life balance by making office life more like home, often with the boss as substitute parent. Business development agency the Fourth Room has offices which are **laid out** like a house. Each morning the kitchen table is set for breakfast and a family lunch is held twice a week. British Airways has designed its head office so that it looks like a corporate village. More worryingly, staff are no longer known as employees, but residents.

The Guardian

4 Work in groups and discuss the following questions.

1. Is it possible for a business to be one big happy family?
2. In your country, how common is it for people to spend their working lives in the same organization?
3. How often do you think *you* will change your career or place of work?

GRAMMAR
Phrasal verbs

> **PHRASAL VERBS**
> A phrasal verb is a verb combined with a preposition or an adverb. This gives the verb a new meaning. Phrasal verbs are idiomatic and they follow a number of grammar rules.

1 We can often work out the meaning of a phrasal verb from its context. Match the verbs in bold in the text to the definitions in the box.

> organize / solve a problem
> finish repaying a debt
> take care of
> keep
> give / distribute
> choose
> have the idea of
> arrange
> remain after normal leaving time
> have a (good) relationship with someone
> develop
> eventually finish

2 Continue 1–6 using the phrasal verbs from the text.

1 She borrowed £8,000 to complete her studies and it took her two years _____.
2 Hi, darling, it's me. Listen, I'm going to be late for dinner. I have to _____ in the office to meet a customer.
3 I never expected to retire as the managing director. I can't believe how my career _____ so well.
4 It's natural for people to leave after a couple of years. You can't expect to _____.
5 These files are in a terrible mess. Please ask Martin to _____.
6 It's time to make a decision. Which design should we _____?

3 Not only can phrasal verbs be idiomatic, but their grammar can vary. Match the phrasal verbs in sentences 1–6 in 2 above to one of the grammar explanations a–c below.

a   a phrasal verb that needs an object
b   a phrasal verb that does not have an object
c   a phrasal verb that needs an object but that does not separate

4 Look at the pairs of sentences 1–4. One of the sentences for each question contains a grammar mistake. Identify the sentence and correct the mistake.

1   a   Our sales have gone up every year.
    b   The value of shares was gone up.
2   a   The application form was sent back because he hadn't filled in it properly.
    b   It had been filled in using pencil, not ink.
3   a   They broke into the market by cutting their prices by 20%.
    b   If we increase our sales force, we'll be able to break the market into.
4   a   We look forward to seeing you next Monday.
    b   I am looking forward to hear from you next week.

See page 142 of the grammar guide.

5 A single phrasal verb can also often have several different meanings. Study sentences a and b below.

1   In which sentence does *take in* mean understand?
2   In which sentence does *take in* mean trick or deceive?

a   She took them in with the lies in her CV.
b   I couldn't take in the instructions because they were too complicated.

6 Now identify how the meaning of each phrasal verb is different within the following pairs of sentences.

1   a   He *picked up* German during his work placement.
    b   Don't worry. Sales should *pick up* after the summer.
2   a   I can't *make* these sentences *out*. Can you ask them to send the fax again?
    b   Even though it was her fault, she *made out* it was our mistake.
3   a   Let's *take* our jackets *off* – it's very hot in here.
    b   The plane *took off* three hours late.
4   a   They have *put up* the price of oil again.
    b   I'm coming to Paris – could you *put* me *up* for a couple of nights?

7 Are there any grammatical differences in how each phrasal verb is used?

Human resources

LANGUAGE FOR
handling interview questions

1 Expand the prompts to form full questions.

1 *What / you / see / yourself* doing in five years' time?
   ....

2 *How quickly / you learn* new skills?
   ....

3 *What / be / most important thing / you learn* from your placement last summer?
   ....

4 *you / rather / be* out and about, or office-based?
   ....

5 *you / think / could* tell us about your greatest weakness?
   ....

6 *you / tell* what qualities you would bring to this job?
   ....

7 *I / like you / describe* a difficult situation you handled well.
   ....

8 *you / mind / tell / us* how much you are currently earning?
   ....

2 🔊 10 2 **Listen and check your answers to 1.**

3 🔊 10 3 **Connect the replies a–h to the interview questions above. Then listen and check your answers.**

a I'd much rather be visiting customers than be stuck behind a desk.
b Certainly. Once some important documents were lost, so I created another set.
c Mm, that's an interesting question. I'm good at learning new programming languages.
d Let me think… I'm thorough and methodical, which is essential for dealing with paperwork.
e In five years' time? I see myself running a large department, or my own business.
f I'd rather not talk about money at this stage, if you don't mind.
g I really enjoyed the teamwork.
h Well, I tend to be slow at dealing with paperwork, but I am improving.

4 Would the replies a–h in 3 impress an interviewer?

5 Work in pairs. How would you answer the interview questions from 1?

SPEAKING

1 Have you ever had a strange interview experience?

2 🔊 10.4 Listen to four people talking about interviews. Match each description 1–4 with one of the interview types below:

- one-to-one interview
- panel interview
- group interview
- serial interview.

3 Which method in **2**:

- is the most stressful for candidates?
- gives the most accurate impression of a candidate?
- is the most common in your country?

4 Work in three groups.

1 Each group should prepare interview questions for one of the posts a–c below. Try to use words and phrases from the Language for section on page 100.
  a a PA reporting to a number of managers in a medium-sized company
  b a graphic designer for a teenage magazine
  c a customer services manager dealing with angry customers from around the world
2 Make new groups and take it in turns to ask each other your questions.

CASE STUDY

1. **Read the details about Drivers Sport. What kind of person is it looking for? What profile do you think would be most suitable for this post?**

Drivers, the sports equipment company, is trying to recruit a talented salesperson to break into the golfing equipment market. It wants to recruit just one person to cover the clubs in Scotland and the north of England. The successful candidate would have to visit specialist sports suppliers and golf courses to sell its goods. They would have to spend up to six weeks a year away from home on short business trips within the sales area, and a further two weeks a year in the US or at hospitality events. The job is demanding but very rewarding.

2. **The Human Resources Manager at Drivers has received four sets of details from the employment agency it used for its initial search. In pairs, read the notes carefully and decide which two people you would like to call for interview.**

3. **Work in groups of four or five. Two / three of you should be interviewers and the other two the candidates you have selected for interview. Interviewers should spend five minutes thinking of questions they might like to ask. Candidates should spend this time inventing further personal details and predicting the questions which are likely to be asked. When you are ready, hold the interviews.**

Catherine Butcher

Age: 33

Marital status
Divorced, two small children.

Qualifications
Diploma in Marketing.

Experience
Seven years working in fashion sales and insurance.

Sales aptitude test: 10 / 10

Expected salary
€60,000 – has also made hints about a golden hello

Initial impressions from interview
Self-confident and dynamic. Very well-presented. Says she loves sales. Claims she can sell anything. However, not very knowledgeable about sport in general or golf in particular.

Notes
Reservations about her family situation. Could she travel?

Mark Paris

Age: 28

Marital status
Single.

Qualifications
BA and teaching certificate.

Experience
Two years' teaching experience – sports and gymnastics.

Sales aptitude test: 5 / 10

Expected salary
€60,000

Initial impressions from interview
Self-confident. Says that he could learn the techniques which would make him a better salesperson.

Notes
Feels that he would be able to exploit his reputation as a nationally known athlete. Successful sportsman with medals. National level. Forced to withdraw because of knee injury. Says he knows what athletes want and can speak with confidence about our different ranges.

Stuart Marsh

Age: 52

Marital status
Widowed, two grown-up children.

Qualifications
Left school at eighteen after A-levels to join army.

Experience
Army officer for ten years. Left with rank of captain. Twenty-three years of sales experience, highly skilled salesman.

Sales aptitude test: 9 / 10

Expected salary
€75,000 plus commission and usual perks.

Initial impressions from interview
Active and dynamic. Likeable. Looks younger than fifty-two. Would be able to bring clients with him. Keen tennis player.

Notes
On your instructions we approached Mr Marsh. Have heard on the grapevine that he does not get on well with the new sales manager of his existing company.

Belinda Behan

Age: 24

Marital status
Married, no children.

Qualifications
BA Ancient history. MBA in export management.

Experience
one year in family import / export business.

Sales aptitude test: 7 / 10

Expected salary
€50,000 plus commission.

Initial impressions from interview
Pleasant and charming. Well-educated and softly spoken. Not really interested in a long-term career in sales: this job may just be a stepping stone for her. Not motivated by money.

Notes
Daughter of Findley Behan, a professional golfer who won lots of competitions in the 1980s and 1990s. Plays golf herself and knows a lot about our equipment. Was found through a headhunter.

Human resources

WRITING

1 The following extracts come from three separate letters: an application letter, an invitation to an interview day, and a job offer. Reassemble the sentences 1–11 in the correct order to make a paragraph from each letter. The first line of each letter has been given on the left.

An application letter
I am writing to express an interest in the post of website analyst which was advertised in last week's edition of Bizztalk.

An invitation to an interview day
Further to your application we would like to invite you to attend an interview day at our assessment centre on 23rd June.

A job offer
I have pleasure in informing you that your job application for the above post has been successful.

1 The day will begin at 9.45 with two one-hour aptitude and psychometric tests.
2 If you still wish to take up this offer please sign and return the letter of acceptance to us by 18th September.
3 I have been searching for exactly this type of opportunity for a long time and I believe that I could have the combination of the right academic background and experience for this post.
4 After lunch there will be a group task which will be observed by members of our team.
5 This is a permanent post subject to the completion of our standard three-month trial period.
6 We should have finished by 17.45 at the latest.
7 I am a twenty-four-year-old Computer Science graduate with two years' work experience.
8 This appointment will be at scale three of our general management grade and the starting salary is currently £23,000, reviewed after six months.
9 At some point in the day you will have the opportunity to discuss your application with a member of the Human Resources department.
10 We would like to make you a provisional job offer depending on the reception of satisfactory references and original copies of your qualifications.
11 I am currently working in a computer start-up.

2 Study this advertisement, and write one of the letters below, using the examples from **1** to help you.

1 A letter from Georgi Petrov, applying for the job.
2 A letter from the Beacon Organization inviting Georgi Petrov to an interview day and explaining the timetable of the day.
3 A letter from the Beacon Organization offering Georgi Petrov the job.

The Beacon Organization seeks enthusiastic people to manage their international summer camps throughout Europe for disadvantaged teenagers. Ideal candidates will have experience of working with young people. They should be fair-minded and enthusiastic, and sensitive to different cultures and expectations. They should speak good English and be ready to lead an international team of co-workers. They should be fit and active, and willing to participate in all aspects of the camp's sporting and cultural activities. Write to the Personnel Manager at PO Box 765.

Georgi Petrov
Twenty-one-year-old Bulgarian. Studies Sports Science at the University of Wales, Swansea (last year of degree). Worked as teaching assistant in school in Burgas before degree.

10 Human resources

VIDEO CD-ROM INTERVIEW

1 **PAUSE FOR THOUGHT:** You are going to hear Ray talking about job interviews. Before you watch, imagine you are attending a job interview. What questions would you ask the interviewer about the job / company?

2 Now watch **10 Human resources, INTERVIEW**. Compare your answer in **1** with what Ray says.

3 Watch **10 Human resources, INTERVIEW**, again. Make notes on what Ray says, under the headings below.

- Suitable job candidates ....
- CVs ....
- Techniques used by interviewers ....
- Advice for interviewee ....

Ray Starkie
An employment and training adviser

LANGUAGE REVIEW

1 Watch **10 Human resources, LANGUAGE: Phrasal verbs**. Write down the seven different phrasal verbs that the speakers use.

2 Write sentences about yourself using four of the phrasal verbs from **1**.

WORDBANK

1 Find collocations from the interview. Match a word from the box below to a word in the Vocabulary notebook opposite.

| adopt | training | underplay | relevant |

2 Complete the sentences below using a collocation from the Vocabulary notebook. You may need to change the form of the verbs.

1 Don't worry too much if the interviewer .... an aggressive ....
2 A variety of .... are available to staff who wish to develop their skills.
3 You will never get a promotion if you always .... your ....
4 Please include details of .... and training courses you have completed.

3 Read the extracts from the interview below. Replace the idioms in *italics* with a phrase of your own that expresses the same meaning.

> ... [candidates] may not really have much knowledge of what is required, so they really have got to *sell themselves* from a position of slight vulnerability ...
>
> ... a candidate who gets through [aggressive questioning] can really *shine* ...
>
> ... the soft approach doesn't necessarily mean that the interviewer *is on your side*.

Vocabulary notebook

Nouns:
.... qualifications
.... opportunities

Verbs:
.... an approach
.... achievements

Click on WORDBANK. Practise the words in 10 Human resources.

Business start-up

TALKING BUSINESS

1 Read the text below about Fabio Russo.

2 Work in pairs. If Fabio makes his big decision, what does he stand to gain? What does he stand to lose?

> For the past twenty-five years Fabio Russo has been a consultant working for a major American multinational. He is a specialist in advising on pay structures. Over his successful career he has built up an enormous contacts book across a broad range of industries all over the world. Now he has decided to draw on his own experience by setting up his own company. In his preliminary plan he will be working alone with a single secretary from two converted rooms in his house.

LISTENING

1 You are going to listen to an interview with Anthea Fowler, who works for an organization called the Franchise Group. Before you listen, read the tip and discuss the questions.

1 In this arrangement, what benefits are there for:
   - the franchisor?
   - the franchisee?
2 How many franchises can you think of which operate in:
   - the fast food sector?
   - the business services sector?
   - the car industry?

Tip

Franchise

A contractual agreement in which one party (the franchisor) sells the right to market goods or services under its name to another party (the franchisee). McDonald's and Häagen-Dazs are examples of retail franchises.
The franchisee is usually given exclusive selling rights in a particular selling area.

2 **11.1** In part A, Anthea Fowler discusses becoming a franchisee. Listen and answer the questions.

1 According to Anthea, what are the advantages of taking on a franchise rather than starting an entirely new business?
2 Complete the following statistics.
   a Percentage of British businesses which are franchises: ......
   b Number of people employed in franchises: ......
   c Amount of business generated: ......
3 Decide if statements a–c are true (*T*) or false (*F*).
   Anthea believes that:
   a Franchises are the perfect way to learn about a new business. ......
   b Franchisors need to be entrepreneurs. ......
   c Franchises are good for older people. ......

11 Business start-up

3 🔊 **11.1** In part B, Anthea discusses how franchisors make their money, and the advantages for franchisees. Listen and answer questions 1–4.

1. According to Anthea, how much money should people be prepared to pay for a franchise?
2. What mistake of the interviewer's does Anthea correct?
3. Anthea describes how franchisors commonly help their franchisees. Study the list, and tick (✓) the areas she mentions. Does she mention anything else?

   national advertising ......   management systems ......
   help with recruitment ......   a logo you can use ......
   promotional material ......   reputation ......
   economies of scale ......   assistance with finance ......

4. What big advantage does a franchise holder have over a nearby, independent competitor?

4 🔊 **11.1** In part C, Anthea gives practical advice for choosing a franchise. Listen and answer the questions.

1. How should people go about finding a franchise?
2. When looking for a franchise, what information should you look for?
3. What should you do if the franchisor tries to make you sign straightaway?

YOUR TURN!

1. If you had to set up a franchise, which big company would you approach?
2. How would you raise the money to get started?

GRAMMAR
Adjective and adverb patterns

1 What is the difference between the grammar and meaning of the words in *italics* in the pairs of sentences 1–3?

1. a The agreement was *hardly* dry before they were making plans.
   b The agreement was *hard* to reach.
2. a I've been *late* quite a few times this week.
   b *Lately* I've been working a lot with middle-aged people who have been made redundant.
3. a *Nearly* always, the system is, the bigger the business, the higher the fee.
   b The exam is getting *near*.

2 Look at the pairs of adjectives and adverbs in the box below.

| actual | real | eventual | short |
| actually | really | eventually | shortly |

1. Find examples of their use in listening script 11.1 on page 157.
2. Create further sentences with these words.

3 Different structures create subtle changes in meaning.

1. Which sentence a or b below seems to express greater disappointment?
   a The price change hasn't made *much* difference in demand.
   b The price change has made *hardly any* difference in demand.
2. Which sentence c or d below seems to express less criticism?
   c The new model is *far less* reliable than the old one.
   d The new model *isn't quite as* reliable as the old one.
3. Which sentence e or f below seems to express more conviction?
   e *It's the easiest* way of going into business for inexperienced people.
   f *There's no easier* way of going into business for inexperienced people.
4. Which sentence g or h below seems to express more frustration?
   g *The longer* we stay in business, *the less* profit we seem to make.
   h *Every extra* year we stay in business, we seem to make *less* profit.

See page 135 of the grammar guide.

4 Decide what you would say in these situations, using as many of the constructions studied in **1** to **3** as possible.

1. You are convinced that the best kind of advertising is by word of mouth.
2. You have interviewed a candidate for a job. Your first impression was that the candidate was perfect, but now you feel he lacks confidence.
3. You think that building new roads will lead to the devastation of the countryside in the future.
4. You had extra memory installed on your computer, but you haven't noticed any improvement in its performance. You are disappointed.
5. You have been travelling to a meeting in a distant city by train. You thought that driving would be quicker, but you will soon be arriving at your destination – an hour quicker than it would have taken by car.

READING

1 Research by Manchester Business School has shown that family firms rarely survive past the first generation. Only a third reach the second generation, and 13% the third. Why do you think so many British family businesses are short-lived?

2 Work in pairs. Student B, turn File 17 on page 130. Student A, read text A on this page and make notes answering these questions.

1. What are the disadvantages of joining the family business as a graduate?
2. What problems can family members face when they join the family firm?
3. What should parent owners of companies do when bringing their children into the family firm?

3 When you and your partner are both ready, tell each about the text you have read. Use your answers as a guide.

A

To join or not to join?

Working in her father's manufacturing company during the school holidays and at weekends convinced Satbir Billen that she did not want to go into the family business. 'I enjoyed working there but I saw the hard work that was needed, the long, unsociable hours, the setbacks and the stress. I also saw the good things – but I had no illusions,' she explains.

After completing her degree, Satbir worked as a scientist, followed by a couple of years in public relations. Satbir's views have changed since working in PR. 'I realized that to be successful in your career, even if you're working for somebody else, you still have to work long hours and deal with stress. That's when I started to rethink my views about working for yourself: at least my father has reaped the rewards from being his own boss,' she adds.

'My brother, Jatinder, joined the family business straight from university, but decided to leave after two and a half years. He felt that because it was our father's company, he would never get the recognition he deserved. He went to work for another company for a year. However, he has now realized that working for himself is what he wants to do and he has started his own company. When my father retires he will see if he can try and run both companies,' she says. So according to Satbir, working outside the family business helps you decide whether it's right for you.

Ben Williams, a corporate psychologist, agrees that it's rarely a good idea for graduates to go straight from university into the family business. He says that graduates who do, can expect 'resentment from other people in the business who feel that they don't have the experience or ability for the jobs they are doing.' Mr Williams advises graduates to work in the outside world before joining the family business so that they can 'learn how to fail and make mistakes. If graduates entering family businesses bring outside work experience, they have something to offer other than the fact they are related to the owner,' he explains.

This is supported by Simon Lees Jones, a surveyor who joined the family business, J W Lees & Co, a brewery, after working elsewhere for several years. 'My father and uncle have a policy that before any family member joins the business they have to have worked outside the business for at least five years,' he says. Simon is now property director, his brother is sales and marketing director, and his two cousins also work in the business. 'When I joined the family business, I had to do every job, including the menial ones like cleaning and delivery. This gave me a good all-round knowledge of the business and helped me to get to know everyone. The workers now respect our dedication to the business,' he explains.

The Guardian

4 Read the other text and find out if your partner forgot any important points.

5 Complete sentences 1–6 with a phrasal verb from the box. All the phrasal verbs appear in either text A or B.

| put off | go into | hand over | step down | end up | sort out |

1 It really is time for Mr Hill to appoint a successor and _____ as Managing Director.
2 Their youngest daughter is going to _____ the business when she leaves university.
3 We need professional help to _____ the accounts – mother left them in a terrible mess.
4 Her father has got a terrible temper – it would _____ me _____ ever joining the business.
5 He should _____ the business _____ to the best person for the job, not just one of his kids!
6 If you don't make a choice, the firm will _____ without any sense of direction.

6 On page 99 of Unit 10 we looked at the grammar of phrasal verbs. What type of phrasal verbs are the ones we have just studied?

7 Find words and expressions in italics in texts A and B which mean the following:

Text A:
problems that stop progress (paragraph 1)
to gain the advantages of something (paragraph 2)
public acknowledgement that you have done something well (paragraph 3)
negative feelings caused by unfair treatment (paragraph 4)
an official and principled way of doing something (paragraph 5)

Text B:
a long-term, unpleasant, and personal argument (paragraph 1)
a bad situation you can easily get into (paragraph 2)
a time in a company where there is no leadership or direction (paragraph 3)
a person who is promoted into another one's old position (paragraph 4)

YOUR TURN!

"I'd like to introduce you to the new production manager – my son, Edward!"

Look at the cartoon on the left. One of the workers in the company has already complained:
'I've worked in this firm for seven years, and now the boss's son walks through the door. He has just finished university and thinks he can tell me how to do my job!' How would you feel in this situation?

LANGUAGE FOR
responding to requests / suggestions

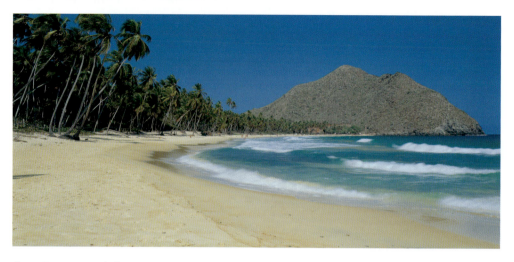

1   Vicente Cordoba is trying to gain investment for a new hotel at a beach resort in Venezuela. He is having a meeting with a potential business partner, James Myall, an investor from the USA.

  1 How will Vicente show James he has a good investment opportunity?
  2 What specific information will Vicente want to keep private?

2   ((11 2)) Listen and check your answers.

3   ((11 2)) Listen again and complete sentences a–h below.

   Part A
   a The thing is, Vicente, _____ that the project is viable.
   b I can _____ our business model is sound, and based on similar hotels in the area. _____ the tourist numbers in the area and the growth that has been forecast.

   Part B
   c All of the figures in the report _____ by the government.
   d And from talking to people in my company, we _____ that other backers would _____ to invest in Venezuela.
   e Our mother company has said that they are _____ reveal these figures.
   f I'm _____ they have to _____ for the moment.

   Part C
   g If you _____, James, I'd like to _____ the discussion of the layout of the hotel _____.
   h Perfect. I was going to suggest _____.

4   Which phrases in sentences a–h are used to:

   ■ express something certain
   ■ agree
   ■ soften a statement / unwelcome information?

SPEAKING

1. Would you like to start up your own business? If so, in which sector? What factors would you need to consider?

2. Read the situation below.
   1. What do you think of the Jubiolation concept?
   2. Would it work in your country?
   3. Would you risk your money in it?

> During a holiday in the USA last year, some young businesspeople were impressed by the number of juice bars which seem to have taken over from traditional coffee shops. On their return, they decided to bring this concept to the fashionable Covent Garden area of London and opened Jubiolation, a New York-style juice bar. Jubiolation sells fruit- and milk-based drinks and high-quality sandwiches. The company also has a policy of only using organic ingredients. Now the founders of Jubiolation would like to expand, and open up further branches in other parts of London, and in Berlin and Copenhagen. They have decided to approach Gravesen Inc., a venture capital organization, for financial backing.

3. Jubiolation have sent an initial business plan to Gravesen Inc. Read the extracts below.

Our concept
- Our drinks are extremely healthy.
- Our concept will help to encourage organic farming and help the environment.
- Modern farming methods and factory farming are to blame for recent food scares in the UK. By using only organically produced ingredients in our sandwiches, we are promising customers a healthy and nourishing alternative to fast food such as hamburgers and fries.

Experience
- One of our partners used to work in financial services for a bank.
- Another partner is a trained chef who has produced some amazing sandwich recipes.
- This chef has also created some unique fruit-juice cocktails and milk-based drinks after months of experimentation.
- Our team has youth and enthusiasm on its side.

4. Work in two groups with two or three students in each group. Group A, you are the founders of Jubiolation. Your role is to convince Gravesen to invest in your business: turn to File 18 on page 131 for your information. Group B, you are Gravesen Inc.'s representatives: turn to File 28 on page 133.

5. When both groups are ready, hold the first meeting. Try to use words and phrases from the Language for section on page 110.

CASE STUDY

1 Read the text about Angela and Maurice Butler. What has happened to both of them quite recently?

> Angela and Maurice Butler, both 47, have both recently been made redundant from their jobs in the City of London. Together, their redundancy payments total £100,000.
> They have both been looking for jobs but after multiple setbacks, they have found that opportunities for 'used' executives in their late forties are scarce. They have both ended up accepting that a franchise could be the best way of starting out again. In this way they could reap the rewards of their experience while avoiding the pitfalls that can come from starting a business from scratch. Their imagination has been caught by two possible franchise opportunities: Top Hole, and Puddings Galore.

2 Read the information about Top Hole golf ranges and the Puddings Galore franchise. Then discuss the following questions.

- What unique selling points does each business concept have?
- What potential customer groups do these franchise opportunities target?
- Which of these two opportunities would best suit Angela and Maurice?

Top Hole builds on a popular concept from Japan based on golf-firing ranges for long-range driving practice.
Players can turn up and practise their drives. These ranges are particularly popular in Japan where space is at a premium. Joining a proper golf club in the Tokyo area can cost around ¥3.5 million plus annual fees of a further several thousand. By contrast, an hour at one of the firing ranges costs just a few hundred Japanese yen. Players drive from under a covered area, and practise their drives without having to bother picking up the balls afterwards. Joining Top Hole is a chance to get in at the beginning of a completely new franchise opportunity. The green-belt area around London has been targeted as the best area for these franchises.

Puddings Galore is a café-franchise chain specializing in desserts. Each dessert is served as a giant individual portion which the average person cannot finish. The company's slogan is: 'A dessert that's a meal in itself'. An international range of desserts including Crème Brûlée, Tiramisu, Crema Catalana, Bread and Butter Pudding, and Mississippi Mud Pie are sent ready-prepared by the mother company to be cooked in the franchisees' ovens. For £4.80, customers get the dessert of their choice plus a large cup of freshly brewed Italian coffee. The company has excellent high street recognition.

3 Angela and Maurice are now seriously considering taking up one of these franchise opportunities. Study the initial details and rough costings they have obtained.

Which opportunity:

- requires the bigger investment?
- has the greatest potential?
- has more chance of breaking even quickly?

4 Would you advise Angela and Maurice to go for one of these opportunities?

Top Hole

- Four franchises are available for the green-belt area around London, one close to where Maurice and Angela live.
- Basic facilities would consist of a covered area for up to twenty players and a fenced 300 m range, as well as a small bar. Maurice and Angela feel they could use part of their land to house the business.
- Average golf clubs in this area cost around £1,000 to join. However, they usually offer a full course of eighteen holes and clubhouse facilities. Coaching is usually available from a professional.
- A lot of businesspeople and executives live in the countryside around London, from where they commute to work.
- British people tend to have more leisure time than the Japanese.

Costs
Franchise fee: £15,000 up-front joining fee for five years, plus 10% of turnover after the second year.
Equipment: £5,000
Build facilities: £200,000
Lighting (for night use): £6,000
Players pay: £10.00 for an hour's driving practice.

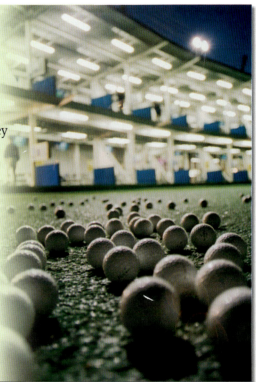

Puddings Galore

Target customers:
- Young people, before or after the movies or other evening events
- Shoppers who fancy a break

There are currently two franchising opportunities available.
- Central London in the West End where all the main theatres are based. This location attracts shoppers and people on their way to theatres and cinemas. The area is also popular with tourists and sightseers.

Costs
Franchise fee: £27,000 for three years and 10% of turnover from the second year
Lease of premises: £22,000 per year
Shop-fitting and kitchens: £30,000
Wages and charges: £12,000 per year per member of extra staff hired

- There is a variable cost of £1.50 for each Puddings Galore portion and coffee.
- Diners pay a flat charge of £4.80.

Business start-up

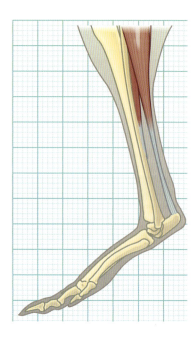

WRITING

1 Inventions sometimes result from an unlikely combination of observations and ideas. Read the information and discuss the questions.

1. How feasible do you think this invention is?
2. How popular might it be?
3. What problems could it face along the way?

> Rudi Jacobson, who has a Zoology DPhil, has come up with an idea for a new kind of shoe. Rudi wrote his thesis on the kangaroo's ability to jump long distances. He has been using this to create a new kind of heel based on the physiognomy of the kangaroo. By mimicking the kangaroo's foot, he has produced a special spring-loaded sports boot. This shoe is to be worn by athletes and other people recovering from a sports injury. The spring heel supports the injured foot and helps strengthen damaged muscle. He has protected his invention with international patents. Now, Rudi needs to raise finance to take his invention to a more advanced stage and into mass production.

2 Rudi is writing to the venture capital organization, Gravesen Inc. Reorganize the jumbled letter a–i according to steps 1–9 below.

1. Who I am and why I am writing.
2. The idea.
3. Developing the idea.
4. Measure of our success so far.
5. Our next step.
6. Why I need your help.
7. What we could achieve together.
8. Enclosures.
9. Willingness to meet and discuss the proposal further.

Dear Gravesen Inc.,

a *In this belief*, I have dedicated the past year to the development of a prototype boot. A crowd gathered around us as soon as we began testing it at a race track in Crystal Palace.

b I would welcome the opportunity to see you in person and discuss my plans and requirements in further detail. In the meantime, I trust that you will respect the confidentiality of all aspects of our discussion.

c I believe that your *financial expertise*, combined with my keen understanding of the technology and mechanics involved, could bring *this dream* to fruition.

d I am writing to you with a business investment opportunity which I feel sure will be of interest. I am a qualified zoologist who has developed a concept which will revolutionize sports and other injury recovery.

e *Having proved* that the invention can work, my ambition is now to bring it to a mass market.

f Enclosed is a preliminary business plan for your consideration.

g *This innovation* has resulted from research in which I concluded that it would be possible to design a boot that aided the recovery of ankle and heel injuries, based on my research into the jumping action of the kangaroo.

h *However*, I recognize that doing so will require the financial backing of an organization such as yours, which shares my vision and enthusiasm.

i *Their interest* demonstrates the device's enormous potential.

Yours sincerely,

Dr Rudi Jacobson DPhil, Oxon.

3 How did the words and phrases in *italics* help you to put the letter in order?

4 To avoid repeating the same word too many times in a text, we can use a synonym or pronoun. How many different words are used to refer to the boots in the letter?

5 Now look back at Speaking on page 111. The founders of the Jubiolation juice bar would also have had to contact Gravesen Inc. before being granted an interview. Write the letter they would have sent.

11 Business start-up 115

VIDEO CD-ROM INTERVIEW

1 **PAUSE FOR THOUGHT:** You are going to hear Catherine and Luke talking about their publishing business. Before you watch, can you think of any innovative ways for a small publisher to promote a new book?

2 Now watch **11 Business start-up, INTERVIEW**. Compare your answer in **1** with what Catherine says.

3 Watch **11 Business start-up, INTERVIEW**, again. Make notes on what Catherine and Luke say, under the headings below, as in the example.

| Hilltop Publishing
small family business | Catherine Croydon
Director | Luke Croydon | Dave Croydon |

| Positive points of running your own business | Difficulties in running your own business | What to do before starting a business |

Catherine & Luke Croydon
A family business

LANGUAGE REVIEW

1 Watch **1 Target markets, LANGUAGE: Adjective and adverb patterns**. Write a summary of what each speaker says, using phrases from the box below. You should use each phrase once.

| some day | not nearly as | in the future | one day | far more |

2 Answer the questions below for yourself. Include one of the expressions in *italics*.

   1 What is your ambition, as far as work is concerned?
      eventually / one day / some day
   2 What false impressions do people have of your country?
      but in fact / but actually
   3 Compare yourself now to yourself ten years ago.
      far less / not quite as / not nearly as

WORDBANK

1 Find collocations from the interview. Match a word from the box below to words in the Vocabulary notebook opposite.

| touch | marketing | independents | level |

2 Write a definition below the collocations in the Vocabulary notebook opposite.

3 Complete the sentences below with a preposition.

   1 If you need to raise capital, there are several avenues open ..... you.
   2 We are aiming to key ..... to the tourist industry, by offering tours of the factory.
   3 ..... hindsight, we shouldn't have borrowed so much money.
   4 I finally decided to plunge ..... with both feet, and start my own company.

Vocabulary notebook

_____ of expertise
= _____
  _____

personal _____
= _____
  _____

small _____
= _____
  _____

_____ plan
= _____
  _____

**Click on WORDBANK.
Practise the words in
11 Business start-up.**

Reputations

TALKING BUSINESS

1 **French champagne producers have successfully stopped other makers of sparkling wine from calling their products champagne.**

   1 How do you think French producers managed to do this?
   2 What products from your country have an international reputation?
   3 How easy is it to build and protect a reputation?

LISTENING

1 **12.1** Charlotte Gadsby, a motoring expert, talks to Gavin Strange. In part A, Charlotte and Gavin discuss how a manufacturer's reputation can change. Listen and answer questions 1–4 below.

   1 How easy is it for a company to regain a good reputation once it is lost?
   2 How bad was Skoda's reputation in the UK?
   3 What was the turning point for the company?
   4 How did Skoda win back the trust of the public?

2 **12.1** Listen to part B of the recording. What is the Skoda Superb? How is it different to other vehicles in the Skoda range?

3 Marketing people sometimes use the VALS classifications to describe consumers.

1. Read the business tip on VALS segmentation.
2. Listen to part B again and explain what kind of car the following groups would buy:
   achievers _____
   emulators _____
   survivors. _____

4 Below are some of the words used to describe reputations in listening script 12.1.

1. Which two words carry a negative connotation?
2. Which two words can be made negative by using the prefix *un-*?
3. Write definitions for the following words from listening script 12.1 on page 158, as in the example. Try to get the meaning from the context.

   luxury: *a luxury item is made of the highest quality and sold at a very high price*
   renowned: _____
   prestigious: _____
   notorious: _____
   legendary: _____
   maligned: _____
   eminent: _____
   reliable: _____
   trustworthy: _____

5 Listening to native English speakers often involves hearing a lot of idiomatic language. Work in pairs. Look at the phrases in *italics* below and see if you can guess the meaning. All of the phrases come from the listening script. Do you have similar expressions in your language?

1. Once a car manufacturer develops a *lousy* reputation, is it possible to live it down?
2. How did they manage to *shake off* the brand's poor reputation?
3. The Skoda Superb has been *resurrected*, hasn't it?
4. One of the reasons these other cars are prized is because they are *status symbols*.
5. So, basically, it *boils down to* the *snob appeal* of the brand name.

> **Tip**
>
> **VALS Segmentation (Values and Lifestyles)**
>
> **Belongers** – people happy to live in a traditional way.
>
> **Achievers** – successful and prosperous people who have reached the top of their profession.
>
> **Emulators** – young people who want to become achievers.
>
> **Societally conscious** – people who belong to groups and wish to work with groups.
>
> **Survivors** – old people, retired people, those who believe they have no future.
>
> **Integrated** – people who are satisfied with their way of living and have a strong inner life.
>
> *Peter Collins Publishing Dictionary of Marketing 2nd Edition*

YOUR TURN!

On your own, quickly fill in the statements with the name of manufacturers of different types of good. Then work in groups or pairs. Compare your answers and explain why you think these companies have good or bad reputations.

1. The best manufacturer in my country is _____.
2. In the next three years _____ will disappear as a brand.
3. It's true that _____ used to have a really good reputation, but that's all in the past.

READING

1 Read the text about Puma quickly and find out what these numbers refer to.

| 26 | 29 | 60s | 250,000,000 | 1993 | 168.71 | 1,500,000 |

2 Summarize the changes that Jochen Zeitz made in these three key areas:
- personnel / management
- marketing
- production.

3 How has the company's philosophy changed under Jochen Zeitz?

4 Is he a business 'hero'?

Focusing on Armchair Athletes, Puma Becomes a Leader

Pelé wore Puma in the 1970 World Cup

Ten years ago, the German footwear maker Puma was on the brink of bankruptcy, struggling under eight years of losses, $250 million in debt, and a warehouse filled with 1.5 million pairs of cheap sneakers. How times have changed. Last month, Puma said that it made a profit for the 10th straight year.

The architect of Puma's turnaround is its chief executive, Jochen Zeitz, who has been labeled a wunderkind in a country of gray-haired chiefs in their mid-60s.

'One of the reasons we are successful today is because we went a completely different route,' Mr Zeitz, who became chief executive in March 1993 at the age of 29, said in an interview. 'This is an industry that started out serving athletes. It's not just about athletes anymore, but about people who like to wear sporting clothing because they like the look.' A crucial element in Puma's revival was Mr Zeitz's decision in 1998 to make footwear and apparel aimed at consumer segments like snowboarders, car racing fans and yoga enthusiasts. Puma morphed into a fashion brand.

Puma's Frankfurt-traded shares have almost tripled in price, to 168.71 euros Thursday, since March 7, 2003. In that period, shares of Nike Inc. listed in the United States rose 56 per cent and the German shares of Adidas-Salomon, 26 per cent.

After becoming chief, Mr Zeitz closed Puma's shoe factory near its headquarters in Herzogenaurach, a town northwest of Nuremberg. He cut the workforce by almost half, eliminating a layer of vice presidents and regional managers, and shifted production to contractors in China, Vietnam and Taiwan. Former colleagues say Puma is benefiting from Mr Zeitz's eclectic, internationalist background by catering to the varying tastes of Asian, North American and European consumers. Besides his native German, Mr Zeitz speaks English, French, Spanish, Italian and Portuguese. Language skills were an advantage when he began his career devising plans to market skin care products at Colgate-Palmolive. He joined Puma's marketing department in 1988.

In March 1993, Puma was far from a challenger when Mr Zeitz, then Puma's marketing head, was chosen by the Swedish-based investor group Aritmos, Puma's majority shareholder, to become the company's fourth chief executive in four years. 'Back then, Puma was a loser, a me-too brand, with a low image and lousy performance in the U.S. and the rest of the world,' said Thore Ohlsson who at the time was chief executive of Aritmos. 'Jochen had a vision he could revitalize the brand … I believed in him, but I had to convince my board to take a chance on a 30-year-old.'

Off the field, Puma was run by production managers reluctant to part with costly German production methods even as profits slipped and Puma lost ground to Nike, Reebok and Adidas. Marketing and brand management was not a priority, said Mr Zeitz.

'When I became CEO, Puma was bankrupt on paper,' Mr Zeitz said. 'The company had been run by people who thought Germany was the center of the universe and that everything made for the German market could be exported to the world. No one thought about the consumer.'

Today, Puma still sells its trademark King soccer spike, but its two best-selling shoes are aimed more at the armchair athlete. Those are the Mostro, a walking shoe with a special sole, and the Speed Cat, modeled on shoes worn by Formula One drivers.

The New York Times

12 Reputations

5 Search the text for the words and expressions which match these definitions.

1. on the edge of financial disaster (paragraph one)
2. a place where you store your goods (paragraph one)
3. transformed itself (paragraph three)
4. moved manufacturing from one place to another (paragraph five)
5. taken from many different styles and ideas (paragraph five)
6. a product copying another company's earlier / more successful product (paragraph six)
7. put new life and energy into something (paragraph six)

GRAMMAR
The definite article

YOUR TURN!

1. When you go shopping how influenced are you by brands' or companies' reputations? Think about:
   - cosmetics and toiletries
   - electronic goods
   - clothes and shoes.
2. Where do companies' reputations come from?

1 Match examples 1–8 to the descriptions a–h of when we use the definite article (*the*).

1. Puma was a loser, a me-too brand, … Jochen had a vision he could revitalize the brand.
2. the U.S.
3. the world, the centre of the universe
4. the latest fashion
5. the armchair athlete
6. the Mostro
7. the fourth chief executive in four years
8. he cut the workforce

a. with superlatives
b. the name of a particular brand or model
c. where something is mentioned for the second time
d. some place names (where there is an 'of' in the name)
e. with ordinal numbers
f. when it is clear what we are referring to
g. where there is only one of something
h. with a singular noun for a general type (*the old, the unemployed*, etc.)

See page 137 of the grammar guide.

2 Complete sentences 1–10 with *a, the,* or ø (nothing).

1. ___ best place to buy luxury items is ___ famous department store like ___ Harrods.
2. After ___ product recall ___ company acquired ___ terrible reputation for ___ unreliability.
3. My father always said that ___ fashion was ___ waste of ___ time.
4. ___ new Mini is popular with ___ over-sixties.
5. Was ___ meeting you went to yesterday ___ success?
6. ___ new product is ___ small hand-held device for ___ businessman in ___ hurry.
7. It's ___ amazing opportunity. In fact, it's ___ best we've ever had.
8. ___ launch was ___ total disaster. ___ public didn't like ___ advertising campaign at all.
9. ___ first time she went to ___ Swiss branch she met ___ Managing Director.
10. It takes ___ long time to build ___ reputation, but you can lose it through ___ single mistake.

LANGUAGE FOR
clarifying

1 Many small businesses have to rent premises or office space. What kind of difficulties do you think could arise between landlords and tenants over:

- rent?
- the lease?
- maintaining and cleaning the premises?

2 Sally Brewer is a graphic designer who has been looking for new office premises. She has just seen a possible new location and is talking to the estate agent, Alan Judd. The problem is that Sally has been warned that the estate agent has a bad reputation. She is asking questions to find out as much information as possible.

1 (12.2) Listen to part A and answer the questions.
  a What does she like about the premises?
  b What is one of her main concerns?
  c What is the misunderstanding?
2 (12.2) Now listen to part B.
  a What is the problem with the property?
  b Do you think Sally will take the office?

3 Turn to listening script 12.2 on page 158. What words and expressions do Sally and Alan use to:

- show they don't understand?
- clarify something?
- check / recap what has just been said?

4 Study the phrases from the listening script 1–7 below and match them to the correct function a–g.

1 So what do you think of the premises …
2 One thing I'm worried about, though, is …
3 You are entitled to ten spaces in the underground car park as part of the lease.
4 As I understood it … / If I've understood correctly …
5 When exactly are they available? The premises, that is.
6 What does 'a bit of work' entail?
7 Would you like to run through anything else before we go?

a Asking for greater explanation
b Checking your own (possibly false) belief
c Explaining a contractual benefit
d Asking for opinion
e Asking for specific information
f Offering further information
g Introducing a concern

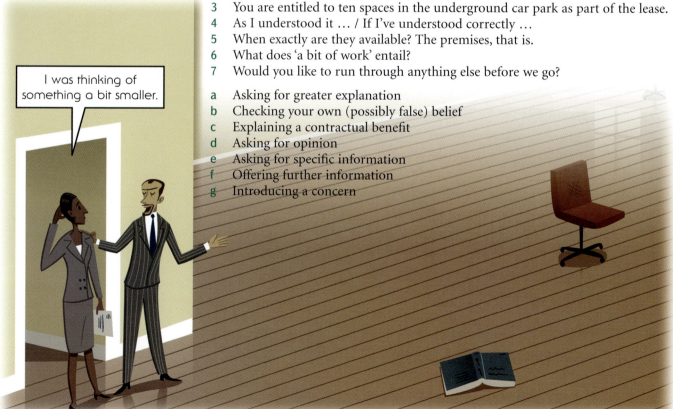

I was thinking of something a bit smaller.

12 Reputations

SPEAKING

1 Work in pairs. You are going to role-play two short meetings where you need to check and clarify information. Try to use words and phrases from the Language for section on page 120. Student A, your information is below. Student B, turn to File 21 on page 131.

2 Prepare your questions based on the information you have. Then have the meeting.

Student A
Meeting one

You wish to rent some office space through a letting agency. Student B is the letting agent. You know the company is reputable, but you want to be clear about every aspect of the contract nonetheless.
You want to know:

Lease	length of contract, renewal terms, notice period.
Rent	current rate, future increases.
Facilities	car parking, who organizes cleaning / repairs?

Meeting two

You work for Sutcliffe's cars. You receive a phone call from Student B, who wants to rent a car.

Type of vehicle	
Family saloon	seats four, air-conditioned. Special weekend rate €120 up to 150 miles (€1 per mile after this)
Insurance	fee includes insurance. For damage hirer pays first €200.
Other	payment by credit / debit card only. Two people can drive. Drivers must be 21+ and have had full driving licences for > 2 years.
Pick up	any time
Return	by 10 am Monday morning.

CASE STUDY

1 Read the details of three court cases on page 123. Decide who is the claimant (the person bringing the case to court), and the defendant (the person who has to answer the accusation) in each case. Write your answers in the second column of the table below.

Case	Participants	Claimant's Arguments	Defendant's Arguments
A	Claimant: Defendant:		
B	Claimant: Defendant:		
C	Claimant: Defendant:		

2 Work in groups and brainstorm arguments for and against the claimants and defendants. Add your arguments to the third and fourth columns of the table above.

3 Which cases do you think could be settled out of court?

4 In groups, select one of the cases and prepare the argument for either the defendant or the claimant. Think of arguments which would convince a judge.

5 When you are ready, act out the case in front of the rest of the class.

12 Reputations

A

Fanshawe Engineering is well known for its apprenticeship training schemes. However, one of its apprentices, seventeen-year-old William Hinton, was blinded in one eye while operating a machine in the factory where he was training. His parents are suing Fanshawe for negligence and failure to supervise their son. They want £1million in damages for William's loss of future earnings. William's foreman Tony Bates maintains that every time he told William to wear the glasses the boy refused because he said they were uncomfortable.

B

Farinelli Fashions sells its designer clothes in selected boutiques and department stores in the USA, Europe, and Japan. Prices are high in line with Farinelli's upmarket image and retailers sign strict agreements with Farinelli to sell at a fixed price. Domus, a large supermarket chain, has obtained large quantities of Farinelli designer jeans on the grey market and is selling them at half the normal price. Domus bought the jeans from wholesalers in less rich countries where the price controls do not apply, and from factories in less developed countries where Farinelli's jeans are made. Domus's managing director says 'We want to give our customers the chance of luxury at a fair price.' CEO Paola Farinelli is furious and alleges that Domus is acting illegally by ignoring their price controls and damaging her brand's upmarket reputation. She is taking Domus to court to make them remove her goods from the supermarket. 'How can we be in breach of contract when we never signed one?' protests a Domus representative.

C

Eventful Events is a pan-European company organizing events such as receptions and entertainment for major companies. Last month it arranged with catering firm Salvo's to supply food and drink for the first night of an important exhibition of Oriental art in a fashionable Vienna art gallery. After contacting several caterers, Eventful Events signed a contract to the value of £4,200 with Salvo's. The day before the launch, the caterer said that it had made a mistake with pricing the contract as the company had requested some very expensive items such as Japanese sushi and that the price was now £8,000. Jane Wilkins, the CEO of Eventful Events, finally agreed to the new price and signed the contract under protest. However, when the invoice arrived, she refused to pay it. Salvo's has taken Eventful Events and Jane Wilkins to court to get its invoice paid in full and claims that Eventful Events acted in bad faith.

Reputations

WRITING

1 Certain adverbs can be used with verbs or adjectives to make your language sound stronger and / or more convincing. Match the beginnings of sentences 1–7 with appropriate endings a–g.

1 Both sides are *entirely* … ……
2 They *wholeheartedly* … ……
3 They apologized … ……
4 The new guidelines are *completely* … ……
5 When I learnt she'd broken the contract, I *immediately* … ……
6 You promised … ……
7 They *deeply* … ……

a … regretted any inconvenience we had suffered.
b … satisfied with the outcome of the negotiations.
c … unsatisfactory and need to be rewritten.
d … withdrew my offer.
e … welcomed the new proposals.
f … *profusely* for the misunderstanding.
g … *faithfully* to deliver our order.

2 In written or more formal English, adverbs are often used to introduce sentences. Replace the words in *italics* with one of the adverbs from the box below.

| admittedly | regrettably | understandably |
| clearly | accordingly | hopefully |

1 *I can appreciate that* the customers were disappointed with the late delivery.
2 *If all goes well*, you should receive the package early next week.
3 *It was a shame that* I didn't receive your message before leaving the office.
4 *It's obvious that* we should have checked their bank references beforehand.
5 *We accept that* we were partly responsible for the misunderstanding.
6 *As a direct result* we decided to introduce new quality-control procedures.

3 Flavia's Natural Foods, FNF, produces a range of bottled sauces and foods which use only organically produced vegetables.

1 Recently Flavia contacted Carrie Phelps, a PR consultant. Read the press release which Carrie has written. What bad publicity has FNF received?
2 How does Carrie try to show that FNF is an ethical organization?
3 Now fill the gaps with adverbs from **1** and **2**.

Press Release

As faithful customers, you will already be aware that we take great pride in our products, which we consider to be 100% organic.

¹ ………………………, we learnt recently that a small quantity of the tomatoes used in some of the pasta sauces in our Partnership range have been contaminated. This contamination was caused by chemical sprays blowing over from a neighbouring farm. ² ………………………, there is no excuse for the occurrence of such an incident, and strict measures are now being introduced to control the distance of our crops from non-organic ones. ³ ………………………, we will be able to ensure that this type of accident never happens again.

Even though 98% of our tomatoes were ⁴ ……………………… unaffected, we ⁵ ……………………… took action and have now withdrawn all the sauces from supermarket shelves.

We, at FNF, would like to take this opportunity to thank Foodwatch for its vigilance and for bringing this story to everyone's attention, and we ⁶ ……………………… support this organization in its quest to improve the quality of our food.

4 Carrie's agency has been asked to come up with a press release defending Quayside Furniture, a company that was recently attacked in a TV documentary. Student A, you have a summary of the documentary's criticisms: turn to File 13 on page 129. Student B, you have Quayside's defence: turn to File 23 on page 132. Read your information and then work together to write a press release explaining the company's position.

12 Reputations

VIDEO CD-ROM INTERVIEW

1 **PAUSE FOR THOUGHT:** You are going to hear Annabel talking about a new variety of lemon which she has helped to promote. Before you watch, guess how this new variety might be different from ordinary lemons.

2 Now watch **12 Reputations, INTERVIEW.** Was your guess in **1** right?

3 Watch **12 Reputations, INTERVIEW,** again. Make notes on what Annabel says by building up the spidergram below.

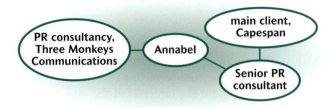

Annabel Dunstan
A senior PR consultant

LANGUAGE REVIEW

1 Before you watch, read the extracts from the interviews below, and write *a / an, the,* or no article in each gap.

> ANNABEL: Well, we've got lemons in front of us. We've just launched [1] ..... first seedless lemon on behalf of Capespan, and it's been [2] ..... fantastic story. We've had coverage in [3] ..... national press, …
>
> MATT: The brief we were given from [4] ..... Management of Post Office was to try and attract [5] ..... new users into [6] ..... post offices. It's a network that's been there since 1850 …
>
> TONY: … [7] ..... new car has just come out which combines [8] ..... electric motor with [9] ..... petrol motor, and it's fantastically economical and has [10] ..... very low emissions, and [11] ..... whole car, beyond that, is beautifully designed, …

2 Now watch **12 Reputations, LANGUAGE: Articles,** and check your answers to **1**.

GLOSSARY

Sainsbury's
one of the largest supermarkets in the UK
The Daily Mail
a popular national newspaper
GMTV
a morning television programme in the UK

WORDBANK

1 Complete the definitions below with words from the box, and match them to the collocations in the Vocabulary notebook opposite.

| magazines | considered | skills | newspapers | industry |

be .... to be a good company
.... and .... containing news about a particular ....
learning the .... necessary for representing an organization in public

2 Complete the sentences below with a preposition.

1 I read trade journals to find out what the competition is up ..... .
2 The publicity emphasizes that the company is looking ..... the future.
3 In an interview you have to get a story ..... in as little as twenty seconds.

Vocabulary notebook

have a good image
= ....

media training
= ....

trade press
= ....

Click on WORDBANK. Practise the words in 12 Reputations.

Information files

1
UNIT 1
Page 13

You have the following extra information about 'Empire':

- It is an old-established product like Sherlock but slightly less successful.
- In danger of going out of fashion.
- Suggestions: Research shows that creating a science-fiction version could be popular. A deluxe version could be produced.
- Developing a science-fiction version will cost $500,000.
- Developing a deluxe version will cost $200,000.
- Updating the game to make it more fashionable will cost $100,000.
- Dropping the game will save $300,000.

2
UNIT 7
Page 73

Student A
You are a member of senior management, working with Student B.

Grievance 1
Sales and marketing staff work longer hours than blue-collar staff. Blue-collar staff work clear shifts and are paid overtime.

It is essential for the company's future that sales staff improve foreign language skills.

Secretarial staff may have to deal with enquiries from abroad.

Blue-collar workers are lucky to have language lessons paid by the company. They are for use on holiday.

Grievance 2
Golfing weekends are part of work. They are to cement relations between suppliers, customers, and Stonebridge. Senior executives have to sacrifice their weekends to do this. Other workers can spend their time with their families.

3
UNIT 1
Page 14

Using the information below and the C1 features on page 14, write some advertising copy for a business magazine. Think about the interests of the target group.

Research shows that the scooter would appeal to young professionals aged 25–35, tired of relying on public transport which is often crowded and sometimes late. Many people in this target group perceive the City Scooter as a 'cool', fashionable form of transport. They like the idea too, of being able to wear smart city clothes, while being protected from the wind and rain. BMW is considered a very high status brand by this group.

4
UNIT 2
YOUR TURN
Page 17

Your Turn!
Work in pairs. Look at the situation below. With your partner find a solution.

Sandra Green
Sandra's business fits new windows. Her firm has a financial crisis. She is unable to pay her staff or her suppliers' invoices.
She increased her staff from six to nine people last summer.
One customer has gone bankrupt owing Sandra £40,000. She has little chance of recovering this debt.
Two other customers owe her £20,000 – she is trying to recover this.
She invested in three new vehicles last year.
She has a large loan from the bank. If the bank demands its money back, she will have to sell her assets or go into liquidation. However, she thinks that the business is basically in good shape and that this is just a temporary problem. She has six months' work on her order book.

Information files 127

5
UNIT 2
YOUR TURN
Page 19

You are going to work with Student B to complete Fred Smith's story. Each of you has four stages in the story.

1. Decide the order of the complete story by describing your stages to each other.
2. When you have finished, retell the story in the past using a variety of past tense forms.

Ten years later, Fred has 20 planes. He wants money for investment.

Fred inherits £20,000 and buys a light aircraft at an auction.

ABC merges with XYZ.

Fred Smith leaves the air force in 2000. He works in an office but dreams of flying again.

6
UNIT 6
Page 61

The team leader / external contact

The quality control team at Harper's Cameras noticed a 10% increase in costs through breakages. Members of the team are now meeting to discuss the problem.

Your role is to:

- keep the meeting running smoothly
- encourage everyone to make a contribution
- be as enthusiastic as you can – you need to motivate the others.

In addition to the breakages, some parcels have been lost on the way to the customer. Sometimes separate invoices and documents, which are sent by post, have also been lost.

7
UNIT 6
Page 64

Study the information below which gives market information about GFV, a pharmaceutical company. Use the information to write a paragraph using the language in 1–3 on page 64.

> **Company issues a profit warning.**
>
> CEO Wilfred O'Leary resigns.
>
> CEO Cheri Carbone appointed. Whizz kid. Good track record. Ex-head of research at JKL Chemicals, recently acquired by GFV. Carbone is a keen tennis player. 38 years old. American of Italian origin. Shares recover slightly.
>
> JKL launches a new anti-ageing cream.
>
> Animal rights protests outside GFV laboratories in Hertfordshire, UK. Poor publicity leads to fall in share value.
>
> Carbone announces takeover of HTY, a cutting-edge biotechnology company. Shares rise to all-time high.
>
> Scare over allergic reaction to anti-ageing cream.
>
> Carbone announces complete recall and runs TV commercials. Confidence restored in GFV. Price recovers.

8
UNIT 7
Page 74

You are the manager of Minty's nightclub. You recently received a letter of complaint from a customer: Heinrich Ball. Heinrich has complained because he recently went to the club to celebrate his eighteenth birthday. When he got there he was asked to prove his age before he could go in. Unfortunately, he didn't have his ID with him and was refused entry. He felt he was treated rudely by the people at the door and unnecessarily humiliated in front of his friends.

Write a letter of apology to Heinrich using phrases from the letter on page 74.

9
UNIT 7
Page 71

Work in pairs. In the second role-play swap roles. One of you should be the call handler, the other the customer. Try to use words and phrases from the Language for section on page 70.

Role-play 2	
Customer	You are calling about a set of kitchen knives you ordered over the Internet. You ordered the knives for $100 a month ago and they still haven't arrived, even though the company has debited your account with the money. You are so angry that you want a full refund.
Call handler	You want to be friendly and helpful. The problem was that the knives were out of stock and were only shipped yesterday. You want to keep the customer so, as a concession, you are willing to give him / her e-vouchers which will give him / her 30% off his / her next purchase. You cannot refund the money, unless the customer returns the knives: but you do not want him / her to do this.

10
UNIT 7
Page 68

1 Read article B below and complete column B of the table on page 69.

People who envy top tennis players should think about their early days on the minor tournament circuit, going from competition to competition, sleeping in cars or depressing motels. I once knew a future top tennis player who had saved enough prize money to buy a second-hand camper van to make her life more comfortable. I went with her when she went to a local dealer.

When he saw us, two girls barely out of high school, he moved into his routine. He progressed from the oldest and cheapest vehicles to the most modern deluxe versions. This locked us into the logic of his pricing. Naturally the one my friend liked best was among the most expensive. Putting on his 'favourite uncle' act he said, 'I know you've fallen in love with this, so I'd really like to help you. There is someone else who's interested, but if you paid cash, I could work out a discount.'

The words 'do it now, otherwise I'll let the other guy have it' hung in the air like an unspoken threat. Now if I'd been her, I'd have paid the money before he changed his mind, but she smiled sweetly, thanked him for his time and walked away. When I asked her why she hadn't bought it, she replied, 'I want it, but I don't want to discuss the price on his territory'.

The following day she rang him up and offered him $3,000, a fortune in those days but still less than the asking price. Naturally, the salesman protested, but he finally caved in and she got the van. He wished he hadn't let her leave the garage, but she had known that if she had tried to get a better price on his home ground, he would have simply referred her to one of the cheaper vans. And on the phone, he couldn't do this. I wish I had such cool determination. Unless you have this gift, you'll never win the big points.

I'm sure it's that which separates a champion from the rest of us. Perhaps if I'd had the same determination, I'd be as rich and famous today.

2 Work in pairs with a partner from the other group and exchange information to complete the second column of the table.

11
UNIT 1
Page 13

You have the following extra information about 'Who's there?':

- It has had an extremely successful first two years.
- It is very popular amongst families with young children.
- A computer game version was considered last year.
- Suggestion: Extend the range with different versions using film stars, sports people, or historical characters.
- Extending the range with new editions will cost $200,000 each.
- Developing a computer game will cost $1,000,000.

12
UNIT 7
Page 73

Student B

You are a member of senior management, working with Student A.

Grievance 2
The social club has caused the problem itself. There have been too many incidents of drunkenness.
The social club is really just a place for drinking: the subsidy is used more to support the subsidized bar than to pay for the football and rugby teams.

Grievance 3
You are shocked by the treatment Steffi has received. She is a highly qualified and skilled manager. It is out of the question that she will be replaced.
Sexist comments have no place in a modern factory. Workers are lucky to have training to upgrade their skills. This shows Stonebridge's commitment to all staff. Workers who strike will be sacked.

13
UNIT 12
Page 124

Student A

Read the criticisms of Quayside Furniture that were made in the TV documentary. Then follow the instructions on page 124.

1. Skilled employees are paid only the minimum wage.
2. Employees do not get proper contracts.
3. Most employees are on short-term contracts of twelve weeks which are then cancelled after a year. These employees receive no pay for public holidays.
4. There is no entitlement to sickness benefit. If an employee is sick, they don't get paid.

14
UNIT 6
Page 61

The critic / inspector

The quality control team at Harper's Cameras noticed a 10% increase in costs through breakages. Members of the team are now meeting to discuss the problem.

Your role is to:

- prevent expensive or impractical ideas
- make sure any new idea is thoroughly tested and analysed before it is put into operation.

You also want to find out where breakages occur. They may be occurring in the company's own packing department, the warehouse, with the carrier, etc.

15
UNIT 1
Page 14

Using the information below and the C1 features on page 14, write some advertising copy for a Sunday newspaper. Think about the interests of the target group.

Readers are A1 and A2 aged from thirty to seventy. They are very quality- and safety-conscious. They like the idea of being protected. Readers with student-aged children know the high accident rate among motor cyclists and would like the protective frame. They could be put off by price and buy a second-hand car instead. Parents in the countryside driving children to activities would welcome a vehicle for their children.

16
UNIT 9
Page 94

How the Internet Works

Here's what happens to a piece of data (e.g. a web page) when it is transferred over the Internet: it is broken up into a whole lot of same-sized pieces called packets. A header is added to each packet that explains where it came from, where it should end up, and how it fits in with the rest of the packets.

Each packet is sent from computer to computer until it finds its way to its destination. Each computer along the way decides where next to send the packet. This could depend on things like how busy the other computers are when the packet was received. The packets may not all take the same route.

At the destination, the packets are examined. If there are any packets missing or damaged, a message is sent asking for those packets to be resent. This continues until all the packets have been received intact. The packets are reassembled into their original form. Each computer connected to the Internet has software called TCP / IP (Transmission Control Protocol / Internet Protocol) which is responsible for receiving, sending, and checking packets. TCP / IP is the 'glue' of the Internet.

17
UNIT 11
Page 108

1 **Student B, read text B in the next column and make notes answering these questions.**

   1 What problems can family members face when they join the family firm?
   2 What should parent owners of companies do when bringing their children into the family firm?
   3 What problems can occur when family members retire?

2 **When you and your partner are both ready, tell each other about the text you have read. Use your answers as a guide.**

When a founder steps down

Handing over the family business often sets off a bitter feud. Tony Bogod, a family-firms consultant, regularly asks psychologists for help. 'Although I trained as an accountant, I now find myself working more with feelings than figures,' he says. 'I really need a leather couch in my office'. One owner-manager had *handed over* the running of his printing business to two sons. But the brothers fought furiously. Bogod says: 'One day the father phoned me up in tears, saying, "all I want is for them to be happy"'. This case follows a general trend for fathers who pass their businesses to sons. 'Father-son succession is much harder than father-daughter', says Bogod. 'When a son *goes into* the business, it is about proving himself, being competitive, and wanting to make his father proud. But with a daughter, it is about support and wanting to be there for him.' Bogod believes that starting an early discussion about passing on the business is the key to a successful handover. Even though talking to parents about retirement is hard, you should start doing it ten years before they retire.

Barbara Murray, a family-business expert, believes that failing to talk is not the only pitfall. 'A common mistake that people make,' says Murray, 'is that when they are nervous about who is going to be the next leader they try to solve the problem very quickly without exploring it properly. So it's automatically the oldest son or the daughter with the business degree who gets the company. What they should really do is have an honest look at what the business needs, then find someone who is not directly involved in the firm. The outsider can say if the skills the business needs are in the offspring.'

Before making a final choice, owner-managers should consider another factor, says Andrew Godfrey of Grant Thornton, the accountant. 'You need to know what you want to do with your business before you select a successor. Until you know where the business is going, you don't know what kind of a leader you need – is it a cost-cutting man or a marketing man?' Leaving the decision on succession to the board spells trouble, says Godfrey. 'If you don't choose, you will end up with a committee. Rule by committee is disastrous. Nothing happens, you get a business vacuum and the firm drifts.' Many families *fall out* when the company founder stays on past retirement, says Godfrey. 'There has to be a plan about how the older generation is going to exit the business. To do this they need to have enough money outside the company to make themselves financially independent.'

But choosing a successor is just too hard for a lot of owner-managers. 'The classic mistake is the father who retires and just cannot tell his children who is going to be managing director. He says, "you can *sort* it *out* when I am dead". This will keep a lid on it while he is alive. But as soon as he dies, you can be sure that the family will have its own version of world war three.'

The Sunday Times

18
UNIT 11
Page 111

You are the founders of the Jubiolation concept. Use the notes below to prepare for your meeting with Gravesen Inc.

The business environment

Target market	office workers aged 20–35. They would pay from £5–8 for a sandwich and drink.
Research	You have surveyed 200 office workers. Results show 67% were worried about the quality of their food at lunchtime. 85% would buy organic food if it was reasonably priced.
Competition	*Su-go* is a juice bar without sandwiches. They have fifteen branches in central London. *Mozzarella* is a quality sandwich bar with branches nationwide. They do not use organic ingredients but do produce high-quality lunches. They have recently experienced some resentment among their customers after the company's founder stepped down and sold the concern to a large, US-based multinational.
Investment	you have invested £50,000 of your own money and borrowed a further £120,000 from two different banks.

19
UNIT 6
Page 61

The coordinator / implementer

The quality control team at Harper's Cameras noticed a 10% increase in costs through breakages. Members of the team are now meeting to discuss the problem.

Your role is to:

- liaise with other interested parties and put the group's ideas into practice
- contact your own transport section and find out from them what the problems are
- find out from different organizations what suggestions they have for tracking deliveries and find out the price of these systems.

20
UNIT 7
Page 73

Student C

You are a union representative, working with Student D.

Grievance 1
The treatment of blue-collar workers is unfair. Sales and marketing staff are already much better paid. Learning a language will help workers to improve their prospects. They can help with technical installations in other countries. Secretarial staff at the same, or lower level, than blue-collar staff can study in work time.

There are a number of ways you could protest if you do not get what you want. You could threaten the company with:
- an overtime ban
- a strike
- work-to-rule.

21
UNIT 12
Page 121

Meeting one

You are a letting agent. You are showing a client, Student A, some office space. Student A has never rented commercial property before, so you will have to explain everything carefully. Use the information below.

Lease	contract is for two years and is renewable. Payment every three months, in advance. Rent increases annually in line with inflation. Deposit is six months' rent. Notice is six months on either side.
Facilities	the occupier is responsible for their own office area. Office has four reserved spaces in office car park. Maintenance and security is the landlord's responsibility.

Meeting two

You work for a company in London. You are looking after some overseas visitors for the weekend. You need a car from Friday evening to Monday morning. You will probably have to drive at least 250 miles. You are telephoning Sutcliffe's cars to do this.

You need to know the following:
Price	special weekend rate? type of car?
Insurance	how much? who can drive?
Details	when to pick up and return car? how to pay?

22
UNIT 7
Page 73

Student D
You are a union representative, working with Student C.

> **Grievance 2**
> The social club is at the heart of the factory. Employees can relax after a hard day's work. It is also an important centre for retired members of staff.
> The club raises money for charity, which is good for the firm's image in the community. Golf weekends cost a fortune.
>
> **Grievance 3**
> You feel Steffi is arrogant and treats older workers with contempt. She is bad-tempered and people are afraid of her. When people criticize her she accuses them of being sexist. She has no respect for workers' qualifications and experience. You want someone who is more sensitive to different cultures and working practices.

23
UNIT 12
Page 124

Read the information that Quayside Furniture had provided to Carrie Phelps, in reply to the criticisms made in the TV documentary. Then follow the instructions on page 124.

1. Quayside is a small, family-run business. It cannot afford to pay its employees more. Competition is strong and the company is struggling to stay in business.
2. The company provides work in an area of high unemployment.
3. The company only employs five full-time staff, who enjoy the same benefits as staff elsewhere in the industry. The other employees are casual workers who are employed as needed.
4. Quayside offers flexible hours to its staff. It provides an ideal solution for people who only want to work part-time, or for students looking for holiday work.
5. The problem with contracts is a temporary, administrative one. The secretary resigned without any warning and the company has not yet been able to replace her.

24
UNIT 1
Page 13

You have the following extra information about 'Bidders':

- It is expensive to produce and quite difficult to play.
- It sold fairly well in its first year but sales have fallen sharply.
- Popular with older, more sophisticated customers.
- Suggestions: Try selling it through museum shops and art galleries. Repackage for art conscious markets like Japan. Aim at the top end of the market.
- Repackaging will cost $400,000.
- Marketing in Japan and elsewhere will cost $200,000.
- Dropping the game will save $400,000 in production costs.

25
UNIT 1
Page 14

Using the information below and the C1 features on page 14, write some advertising copy for a magazine aimed at students. Think about the interests of the target group.

> This magazine appeals equally to male and female students. Many students appreciate that the scooter is very economical to run, and green. The style of the scooter would be an important aspect for this group, although part of the male readership would not like to feel over-protected.

Information files

26
UNIT 2
YOUR TURN
Page 19

You are going to work with Student A to complete Fred Smith's story. Each of you has four stages in the story.

1. Decide the order of the complete story by describing your stages to each other.
2. When you have finished, retell the story in the past using a variety of past tense forms.

Fred starts ferrying business people to Holland and Germany.

Profits fall at ABC. American rival XYZ enters European market.

ABC goes public and shares rise. Fred is now a public figure and the company is winning awards.

Fred has the idea of transporting parcels. ABC parcels is formed.

27
UNIT 6
Page 61

The ideas person

The quality control team at Harper's Cameras noticed a 10% increase in costs through breakages. Members of the team are now meeting to discuss the problem.

Your role is to come up with new ideas and creative solutions to problems. You have had the following ideas:

- use computer tracking through bar codes on all invoices and envelopes. There have been important developments in satellite tracking.
- encourage customers to pick up their own consignments by offering them a discount for doing this.
- introduce a system where a certificate has to be signed by the employee who does the packing for each shipment.

28
UNIT 11
Page 111

You are the representatives of Gravesen Inc. You are always looking for potential clients and you are interested by Jubiolation. Remember that you are a big investor: Jubiolation need you more than you need them.

The founders of Jubiolation have approached you for venture capital of £800,000. This is a small sum by your standards, but is this a market you want to go into?

You want to know:

- how convincing their business concept is
- the research they have carried out
- how much money they have invested themselves
- what Jubiolation would give you in return: you want a share in the company of around 50%. Are they prepared to hand over this degree of control?

What other questions might you ask?

29
UNIT 2
Pages 22–23

24 Your website attracts hardly any business. You realize too late that people will only buy well-established brands over the net. You become a victim of net fraud and become insolvent: debts force you out of business.
DISASTER

25 Your new range is a huge success. One of the world's foremost luxury labels offers to buy you out. You wonder if you can go even further on your own.
You decide to take the offer. **Go to 29.**
You stretch your brand to cover clothes and fragrances. **Go to 3.**

26 Your new customer places big orders but, as you expected, your profit margin is quite low. Somehow you need to reduce your outgoings.
You see some low-cost, high-quality samples from a Far Eastern jewellery manufacturer. You let them produce your designs for you. **Go to 22.**
You explain your position to your customer and try to negotiate a better deal for his / her next season's order. **Go to 7.**

27 Your previous actions have cost you a lot of money and put the future of the company in danger. Now you need to rethink your operation completely. With a new business manager you choose between these options:
You start a jewellery-making franchise teaching manufacturing techniques and supplying materials to your franchisees. **Go to 31.**
You adapt your designs as cheaper dress jewellery. Your sales strategy is to hire people to sell the products at parties of their friends. **Go to 32.**

28 The bank is horrified that you have wasted its money. It makes you liquidate all your assets to get its money back. You also have no more money to pay the mortgage on your house. You have a personal and business
DISASTER

29 The offer makes you rich and you decide to leave the rat race. You move to the South of France and become a member of the international scene. Sometimes when you see your designs advertised in expensive fashion magazines you wonder if you could have made it even bigger!
TRIUMPH

30 You know nothing about operating shops in the USA or Russia. You are wiped out and lose everything.
DISASTER

31 You underestimate the difficulty of turning ordinary people into craftspeople capable of producing high-quality jewellery which sells well.
You persevere with the franchise and improve your training. **Go to 6.**
You abandon the franchise and look for new opportunities at the San Diego Jewellery Fair. **Go to 8.**

32 The direct marketing concept is a brilliant success. Many women have been searching for bold, well-produced dress jewellery at a reasonable price. You become rich and are the topic of many business magazine articles.
TRIUMPH

33 A bad move. The customer angrily rejects the entire consignment. You are unable to find another buyer and suffer a cash-flow crisis. You cannot satisfy your creditors and go bankrupt.
DISASTER

34 The customer is not very happy but at least they accept you have acted honourably. However, you doubt whether they will place any further orders. You need to rescue your business fast!
You go to the San Diego Jewellery Fair in an attempt to make new contacts. **Go to 8.**
You decide to appoint a new business manager to help you investigate other business openings. **Go to 27.**

35 The department store rejects your new designs as too *avant-garde*. Tired and fed up, you sell your business to another jewellery manufacturer.
DISASTER

Grammar guide

ADJECTIVE AND ADVERB PATTERNS

Comparatives

Comparative adjectives are formed by adding *-er* to short adjectives; and using *more* or *less* with longer adjectives. Use comparative adjectives:

- to compare and contrast people or objects.

  *The new model is **smaller** and **less expensive than** the old one and **more convenient** to use.*

- with *the* to talk about the progressive link between actions and their results.

  ***The harder** I try, **the less** I succeed.*

- instead of the superlative.

  *Is there a **cheaper** / **less expensive** laptop **than** this one? (= is this the cheapest?)*

Use *as* + adjective + *as* to compare the way in which two things are similar.

*It's not **as heavy** / **comfortable as** the other one.*

Superlatives

Most superlatives are formed by adding *-est* to short adjectives and *the most* / *least* to long ones.

*It's **the cheapest** model but also **the least reliable**.*

Use the superlative:

- to talk about memorable experiences or events (with the present perfect + *ever* / *never*).

  *It's **the most stressful** week I've ever had.*

- to state the highest possible degree of comparison.

  *I'm expecting this interview to be **the toughest**. (tougher than all the rest)*

Adverbs are generally formed by adding *-ly* to the adjective.

To make them comparative, use *more* or *less*.

*Our ordering system has been working **more** / **less smoothly** since we made the changes.*

Note these exceptions:

ADJECTIVE	COMPARATIVE	SUPERLATIVE	ADVERB
good	better	best	well
bad	worse	worst	badly
hard	harder	hardest	hard
fast	faster	fastest	fast

Modifying adjectives and adverbs

Comparative adjectives and adverbs can be made stronger or weaker by using words like *quite, slightly, a little, a lot, considerably, substantially*.

*Our chances of getting the contract are **substantially** better than two weeks ago.*

Further patterns

too and enough

Use a positive form + *too* + adjective; or a negative form + adjective + *enough* to provide an explanation.

*She's **too young** to do the job. She is**n't old enough** to do the job.*

so and such

Use *so* and *such* clauses to express a causal relationship between clauses.

*He drove **so slowly that** they missed the beginning of the meeting.*

*He was **such a slow** driver **that** they missed the beginning of the meeting.*

Remember:

- *hardly* is an adverb meaning 'just a little'.

  *There was so much noise I could **hardly** hear a thing.*

- When certain adverbs with a negative sense begin a sentence, the subject and verb which follow are inverted.

  ***Not only does she** speak Arabic but she speaks Russian too.*

  ***No sooner had we** left than the car broke down.*

Note that some adjectives and adverbs have different meanings despite their similarity of form.

late = not on time; lately = recently
short = not tall; shortly = soon
hard = difficult, not soft; hardly = almost none

Use adverbs:

- with verbs to show how, or to what extent an action is performed.

  I **completely agree** with everything you've said.
  She **apologized profusely**.
  All our ingredients **are organically grown**.

- to modify or emphasize adjectives or other adverbs.

  I was **absolutely furious** when I heard the news.
  He drives **really quickly**.

- at the beginning of phrases or sentences to comment on what comes next. They are often used in more formal speech or writing.

  Hopefully, your car should be ready by this evening.
  (= if there are no problems)
  Clearly, we need to reconsider our credit terms.
  (= it's obvious that …)
  Regrettably, your order was damaged in transit.
  (= I'm sorry to say)

Adverbs such as *incidentally, consequently, understandably* are often used in this way.

CONDITIONALS

Zero conditional

Use the zero conditional:

- to describe a simple cause and effect.

  If you **use** that door, it **sets off** an alarm.

- to describe a scientific truth.

  If you **mix** blue with yellow, you **get** green.

First conditional

Use the first conditional:

- when you think it is likely that something will happen as the result of a future action.

  If we get the contract (condition), we**'ll celebrate**. (result)

- to make a promise or threat.

  If you **can't meet** our deadline, we**'ll have to find** another supplier.

Use *when* and *as soon as* when the first action is sure to happen.

I'll tell you **when / as soon as** we have some news.

Use *unless* meaning 'if … not' in the condition clause. Use *otherwise* before the likely result.

We'll lose the contract **unless** we give them a discount.
We'd better give them a discount. **Otherwise** we'll lose the contract.

Use *provided / as long as* to make the condition stronger.

I'll lend you my car **provided / as long as** you fill it up with petrol.

Second conditional

Use the second conditional:

- to describe a future event or outcome which we think is not very likely to happen.

  If the post **were** more reliable, we **wouldn't have to depend** on couriers.

- to express something in the present or the future which is entirely imaginary.

  If I **owned** the company, I**'d run** it differently (but I'm just an employee).

- to appear more polite in making a request.

  Would you **mind if** I **came** to work an hour late on Monday?

- to make a more delicate or indirect offer.

  What **would** you **say if** we **improved** our delivery time?

Remember:

- *could* can be used instead of *would* in second conditional sentences.

Third conditional

Use the third conditional:

- to talk about 'unreal' or imaginary past situations.

  If he **hadn't made** the phone call, he **wouldn't have heard** the news. (but he did make the call so he did hear the news)

- to express regrets.

  If I**'d known** the truth about the company, I **wouldn't have taken** the job.

If only … or *I wish …* are commonly used when we assume the listener knows the rest.

If only / I wish I'd known the truth about the firm.

Mixed conditional

The mixed conditional uses the third conditional in the condition clause and the second conditional in the result clause.

Use the mixed conditional to describe a past action with a consequence in the present.

If we**'d listened** to his advice, we **wouldn't be** in this mess now.

DETERMINERS

Determiners are used to introduce nouns. They include the articles *a / an* and *the*; *some / any / much / many / little / few / each*, and *several*.

Use the indefinite article *a / an* before a singular countable noun used in a general sense.

*They made us **an** offer.*

Use the definite article *the*:

- when mentioning something for the second time.
  *There was a letter in her postbox. It was **the** letter with details of her appointment.*
- when referring to a particular thing.
  *I'm still waiting for **the** reply from the bank.*
- for many, but not all, geographical names, titles, and names of organizations.
  ***the** Amazon; **the** Managing Director; **the** United Nations.*
- with adjectives to refer to a particular group or class.
  ***the** jobless, **the** well-off*
- for some places and amenities.
  *I'm going to **the** post office / **the** hospital. (the buildings)*

But:

I'm going home / to work. (no article)

Don't use articles:

- for plural countable nouns in a general sense.
  *I enjoy dealing with **customers**.*
- to refer to uncountable nouns.
  ***Money** is the root of all evil.*
- with abstract nouns like *information*, *help*, and *business*.

But:

For specific nouns, *the* is used.

*I hated dealing with **the** customers who came in this morning.*
***The** money she stole proves the point.*

Some and any

Use *some*:

- with plural countable nouns [C] and uncountable nouns [U].
  *We went to **some** interesting presentations [C] at the conference.*
  *She gave me **some** useful advice [U].*
- in offers and requests.
  *Would you like **some** more copies of our brochure?*
  *Could I have **some** information, please?*
- when we see what we want or when we expect the answer to be 'yes'.
  *Could you pass me **some** milk please?*
  *Are there **some** of those nice biscuits left?*

Use *any*:

- to express the idea of *all* or *nothing*.
  ***Any** decision (= all decisions) must be approved by the union.*
  *There isn't **any** reason (= is no reason) to be worried.*
- to check whether something exists or is available.
  *Are there **any** copies of last year's brochure left?*

Much and many, a lot of and lots of

Use *many* with countable nouns, and *much* with uncountable nouns.

***Many** business people have criticized the government's economic policies.*
*The new regulations have caused **much** confusion.*

A lot of / Lots of are used with countable and uncountable nouns and are commonly used instead of *much* and *many* in positive statements.

***A lot of** / **Lots of** business people take the 7.30 train.*
*The mistake caused **a lot of** / **lots of** confusion.*

Remember:

Lots of is more informal than *a lot of*.

*I've got **lots of** ideas.*
*He put made **a lot of** suggestions at the meeting.*

Much and *many* are more commonly used in questions and negative statements.

*How **much** time do we have before the others arrive?*
*We don't have **much** time left.*
*How **many** people do we expect at the meeting?*
*We're not expecting **many** people at the meeting.*

Few and a few, little and a little

Use *few / a few* with countable nouns and *little / a little* with uncountable nouns. *A few* and *a little* mean 'some', while *few* and *little* mean 'not much / many', or 'less than usual'.

***A few** (= some) managers know how to inspire trust and loyalty from their employees.*
***Few** (= not very many) managers know how to inspire trust and loyalty from their employees.*
*There's **a little** (= some) time left, so let's go through the figures again.*
*There's **little** (= not much) time left, so we'll have to go through the figures when we next meet.*

Use *a great / a large number of* with plural countable nouns and *a great deal of* with uncountable nouns to mean 'many' or 'much'.

FUTURE FORMS

English has several ways of expressing the future. The form we use depends on the circumstances and how we view the future event.

Present continuous

Use the present continuous to talk about personal arrangements and plans, particularly when we know the time and place.

*She's **leaving** for Madrid in the next few days.*

Present simple

Use the present simple to talk about schedules and timetables.

*The next flight to Amsterdam **leaves** in half an hour.*

Be going to

Use *be going to*:

- to talk about things we plan to do, or have planned to do.
  *We're **going to** expand our overseas operation next year.*
- to make predictions based on what we can see now.
  *Just look at these sales figures. We're **going to** make a loss this year.*

Future simple (will)

Use *will* (the future simple) for facts and predictions.

*Production of the new model **will** begin in June.*
*More and more countries **will** tie their currencies to the US dollar.*

- to predict the present; i.e. make a deduction based on normal behaviour
  A: *This parcel has just arrived.*
  B: *That **will** be the books I ordered.*

Be to …

Use *be to …* for news and announcements.

*The new terminal **is to** open in 2009.*

Future continuous

Use the future continuous (*will be +-ing*) to describe actions which will be in progress at a time in the future.

*Don't worry. I'**ll be waiting** for you at the airport.*

Future perfect

Use the future perfect to describe something that will have happened by a point in the future.

*We'**ll have had** our two millionth passenger by June.*

Future in the past (was going to)

Use *was going to* to introduce something which was still in the future when viewed from an earlier event.

*How could I have known that they **weren't going to** pay their bill?*

Adjectives with a future meaning

Use *bound to* when you are certain that a future event will happen.

*He's **bound to** be late – he always is.*

Use *likely to* when we think there is a high probability that something will happen.

*Unemployment is **likely to** rise next year.*

Use *due to* when something has been planned for, or is expected to happen.

*Work on the new office block is **due to** begin next month.*

GERUND AND INFINITIVE

The gerund

The gerund is a noun formed from a verb by adding *-ing*.

Use the gerund:

- after certain verbs such as *detest, involve, avoid, mind*.
  *I detest **filling** in these stupid forms.*
- as the subject or object of a sentence.
  ***Eating** and **drinking** are not permitted in the computer room.*
- after prepositions, expressions, and phrasal verbs ending in a preposition.
  *Turn off the lights **before leaving** the premises.*
  *Are you **interested in reading** this report?*
  *He was forced to **give up playing** football after the accident.*

The infinitive

Use the infinitive without *to* (base form of the verb):

- after modal verbs.
  *We **could make** the advertisement bigger.*
- after *make* (someone) and *let* (someone).
  *They can't **make us accept** their offer.*

Use the full infinitive (*to* + base form of the verb):

- to express a reason or purpose.

  She went to the bank **to take out** some money.

  They took a taxi **so as not to be** late for the appointment.

- after certain common verbs such as *want, manage, seem*.

- with verb patterns with two objects such as *encourage, request*.

  They encouraged her **to apply** for the job.

Remember:

Some verbs can take either the infinitive or the gerund: *stop, remember, try.*

This can produce:

- a small, or subtle change in meaning.

  I like to have a clear desk at the end of each day. (It's a habit of mine)

  I like helping customers find solutions to their problems. (I find it pleasurable)

  We tried to get the desk into the building. (This was our objective)

  We tried turning it and taking off its legs. (This was our method)

- or an important change in meaning.

  I remembered to cancel the appointment. (I did not forget)

  I remembered writing down their address. (I wrote the address down, then I remembered later)

  We hated telling her the news. (it was difficult for us but we did it)

  I hate to tell you this. (I haven't told you yet but I'm going to)

MODALS

Modals are auxiliary verbs which let us express concepts such as 'ability' and 'obligation', or allow us to perform a wide range of practical tasks such as making suggestions or speculating. Each modal has a number of different uses.

Can

Use *can*:

- to talk about general abilities.

  He **can speak** three languages fluently.

- to ask for permission.

  Can I **use** your phone?

- to make simple requests.

  Can you **take** me to the station?

Remember:

The simple past of *can* is *could* or *was / were able to*. The future of *can* is *to be able*.

Could

Use *could*:

- to talk about general past abilities.

  In the old days, a skilled worker **could produce** two shirts a day.

Remember:

If we want to say we managed to do something on one occasion, or after a lot of effort we tend to use *be able to*.

  *After three hours, I **was able to** make the printer work properly.*

- to discuss possibilities or options.

  We **could try** changing the colour of the packaging.

- to make more polite or formal requests or offers.

  Could we **have** a table by the window, please?

  Could you **speak** a little more slowly, please?

Must

Use *must*:

- for orders we give to ourselves.

  I **must send** in my tax form, otherwise I'll get a fine.

- for a strong prohibition or rule.

  You **mustn't smoke** anywhere in the building.

Remember:

- *Must* can sound very strong. Use *have to* or *should* to describe duties, and use *Could you* … ? to soften orders into more polite requests.

- We generally use *have to*, not *must*, in a question.

  Do I **have to** wear a uniform, or can I wear what I like?

- for a strong recommendation.

  You **must** see that film I told you about – it's brilliant.

- for making deductions and intelligent guesses.

  He **must be** Bill's son, they look so alike.

Remember:

- For a negative deduction we use *can't be*.

  Six thousand euros for that old car! They **can't be** serious (Not: ~~They mustn't be serious.~~)

- For past deductions we use *must have been / can't have been*.

  They **can't have been** happy with the news. They **must have been** quite shocked.

Have to

Use *have to*:

- to talk about duties or responsibilities.
  *When visitors come I **have to check** their ID and issue them with a badge.*
- to indicate an absence of obligation or necessity.
  *You **don't have to take** notes – I'll give you a handout at the end of the talk.*

May

Use *may*:

- to express possibility.
  *He **may** arrive ten minutes late today.*
- to ask for permission. This is generally considered more polite than *can*.
  ***May** I ask a question?*

Might

Use *might*:

- to speculate, or express a more remote possibility than *may*.
  *You **might have** some trouble clearing those goods through customs.*
- to ask a polite question or make a request.
  ***Might** I **make** a suggestion, here?*

Will

Use *will*:

- to express the future and make predictions. See **Future forms**.
- to make a spontaneous offer or decision.
  *Don't call for a taxi, **I'll give** you a lift.*
  ***I'll do** it straightaway.*
- to describe an habitual action. See Routines and habits.
- to make a request / give an order.
  ***Will** you **post** this letter for me?*

Remember:

- *Will*, like *must*, should be used with care when giving an order.
- *Shall* is only used to make offers or ask for suggestions.
  ***Shall** I **order** the tickets? What **shall** we **do** with our obsolete computers?*

Would

Use *would*:

- to make requests or give polite orders.
  ***Would** you **bring** me the bill, please?*
- to describe past habits. See Routines and habits.
- in conditional sentences. See Conditionals.

Should and ought to

Use *should* and *ought to*:

- to give advice.
  *At an interview, you **should / ought to wear** clothes you feel comfortable in.*
- to talk about what we think is morally right or correct.
  *We **should** help those less fortunate than ourselves.*
- to criticize past actions.
  *You **should / ought to have checked** their bank references before supplying the goods.*
  *You **shouldn't have let** them come in without written permission.*

We generally don't use *oughtn't to / oughtn't to have* as these phrases are difficult to say.

- to make predictions, or predict events that happen normally or regularly.
  *If we leave now, we **should get** there on time.*
  *Jane **should be** here any minute. She usually gets in around this time.*

Need

Use *needn't* to say that something is not necessary.

*You **needn't buy** any tools – the company provides everything.*

Remember:

Need can also be used as a full verb.

You don't need to buy any tools.

In the past, there is an important difference between *need* as a modal and as a full verb.

*I **needn't have bought** my tools because the company provided everything. (modal = I bought the tools but it wasn't necessary.)*

*I **didn't need to** buy any tools because the company provided everything. (full verb = it wasn't necessary to buy any tools so I didn't.)*

PASSIVE VOICE

The passive voice is used to indicate what happens to people, whereas the active voice says what people do. Use the passive:

- when the person / people who performed the action (the agent) is assumed, unimportant, or unknown.
  *The goods **were transported** to our main warehouse.*

- to change the emphasis of a sentence.
  *Ms Meredith **was elected** salesperson of the year by her customers. (not Ms Jones)*
- to describe a process.
  *Mail **is collected** before midday. This **is** then **taken** to one of our sorting stations. Where necessary, it **is flown** by light aircraft to one of the main international distribution centres.*
- for official or impersonal notices.
  *Any form of photography **is** strictly **forbidden**.*
- with a modal, without naming the agent.
  *The piracy of intellectual property **should be stopped**.*

Use *need* in a similar way with either the gerund or the passive.
  *My office **needs decorating**.*
  *My office **needs to be decorated**.*

Use reporting verbs and verbs of cognition to present claims and general opinions.
  *It **is said** that your client failed to honour the terms of the contract.*
  *The factory **is known** to produce the best glass in the whole of Bohemia.*

Remember:

The present and past perfect continuous do not have a passive form.
  *She **has been working** on her report all day. (active)*
  Her report has been being written all day.
- Intransitive verbs do not have a passive form. See **Transitive and intransitive verbs**.
- With an instrument, we often use the preposition *with*, instead of *by*.
  *The drawer was opened **with** a screwdriver (Not: by a screwdriver)*
- Past participle adjectives have a passive sense.
  *I was really bor**ed** by the presentation. (The presentation was bor**ing**.)*
- *Get* meaning 'become' + past participle can be used with a passive sense.
  *The equipment **got broken** during transit.*

Have something done (causative)

Use *have* something *done*:
- to talk about services we ask other people to perform for us.
  *We **had** the photographs in the brochure **taken** by a professional.*
- to describe misadventures and accidents.
  *He **had** his pocket **picked** on the underground.*

PAST FORMS

Past simple

Use the past simple to describe:
- a single past action or a series of completed past actions.
  *He **signed** the invoice, **put** it into an envelope, and **posted** it.*

Remember:

We can omit repeating the subject, as in the above sentence.
- past habits and states.
  *She **took** the same train to work for fifteen years.*

Past continuous

Use the past continuous:
- to set the scene at the start of a narrative.
  *Commuters **were pouring** off the trains. A lot of people **were** impatiently **waiting** for taxis and two stallholders **were** busily **selling** souvenirs.*
- to show an action was in progress when another action occurred.
  *They **were preparing** the accounts when the computer crashed.*
- to show two or more actions were in progress at the same time.
  *While we **were packing** the boxes, the secretaries **were writing** out the labels.*

Remember:

We can often omit the verb *be* and use the present participle on its own.
  *Commuters were hurrying along, (they were) **ignoring** the street vendors (who were) **trying** to catch their attention.*

Past perfect

Use the past perfect:
- to show that an action happened earlier than an action which followed.
  *When we arrived, the meeting **had** already **started**.*
- as part of a sentence expressing a past wish or regret. See Conditionals (the Third Conditional).

Remember:
- Using *after* or *before* can mean we have to use the past perfect or the gerund. *After* refers to an earlier action.
  ***After we had eaten / After having eaten** we continued the negotiations.*
- *Afterwards* introduces the next action in a sequence.

*We had lunch, and **afterwards** we continued the negotiations.*

Past perfect continuous

Use the past perfect continuous:

- to show that an action had begun and was still in progress before another action or event took place.
  *He **had been waiting** patiently for promotion for seven years before an opportunity finally came.*
- to describe repeated actions up to a point in the past.
  *Colleagues **had been taking** her biscuits and **borrowing** her stationery for years before she finally lost her temper.*

PHRASAL VERBS

Phrasal (or multi-word) verbs consist of a verb plus one or two particles. A particle can either be a preposition or an adverb, although this is not always obvious. Its meaning may not be clear from its separate parts.

Compare:

*She **looked up** the number in the phone book. (phrasal verb = consult)*

*She **looked up** when her boss came into the room. (not a phrasal verb = this simply tells us about the direction in which she looked)*

There are four main types of phrasal verb:

Type 1: intransitive (no object), e.g. *turn up*

He turned up.

Intransitive phrasal verbs do not have an object but can be followed by an adverbial or prepositional phrase.

*He turned up late **for the meeting**.*

Type 2: transitive (with object) separable, e.g. *fill in*

Transitive separable phrasal verbs have to take an object.

A full object such as a noun or someone's name, can either go *between* the verb and the particle, or *after* the particle. However, if a pronoun is used then it must come between the verb and the particle.

*He **filled** the application form / it **in**.*

*He **filled in** the application form. (Not: He filled in it.)*

Most type 2 phrasal verbs can be used in the passive.

*The form **was filled in** incorrectly.*

Remember:

Some transitive phrasal verbs cannot be used in the passive.

They came across the documents. (Not: The documents were come across.)

Type 3: transitive inseparable, e.g. *look after*

*Can you **look after** our guests / them?*

The direct object and object pronoun always follow the particle.

(Not: Can you look our guests / them after?)

Type 4: three-part transitive (phrasal prepositional), e.g. *put up with*

*I can't **put up with** it / this noise any longer.*

Remember:

The same phrasal verb can have a different meaning and a different grammar.

*The plane **took off** three hours late. (Type 1 intransitive)*
*They **took** fifty euros **off** the price as a discount for cash. (Type 2 transitive separable)*

PRESENT TENSES

Present simple

We use the present simple:

- to talk about facts, routines, and habits.
  *The factory **produces** circuit boards.*
  *I **leave** the office at half past five.*
- with adverbs of frequency, or other time expressions.
  *They **often** take on extra staff at Christmas.*
  *We eat out **from time to time**.*
- with verbs of 'having' and 'being', perception, opinion and 'thinking', and verbs expressing emotion: *be, have, need, understand, know, like, want, wish*.

Present continuous

We use the present continuous:

- to talk about activities which are happening right now.
  A: *What **are** you **doing**?*
  B: *I'**m looking** for his phone number.*
- to talk about activities which are happening around now.
  *Peter is based at the London office but he'**s helping** us out here for a few months.*
- to express a future meaning. See **Future forms**.

Remember:

Some verbs generally used in the present simple (*be, have, think*) are used with the present continuous when we want to emphasize their temporary nature.

*What **do** you **think** about globalization? (general opinion)*

*You look worried. What **are** you **thinking** about? (at this moment)*

PRESENT PERFECT

Present perfect simple

Use the present perfect simple:

- to refer to something which started in the past and continues into the present.

    They **have been** in business for ten years.

- to talk about past events when no specific time is given or implied.

    Jack **has travelled** all over the world.

- to talk about recent events where the result is still visible.

    The new model doesn't look the same. They **have changed** the shape of the body.

- with adverbs such as *yet*, *just*, and *already* (especially in British English).

    Have you **finished** that report yet?

- to refer to results.

    They **have taken** away six of our most important customers.

- with stative verbs.

    … if I **have understood** you correctly.

Present perfect continuous

Use the present perfect continuous:

- to describe continuous activities which started in the past and continue into the present.

    I've **been working** hard all day.

- to describe repeated actions up to the present.

    I've **been trying** to send this fax all day, but each time I try it won't go through.

- to emphasize an activity rather than a result.

    We've **been exporting** to the USA for years.

- to talk about a recent activity where a result is still visible.

    A: Why are your clothes all dusty?
    B: I've **been looking** for some files in the basement.

ROUTINES AND HABITS

Adverbs of frequency

Use adverbs of frequency and frequency expressions to talk about routines and habits.

- Individual adverbs (*never, rarely, seldom, sometimes, often, always*) can go between the subject and the verb.

    We **rarely** have complaints from customers.

- Longer expressions (*as a rule, most of the time*) go at the beginning or end of the sentence.

    (*Once in a while*) we have complaints from customers (*once in a while*).

Remember:

Always can be used with the present or past continuous to express annoyance or disapproval.

He's **always** upsetting her. (I wish he wouldn't)

Will and used to

Use *will* to describe expected behaviour.

A: Mr Brown kicked the photocopier.
B: Oh, yes, he **will** do that.

Use *would*, or the auxiliary *used to* + infinitive to describe past habits or routines.

After work he **would** / **used to read** the newspaper; then he **would** / **used to watch** the news.

Remember:

Only use *used to* to describe past states.

He **used to be** (Not: ~~would be~~) much more enthusiastic in the old days.

Use the adjective *used to* + gerund to say someone is accustomed, or is becoming accustomed to, something.

They're **used to living** in the city; the traffic doesn't wake them any more.

I'm getting **used to working** with him.

Transitive and intransitive verbs

Intransitive verbs only involve the performer of the action (the subject) and the action (the verb).

The train arrived.

Intransitive verbs include: *go, come, sleep, disappear*.

However, intransitive verbs can involve another person or thing through the introduction of a prepositional phrase.

The train arrived **at the station**.

Many verbs which are intransitive are commonly used with a preposition.

We **waited for** the bus.
This bag **belongs to** me.

As intransitive verbs do not have an object, they cannot be made passive.

He **arrived** last night. (Not: ~~Last night was arrived by him.~~)

Transitive verbs involve or affect another person or thing (the object).

The president **opened** the new factory.

A transitive verb needs an object.

(Not: ~~The president opened.~~)

Transitive verbs, by contrast, can be made passive.

*The new factory **was opened** (by the president).*

Transitive verbs include: *see, do, make, own, believe.*

Most transitive verbs can be used intransitively.

A: What **happened** at the match?
B: We **lost**.

Remember: some intransitive verbs have a transitive equivalent and should not be confused.

Transitive = kill; intransitive = die.
Transitive = raise; intransitive = rise.

SENTENCE FORMATION

Contrasts and concession

We use *although / even though, despite / in spite of,* and *however / nevertheless* to show that there is a contrast between the ideas in two connected clauses. We also use them to make a concession.

Although / Even though and *despite* are similar to *but,* but emphasize the difference between the contrasted ideas.

***Although / Even though** he is only 23, he is our top financial analyst.*
*He is our top financial analyst, **although / even though** he is only 23.*

Although / Even though act as conjunctions, and are followed by a complete independent clause: subject and verb. *Despite* is a preposition so we must follow it with the gerund or a noun.

***Despite being** very young, he is our top analyst.*

In spite of follows the same grammar structure.

***In spite of** being very young, he is our top analyst.*

You can follow *despite* with an independent clause if you use *despite the fact that.*

***Despite the fact that** he is only 23, he is our top analyst.*

Use *however* and *nevertheless* to qualify something which has just been stated.

*It is true that <u>Rebecca isn't very imaginative</u>. **However**, she is reliable and conscientious.*
*We realized that the product wasn't ready for the market. **Nevertheless**, we decided to go ahead with the launch.*

Notice that *however* and *nevertheless* are sentence adverbs, not conjunctions. They are used to begin a new sentence, coming *between* the two contrasting statements.

THE PHONEMES OF ENGLISH

Consonants

Symbol	Key word	Symbol	Key word
p	**p**rice	b	**b**id
t	**t**ake	d	**d**ate
k	**c**ost	g	**g**ood
f	**f**ew	v	**v**ery
θ	**th**ink	ð	**th**ose
s	**s**ell	z	**z**ero
ʃ	**sh**op	ʒ	mea**s**ure
tʃ	**ch**oose	dʒ	**j**udge
h	**h**ere	l	**l**et
m	**c**o**m**e	r	**r**ise
n	su**n**	j	**y**et
ŋ	you**ng**	w	**w**on

Vowels and diphthongs

Symbol	Key word	Symbol	Key word
iː	sh**ee**t	eɪ	m**a**ke
ɪ	sh**i**p	ɔɪ	b**oy**
e	l**e**tter	eʊ	wr**o**te
æ	b**a**d	ɪə	h**ere**
ɑː	c**a**lm	aɪ	l**igh**t
ɒ	n**o**t	eə	th**eir**
ɔː	c**our**se	ɜː	th**ir**d
ʊ	p**u**t	aʊ	n**ow**
uː	f**oo**d	ʊə	t**our**
ʌ	c**u**t	ə	butt**er**

IRREGULAR VERBS

Irregular verbs can be organized into similar groups.

No pattern

be	was / were	been
do	did	done
go	went	gone / been
see	saw	seen

Past simple and past participle the same -t or -d

find	found	found
get	got	got / gotten (US)
have	had	had
hear	heard /hɜːd/	heard /hɜːd/
hold	held	held
learn	learnt	learnt
lend	lent	lent
make	made	made
mean	meant	meant
meet	met	met
pay	paid	paid
say	said	said
sell	sold	sold
send	sent	sent
sit	sat	sat
spend	spent	spent
stand / understand	stood / understood	stood / understood
tell	told	told
win	won	won

Ending in -ought or -aught

bring	brought	brought
buy	bought	bought
catch	caught	caught
seek	sought	sought
think	thought	thought

Change from -eep, to -ept

creep	crept	crept
keep	kept	kept
sleep	slept	slept

Present simple and past participle the same

become	became	become
come	came	come
run	ran	run

Past participle in -en

beat	beat	beaten
break	broke	broken
choose	chose	chosen
eat	ate	eaten
fall	fell	fallen
forget	forgot	forgotten
give	gave	given
hide	hid	hidden
rise	rose	risen
speak	spoke	spoken
take	took	taken
write	wrote	written

Change from -i to -a to -u

begin	began	begun
ring	rang	rung

Change from -ear to -ore to -orn

bear	bore	born
wear	wore	worn

Change from -ow or -y to -ew to -own or -awn

draw	drew	drawn
fly	flew	flown
grow	grew	grown
know	knew	known

No change

cost	cost	cost
cut	cut	cut
forecast	forecast	forecast
hit	hit	hit
read /riːd/	read /red/	read /red/

Listening script

Unit 1

1.1

Part A

Interviewer Joan Howard is a director at Howard and Skinner. She has worked with some major clients during her career. She is currently working at the organization's New York office. So, Joan, what are the different roles in a big agency like yours?

Joan Howard Well, there's the creative side. This includes copywriters: the people who come up with the ideas and write the ads and slogans. The art directors work alongside them to create the advertisement. Then there are the people who buy the media, and finally, the account managers like me. We plan the campaigns with the client and make sure that everything goes smoothly.

Interviewer This sounds interesting, but isn't it very stressful too?

Joan Howard Absolutely, there's a lot of pressure.

Interviewer Have you had any difficult moments?

Joan Howard Actually, I'm trying to sort out a problem right now. We've booked studio time to record a radio spot. But the actress we'd picked to do the voiceover called a couple of hours ago to say she couldn't come, so we've been looking for a replacement. We've been playing new voices down the phone to the client all morning.

Interviewer They must be pleased.

Part B

Interviewer Tell me, how scientific is advertising, and how much is based on instinct?

Joan Howard I'd say it's a mixture of both. When we start we need to know exactly what segment of the market the client wants to aim for, because that will shape the advertising. For instance, the type of person we might choose to endorse a product has to appeal to that segment.

Interviewer I see.

Joan Howard It'll also determine which media we select. Take an airline with an upmarket image which wants to target A-B business travellers. Well, we know the kind of magazines those customers are likely to read and what sort of programmes they watch.

Interviewer I see. That's the scientific bit. And what about the ads themselves?

Joan Howard Well, clearly, the ads and the messages they put across have to be tailored to appeal to your target audience, but the angle, the, the ah, the genius, if you like, behind the ad, is what the creative side of the agency is all about.

Part C

Interviewer How do you know whether the ad has actually reached the people you were aiming at?

Joan Howard Through tracking studies. That's where you ask a sample of people if they've seen an ad or read a commercial, and, if so, how many times.

Interviewer And following on from that, how can you prove to a client that your campaign has been successful?

Joan Howard Obviously, the long-term aim of any campaign is to sell more of a particular product or service. But this doesn't mean people are going to immediately travel on an airline because they've seen an ad a couple of times.

Interviewer So how can you show the client that a campaign has worked, then?

Joan Howard Through 'before and after' studies. You interview, say, a group of business travellers before the advertising campaign. Afterwards, you repeat the procedure and hopefully discover that they have been favourably influenced by the ads they've seen. If their attitudes have changed, this could determine their choice of airline in the future.

1.2

Martin So what's your view on this kids' commercial, then?

Carol I think it's absolutely ridiculous. It's a lot of fuss about nothing.

Martin Yeah, I agree. As far as I'm concerned, advertising is just a bit of fun.

Carol Yes, in my opinion, we should be much more worried about the TV programmes themselves.

Martin Don't you agree, Megan?

Megan Well, I suppose so, up to a point. I mean, I hear what you're saying, but don't you think advertisers should be more careful? Kids can be very influenced by advertisements.

Martin Come off it! Even children don't believe everything they see on TV.

1.3

Julia What's the status of Gangstaz?

Ludovic Well, it's been a disaster since the beginning. It cost us a fortune to develop but, it just never really took off.

Julia Do you think we could try relaunching it?

Ludovic I really don't think it's worth it. It didn't fit in with the rest of our range either. It's over.

Alex Couldn't we find a buyer for it?

Ludovic I'm not sure who would be interested.

Alex Oh, well. So what about Wordsters? It's been out two years now, hasn't it?

Julia Mm, well, it's done quite well already. But there are so many rivals in the word game sector. I think we need to wait and see.

Ludovic Yes, but we can't be sure it's going to take off. Now, we mustn't forget Sherlock. Good old Sherlock, what would we do without it?

Julia Absolutely, it's been around for years but people keep coming back for more. It's great: serious murder mystery but with irony too. It's extremely profitable. OK, it is beginning to decline, but we're planning a fiftieth anniversary edition for next year which should generate additional sales.

Ludovic We might need to think of a new tagline for that edition. It needs a big campaign.

Alex And last, but not least, Sketchit.

Julia Well, it has done very well in its first year so far. As far as we can tell, we've got 40% of the market. I'm sure that slick presentation helped.

Alex That's fantastic! And the market is still growing. It's easy to convert to different language editions. There's a great deal of potential here – I hope it's going to be the new Sherlock.

Julia Sure, but we shouldn't forget that we've had to spend a lot promoting it.

Unit 2
2.1

First of all, there are ways of payment. If you want to buy a house, you can secure a long-term loan on special conditions. This is known as a mortgage and is popular in English-speaking countries.

Another kind of loan is hire-purchase. You buy a product and then pay back the money in instalments, a certain amount each month. When you've paid back all the money, but not before, you own the product.

Now, debt can cause all sorts of problems. As a business, companies need to keep an eye on their cash flow: the amount of money coming in and going out. If the company has cash-flow problems and they have borrowed a lot of money, they could become insolvent. This means the company does not have enough money to pay back their debts.

In the worst-case scenario, a company unable to pay back debts will go bankrupt: the business closes because the owners have no money left. The owners will have to close, to wind up their business.

So it is important for a business to be very aware of their outgoings, the money that goes out to pay suppliers, debts, rent, and overheads. Overheads being things like heating and water. This is how a company meets its liabilities – how it pays what must be paid.

2.2

Interviewer When businesses go bankrupt, is this because the business idea was bad in the first place?

Fenella Not necessarily, even businesses based on good ideas fail if they don't have enough money to deal with their immediate financial commitments. Becoming insolvent results from cash-flow problems.

Interviewer What's the most dangerous point for small businesses?

Fenella When they start to grow. They move into bigger premises, take on extra staff, and their overheads and outgoings rocket.

Interviewer So you need to generate a lot of extra business.

Fenella Yes, but unfortunately, firms invest heavily in equipment on the strength of one or two big customers. Then one of them finds another supplier or doesn't pay his bills, and soon, they're heading for bankruptcy.

Interviewer Ah. What else do small businesses need to think about?

Fenella They should be very aware of the business environment in which they're operating. I had some clients who owned a CD shop in a small town. They were doing well, until a big chain opened next door. They thought their customers would stay loyal but of course they didn't. In the end, they went bankrupt. Now they should have sold up as soon as the chain arrived.

2.3

Interviewer James Fraser, you're a debt counsellor dealing with individuals. How do people manage to get into such a mess?

James Well, there are those who go mad with their credit cards or gamble, but more commonly, it's when something unexpected comes along, like losing a job. People who were managing to live within their means can't pay the bills any more.

Interviewer But there are plenty of jobs about, aren't there?

James True, but a skilled factory worker who was making good money with overtime may not be able to earn the same elsewhere. Now he can't make ends meet any more. He falls behind with the mortgage and the hire purchase, and ignores the unpleasant letters.

Interviewer Oh dear. So what can you do, in a concrete sense, to help?

James Mm, well, I help them to prioritize their debts, starting with the most important things like the rent or mortgage, and electricity and water bills.

Interviewer And what about the things they've bought on hire purchase, or with credit cards?

James One option, for example, is to let the company take the products back. Another option is to offer a smaller repayment. Say the instalments on a washing machine are thirty pounds a month, then you offer the company ten pounds.

Interviewer So do these problems mostly affect ordinary working people then?

James Far from it. I've dealt with managers with well-paid jobs in hi-tech industries. They're the same as ordinary working people except the amounts are larger.

Interviewer I see. And is there any other group which is particularly vulnerable?

James Small businesspeople like builders. Most people borrow to finance a building project, and if interest rates go up, they'll wait. One builder I helped was doing very well but a big interest rate rise meant that the work stopped overnight.

Interviewer So what did he do?

James He sold the BMW and moved to a smaller house. It was either that or go bankrupt.

Unit 3
3.1

Part A

Interviewer Franco, what sort of construction are you involved in?

Franco Well, we mostly deal with big civil engineering projects: dams, power stations, that sort of thing. Most of our work is outside Europe.

Interviewer So enormous infrastructure projects? It's staggering to think of how much work goes into building something like a dam. How do you organize a schedule?

Franco With great care! Customers always want the project to be completed as soon as possible. You have to insist on a realistic time-scale. You must never say in a meeting or whenever, 'No problem, we'll do it', without thinking carefully. It sounds obvious but some companies will say, 'We'll build you a new football stadium in x amount of months', without any experience of such a project.

Interviewer What happens if these constructors don't meet their targets?

Franco Contracts contain targets linked with penalty clauses. These can really hurt you if you fail to deliver. You must never sign a contract with a schedule you think you won't meet. That's why the planning stage is so vital.

Interviewer How is your latest project going?

Franco Hold on, I'll show you the schedule. Here we are. So this is an airport project we're working on, which was planned many years ago. The actual construction started three years ago and the project ends on 17th November next year. So you can see that by January we'll have finished the control tower. In March we'll be laying the runways and by the end of the year we should have finished the entire project. If, of course, everything goes to plan, which is hardly ever the case!

Part B

Interviewer What can go wrong with projects?

Franco Anything and everything! Tomorrow we're starting to build a tunnel by dynamiting a hill. We don't know if we are going to hit rock or water but we're bound to meet at least one or the other.

Interviewer How does this affect the penalty clauses you talked about?

Franco Well, they don't apply if something totally unexpected happens. For instance, a port-building project has been held up because we discovered an archaeological site. Now we'll have to wait until the archaeologists have finished.

Interviewer So obviously you didn't know that was going to happen. What else can go wrong?

Franco Well, projects go over budget. Things take longer than anticipated, or else the price of raw materials goes up. It's difficult, particularly for a very large project which lasts several years.

Interviewer And what about people problems?

Franco Oh, yes – those too. There are rumours that the electricians' union is going to go on strike. I hate to think what effect that'll have. But we are due to meet the union leaders on Thursday. I think it's likely that we'll be able to stop the strike.

3.2

1 I was wondering if you could spare me two minutes.
2 Do you think you could help me sort out these invoices?
3 Can you ring Richard to organize coffee and biscuits for the conference?
4 Would you mind organizing the collection for Melissa Bevan?
5 I'd like you to deal with this straightaway.
6 So if you'd like to organize your own flight and we will reimburse you.

3.3

1 I **am** rather busy. Could we meet later?
2 I **could**, but he doesn't like taking orders from me.
3 Actually, I **would** mind. I hate asking people for money.
4 I **will**, just as soon as I've finished this.

3.4

1

Hi, are you sitting down? I've got some bad news… Well, you'll never believe this, but Sammy Webb's agent has just rung to say that he won't be able to host the ceremony after all … Yeah, yeah, I know. He's just been offered this multi-million-dollar role in a new comedy. Yeah, I guess we could sue him, but I'm pretty sure he won't change his mind. In any case, we've no time to waste. We've got to bite the bullet and look for a replacement.

2

Hello. Hi, erm, there's a little hiccup with the programmes, I'm afraid. Someone has just spotted that there's a bad spelling mistake on pages three and five. They've spelt the name of the hotel wrongly. In 'The Three Kings hotel', they put an apostrophe between the 'g' and the 's' of 'Kings'… I know, I know, we should have noticed it earlier but what can we do? Do you think anyone will notice? If we print them again, it'll be on a really tight schedule.

3

Hi, there's a snag with the fire department. We've had an inspector round and he says that the capacity of the room is six hundred and we have eight hundred guests. What do you think we should do? Can you think of any way around it?

4

There's a problem with the caterers. I've just heard that they're in real financial trouble. I'm not even sure whether they're going to stay in business. What do you think we should do about it? They've given us a really good price, but I think it's probably too good. I mean, should we anticipate problems…

Unit 4
4.1

Part A

Interviewer In every business school people talk about the benefits of globalization, but they hardly ever consider its downside. Doesn't it simply exploit the poor? Isn't it just the new face of colonialism?

Indira On the contrary, research always shows that globalization is a good way, the best way even, of fighting poverty. As a rule, poorer countries benefit when they open up to foreign trade and encourage foreign investment.

Interviewer But what about child labour, and all those people who are forced to work in sweatshops?

Indira Old arguments. Think of the social conditions which used to exist in early US and UK factories. People would work fourteen, fifteen hours a day, six days a week. Eventually, workers will demand social reforms and things will get better. You can't use globalization as a scapegoat. The root of the problem in these countries is often society itself: there is corruption – poverty is there already.

Interviewer So for you globalization can do no wrong.

Indira That's not exactly what I'm saying. Take commodities, raw materials like rubber or coffee. Most of the time, western firms dictate prices and take advantage of producing countries. The producers rarely see the larger part of the value added.

Part B

Interviewer In your view, globalization isn't dangerous for poor countries.

Indira Absolutely, in fact I'd say the opposite. It's people in developed countries who should be worried.

Interviewer You're right there: parents now are worried that our children's lives will be harder than our own.

Indira People in the West have all got used to working less and earning more.

Interviewer And then there are all those people who have been made unemployed because their jobs have gone abroad.

Indira The reason for job losses in the US, for example, is generally labour-saving efficiencies – not jobs moving abroad.

Interviewer But companies do move abroad.

Indira From time to time, but it doesn't happen as often as people think.

Interviewer But even if the companies are downsizing and not moving, people have still lost their jobs.

Indira Yes, but the standard of living of an unemployed person in Germany is still beyond the wildest dreams of the average worker in the developing world.

Part C

Interviewer So if everything's OK, why should rich countries be worried?

Indira It's fine to export manufacturing if you keep the creative knowledge in your own country. That is where your comparative advantage lies. But once this know-how is exported as well, then the advantage is lost. If everyone has the same know-how, poorer countries can overtake the rich because their labour costs, etc. are always cheaper.

Interviewer But is manufacturing really that important? We have seen that people in developed economies are moving into services.

Indira Developed economies. Some would call them 'decaying economies'. An economy needs more than hairdressers. A developed economy just doesn't work like that. It has to make things too. At the moment people are used to buying consumer products from the East at low prices. But it can't last – it won't last. The West is living on borrowed time. Once know-how and design leave a country then it starts to get into trouble.

Interviewer So what advice would you give, to developed economies, I mean?

Indira They must keep investing in innovation. As they did with computer technology: it was that which saved the West before. But a driving force for economic growth like that powered by the IT boom only seldom appears. The world's poorer economies are developing fast: if the West doesn't keep up with the pace of growth, it will find itself in serious trouble.

4.2

So what does the Internet really mean for our everyday working lives? It means hours wasted by junk email, the loss of human contact, and drowning in a sea of information.

And as a medium for conducting business with the outside world, we could even say that it's disadvantageous. Many so-called international businesses are tiny operations with hardly any resources. I strongly believe that most natural business relationships are face-to-face, not virtual. This is surely the only way to measure and judge any future partner.

It's true that there are millions of impressive websites which provide useful information, but who knows what is lurking behind them? The Web is susceptible to piracy and plagiarism. It's difficult to control the flow of information. Security can be a problem. And providing personal details is risky if they fall into the wrong hands.

And finally, if we ask ourselves the question 'What does the Internet actually produce?', the answer is, 'nothing'. It's only a source of information, like a giant filing cabinet, but much less reliable.

Unit 5
5.1

A

Well, there is a hierarchy here I suppose, but it doesn't affect me all that much. Er, I do have a line manager I have to report to and who gives me my assignments, but I don't see her all that often. Most of the time, I work in teams on specific projects. Each member – everyone's an expert in his or her own way, so we're all pretty much on the same level. We generally get on OK, but you don't bother to get to know each other because, well, you know, you'll be working with a different bunch of people this time next month. The main thing is that the work is really interesting and you know when you've achieved something.

B

I guess I don't really have a job – it's more a way of life. I can't really tell you where my working life ends and my social life begins. Terry's the boss I suppose, I mean the one who had the original idea for the start-up, but the rest of us have bought into her dream. We certainly don't count the hours – a lot of us have even slept at the office at one time or another. We send out for pizzas and keep at a problem until we've solved it. We've all got stock options, so if we do manage to launch it, then a lot of us will make a fortune.

C

If you look at that organizational chart on the notice board, you can see the different departments and how they relate to each other. That's me here. Everybody knows exactly what they have to do and where their responsibilities begin and end. A lot of people might find it a bit stiff and formal but to tell you the truth, I like it this way. I'd hate to work somewhere where everything depended on the wishes and moods of one person. And working relationships which get too familiar usually finish in tears, you know what I mean?

D

Some of the time there is some fighting and things can get very unpleasant, but it's really Mr Jones who keeps everyone together. I suppose you might say we're all part of his gang and it's very paternalistic. It's quite old-fashioned, a bit conservative. He's quite authoritarian, and I'd never dare to use his first name to his face, but people here really do care about each other. It's quite hard for newcomers, but once you're trusted, that's it. You might think it sounds unfriendly, but we do socialize outside work and have celebrations on birthdays, and things like that. Sometimes it can be too intense, almost suffocating.

5.2

Gavin Wilson So, what's the dress code here? I had to wear a jacket and tie in my last job. It was quite conservative.

Judith Parker Really? Well, you needn't do that here. It's smart casual I suppose. We're quite informal. Also, you've really got to wear your ID tag. In fact, you're expected to challenge anyone who isn't wearing one.

Gavin Wilson I didn't need to do that in my old job.

Judith Parker We never used to but we were made to tighten up on security after we had a series of thefts. Now this is the staff restaurant.

Gavin Wilson Mm, it looks very nice. And is there a smoking area at all?

Judith Parker Actually, no. You're not allowed to smoke on the premises. It's also banned outside the building as you come into reception.

Gavin Wilson So, where do people go, then?

Judith Parker The company just has an anti-smoking policy. It doesn't have an alternative.

Gavin Wilson We had a smokers' room in my last place.

Judith Parker It's different here. Oh, and another thing, there's a pay phone on each floor for staff.

Gavin Wilson So they won't let us phone from our workstations?

Judith Parker Well, you're supposed to use the pay phones, but nobody makes a fuss if you keep calls short. Anyway, now we're coming to Research and Development. Access is limited and you mustn't ever bring anyone in without senior management approval. It does sound a bit authoritarian but …

Gavin Wilson No, no, I can see why they want to do that.

5.3

1. Someone sent you a CV with their application form. Tell them it wasn't necessary to send their CV.
2. Tell someone that boots and hard hats are essential for all visitors.
3. Tell someone that the canteen is a no-smoking area but that a lot of people do it anyway.
4. Tell someone staff must wear ties.
5. Tell someone that staff are completely prohibited from taking home confidential documents.
6. Staff have ID tags. Tell someone it's not necessary to wear them all the time.

5.4

Frank I used to look forward to coming into work but the old team spirit has disappeared. It's hardest for the newer staff. We used to have a mentor system – you know, an experienced member of staff would look after a less experienced person. But nowadays all we really care about is meeting the sales targets. And paperwork's a nightmare since we lost the back-up staff. OK, I'm earning a lot more money, but money isn't everything you know.

Helen Some of the older staff can be quite intimidating, particularly Melanie! I'm still learning the ropes but I find it hard to approach some of the others. And when I'm on my own, in my little cubicle, I feel really quite isolated. It's not that people are unfriendly but … the office is a bit impersonal. Anyway, I'm selling better as I gain experience, but I don't know how much longer I'll last.

Trudy Thorne Sales is a grown-up job for grown-up people and my role is to get the best from them. If my salespeople want to cry on someone's shoulder, they'd better not come to me. They should spare a thought for all the people in the factory whose jobs depend on them. Most of them earn a quarter of what a good salesperson can make.

Ralph Now they've taken away the basic salary, I never know if I'll be able to pay the bills. I'm finding it difficult to make ends meet – I've got a young family too. I also preferred it when we set up our own meetings with customers. You could get a better feel for the client and build up more of a rapport. I can't seem to close the sales any more. And the harder I try, the worse it gets.

Melanie We used to achieve an average of one sale for every four leads, but now it's fallen to one in six. Sickness and absenteeism are up. Morale among the sales force is low. Staff turnover has risen dramatically. Other than that, everything's great!

5.5

Simon Jones I'm really fed up, Andrea. We've got this no-smoking policy but nobody seems to respect it. You know, in June 75% of staff were for a total ban. But the other day I noticed that there were lots of cigarette ends around the front door and even in the plants at reception.

Andrea Fox Yes, you're right, it really does create an awful impression.

Simon Jones And the toilets smell of smoke too. There are some people who are ignoring the rules completely. Do you have any idea who it could be?

Andrea Fox I've got my suspicions. We've taken on quite a few people lately and there are one or two serious smokers among them. We need to make our no-smoking rules clear when we're recruiting.

Simon Jones Well, there's always the car park.

Andrea Fox Come on, Simon, you can't expect people to go all the way to the car park for a smoke. Think of all the time it wastes, as well.

Simon Jones I suppose so. What shall we do?

Andrea Fox There's a small room next to the coffee lounge. How about setting that aside for smokers?

Simon Jones The insurance?

Andrea Fox I think it will affect our insurance.

Simon Jones OK then, but from now on, people who don't respect the new rules will really have to go! And I don't care who it is. I'll get Jo to email everyone.

Unit 6
6.1
Part A

Jay Thomas What do you think of this idea that there is a fair price for everything?

Tara Williamson Well, as an ordinary person, I tend to agree. But as an economist, I would say it all depends on the market.

Jay Thomas How do you mean?

Tara Williamson Well, do you remember the fuel crisis of a few years ago?

Jay Thomas The petrol shortage?

Tara Williamson Yes, well, the owner of our local petrol station doubled his prices. Now, as a motorist I was furious, but as an economist I admired him.

Jay Thomas Admired him!

Tara Williamson Because he acted in a rational way. It was the law of supply and demand in action. He got the maximum income from his remaining stock. Look, just think, if he had sold at the normal price, he'd have run out in a couple of hours. By raising his price, he controlled demand. It was a good example of price elasticity in action.

Jay Thomas But weren't his prices predatory. You know, unfair?

Tara Williamson Predatory, no. It wasn't a captive market, and people could go elsewhere. But, his old, regular customers have never forgiven him. I certainly haven't been back since.

Part B

Jay Thomas What determines how a company sets the price of a new item?

Tara Williamson Well, obviously a lot depends on the price of competing articles. But after that, the price is basically what they think the market will bear.

Jay Thomas I must say, I was upset last year when I bought a new computer. I paid full price for it, round about €1,500. Six months later it was down to about €800, virtually half the price.

Tara Williamson Ah well, with articles such as the latest hi-tech equipment, they'll use a two-stage strategy. They'll skim the market first …

Jay Thomas Skim the market?

Tara Williamson Yes, they'll set the price as high as they dare, knowing there are customers, early adopters, who will happily pay the asking price to be the first to enjoy the benefits of the new product. Particularly if it's scarce, in short supply.

Jay Thomas I see. I suppose at the time, I was prepared to pay a high premium to do that.

Tara Williamson It makes good business sense too: it lets the manufacturer break even and recover his development costs early on. Once this level of demand has been satisfied, they can attract the next level of consumer by putting it into a more affordable price range. That way, they can achieve greater market penetration.

Part C

Jay Thomas But how much control can manufacturers have over the retail prices of their goods?

Tara Williamson Well, big brand names are keen to dictate the price at which their goods sell. Department stores can be made to respect the price lists and guidelines. And the image of designer labels and other luxury goods can be damaged if they're sold, at discounted prices say, through supermarkets.

Jay Thomas But how could a supermarket get hold of them in the first place?

Tara Williamson Through the grey market. Most branded goods will fetch different prices in different markets. So, the supermarket will locate a supply in a lower-cost country, and then import them to sell at a cut price. The big brands don't like it because it makes a mess of their pricing structure and upsets the exclusive retail outlets. They may even take the supermarket to court.

Jay Thomas So what's in it for the supermarket, then?

Tara Williamson Well, it gets people into their store, where they'll buy other goods at regular prices.

Jay Thomas So, do they sell these luxury brands at a loss?

Tara Williamson They'll work at a much lower margin than a department store, much less than the list price – they will still make a profit on them though. Other products, like washing powder, can be loss leaders, which they'll sell at cost price or even at a small loss, to get the customers through their doors.

Jay Thomas OK, but if that's the case, why do most retailers all seem to charge around the same price for the same goods? I remember shopping around for kitchen appliances, and finding very little variation.

Tara Williamson Well, retailers won't actually sit around a table and fix prices with their competitors. But what they will do, is keep an eye on each other's prices and try to match them. It's not in their interest to get involved in a price war.

6.2

A So, to recap, we all feel that these costs have risen too high and this could have a negative outcome.

B What does 'a negative outcome' mean exactly?

A It means that if the money we're spending on paper, ink, and printing, etc. increases, we'll be going over budget. That could affect staff bonuses for this year.

C But is this the right time to discuss this? I mean, it's an interesting point but I'm not sure how relevant it is to our discussion. I'd just like to say that we have very little time.

A It is important, because the bonuses will be calculated very soon and …

C What I meant is we should wait and see what happens.

A But we can't wait: we can already see …

B OK, costs are a problem but here's some news. There is a good chance that the distributor in Germany will be replaced by one in Vietnam. That would reduce the amount we're going to spend.

C That's a good point.

A Can I just finish off what I was saying? Regardless of what happens in Vietnam, the projected production alone will send our costs over budget. This is a serious and immediate issue.

C Right.

B Yes.

D Does anyone have anything further to add?

6.3

So, here you'll see our sales chart of sales of monitors to Egypt over the last financial year. You'll see that this includes both our fourteen- and fifteen-inch screens.

So, as the year began, sales remained steady until June. Then they crept up for two months until in September things started to go a bit crazy. Sales really fluctuated for three months, as you can see. They slumped by a hundred units in September but then soared in November, peaking at 450 in December – a level we had never seen before. After a peak you have to expect a dip but this was amazing: they plummeted to fifty units in January! There are various reasons for this but the big worry is they have levelled off at that low level.

Unit 7

7.1

Part A

Interviewer What's the key to a successful negotiation, Eric?

Eric Perrot The most important thing is to be very well prepared. This means, firstly, understanding the buyer's expectations, and secondly knowing exactly what is and isn't negotiable. A customer will always try to beat you down, it is part of the dance, you know, the game. But you have to know what your final figure is, and how far you can go to reach a compromise both sides are happy with.

Interviewer I see. And what are your aims when you're negotiating with a client?

Eric Perrot The ideal outcome is to make a deal both sides are happy with and to get an order.

Interviewer But doesn't there have to be a winner and loser?

Eric Perrot That's the worst kind of deal if you want to develop a longer term relationship. I always want to move from being a supplier to a partner.

Interviewer How do you mean?

Eric Perrot Well, if you know and trust each other, you can do business more quickly. The other day I negotiated a million euro contract in four minutes!

Interviewer But what happens if the buyer changes?

Eric Perrot You start all over again. Most companies rotate buyers so that someone new takes over. They don't want relationships to become too cosy!

Part B

Interviewer What skills does a good salesperson or negotiator need?

Eric Perrot To be a good listener and a bit of a psychologist too. You need to be able to recognize the 'buy signs'. For instance, when the buyer starts to talk about possible delivery dates, or specific schedules, you know you can take the initiative and close the deal.

Interviewer And do you have to be persuasive?

Eric Perrot Not really, I never try to force, or talk anyone into a contract. Sometimes of course, you have to have arguments to overcome the customer's objections, but if they are satisfied by the overall proposal then they'll go for it.

Interviewer I see. And what about the customers, which ones are the hardest to deal with?

Eric Perrot The quiet ones. If there's no dialogue then it is hard to build a relationship.

Interviewer How do you get round that?

Eric Perrot I leave doors open. I leave out information, or put some obvious holes in my presentation which will get them to ask a question I can answer.

Interviewer I see. And what about aggressive customers?

Eric Perrot They're much easier. They're usually aggressive because they're insecure. So I reassure them and make them think they are the boss. Things go better after that.

Interviewer So you never get angry yourself?

Eric Perrot Never. Confrontation and losing your temper lead absolutely nowhere.

Part C

Interviewer And do clients ever ask for incentives?

Eric Perrot Oh, yes, all the time. Last month a big supermarket chain asked for help with an advertising campaign. I said something like 'We'll contribute €20,000 provided you order another two tonnes of chips a month'.

Interviewer So you never give something for nothing?

Eric Perrot Never. If you make concessions without getting something in return, you leave yourself open to abuse.

Interviewer And one last question. How flexible are contracts if market conditions change?

Eric Perrot Ah, well, let me tell you a story. Last year the price of potatoes rocketed but unfortunately I'd already undertaken to supply a major customer for three months.

Interviewer So did you try to get out of the contract?

Eric Perrot No, of course not. We lost a lot of money but we didn't try to re-negotiate the contract. But I am certain the customer respected us for it.

7.2

Receptionist Hello, Great Outdoors.

Customer Could you put me through to Customer Services, please?

Customer Services Customer Services, can I help you?

Customer Yes, please. It's about a waterproof jacket I bought last year.

Customer Services And what seems to be the problem?

Customer I washed it according to the instructions on the label and now it's leaking.

Customer Services Hmm. How long have you had it?

Customer I realize it's no longer under guarantee but I don't think a quality item should wear out so quickly.

Customer Services Well, you'll need to bring it into the branch so that we can have a look at it, and give you a credit note or a refund.

Customer I bought it in your branch but I don't live in the area. Can I return it to my local branch?

Customer Services Yes, that's no problem at all, just as long as you've kept the receipt.

Customer Thank you for your help.

Customer Services Thank you. Goodbye.

7.3

Customer Services Customer Services, how may I help …

Mr Miller At last! It's taken me so long to get through to you!

Customer Services How may I help you, Mr…?

Mr Miller Miller. Now listen, I was just on holiday in the USA and my flight ticket was stolen. I phoned your office here in the UK and I got the most useless staff that I have encountered in my life.

Customer Services I do apologize for any inconvenience you've suffered, Mr Miller. Would you like me to enter a complaint on the system?

Mr Miller Yes, I would. I'm – I'm just so angry about the whole thing. The treatment I received was appalling. I didn't pay £700 for that!

Customer Services I can fully appreciate your frustration, Mr Miller. Do you happen to have a reference number?

Mr Miller It's right here. JH/111.

Customer Services If you'd like to bear with me a moment, I'm just accessing your details on my screen. When I have it, I'll enter your details straightaway.

Unit 8
8.1

Part A

Interviewer Why do organizations call in consultants?

Bill Watts Usually, because they've realized that their competitiveness has started to suffer or that their market position is being challenged. Basically, the organization has identified that something needs to be done.

Interviewer But if the company has identified the problem, why do they need consultants?

Bill Watts Because they need an objective look from people who aren't involved in inter-departmental rivalry or company politics. People are too busy with the day-to-day running of the business to stop to think about strategy.

Interviewer What kind of strategic decisions do you mean?

Bill Watts Well, things like moving into new markets, mergers and acquisitions, that type of thing. Sometimes consultants will give management the courage to diversify or launch, say, a takeover bid by confirming what it already believes.

Part B

Interviewer How did it feel going into a company and advising people who had been in business all their lives?

Bill Watts Quite intimidating, particularly as most of the clients and senior managers were much older than me – I was in my late twenties when I joined.

Interviewer So how did you cope?

Bill Watts Well, I was trained in management techniques from the United States – these were unknown in Britain – so this gave me self-confidence. We were also experts in gathering market intelligence.

Interviewer How did people react to you and these techniques?

Bill Watts Well, I'll never forget going to some companies and being looked at like a man from Mars.

Interviewer Ha, ha! And did companies usually follow your recommendations?

Bill Watts Yes, because they had been involved in formulating the strategy. When a consultancy tries to introduce change, it means working closely with the people who will carry it out. Consultants can only give advice, so what we do is ask the question 'What if?' or 'Why don't we try doing it this way?' and develop different plans to meet changing circumstances.

Part C

Interviewer Tell me, Bill, what exactly is McKinsey's 'up-or-out' policy?

Bill Watts If a junior consultant isn't going to become a partner then they are told to leave.

Interviewer Ouch! That's rather brutal, isn't it?

Bill Watts It sounds more brutal than it is, and it's made clear during the recruitment process. Anyway, once someone has spent a couple of years at McKinsey, they have some useful and marketable experience.

Interviewer So what happens to them?

Bill Watts Frequently they're headhunted or they join a business they have already advised. A lot of consultants are happy to have a conventional job and escape the pressure of long hours and lots of travel, and the stress of preparing and giving presentations. Clients pay high fees and demand total commitment and professionalism in return.

Interview Any regrets?

Bill Watts About my career? None at all. You get a fascinating insight into all sorts of organizations, more than in a normal working life. It's stimulating and challenging and the money's good. It's also a great way of getting noticed by some of the top firms in the world.

8.2

1 Let's take a look at the evidence, shall we?
2 If you'd like to open the report on page four.
3 As you can see, this pie chart reveals two other worrying features.
4 I'd like to draw your attention to the following market intelligence.
5 Right, I'm going to begin by running through our main findings.
6 So what can we learn from all of this?
7 I'd like to hand you over to my colleague, Sylvie Grey.
8 Sylvie will be talking you through our short-term recommendations.
9 This brings me to the other key issue, namely, the company's image.
10 Finally, I shall attempt to outline a longer-term strategy for growth.

Unit 9
9.1
Part A

Peter Fagin What's the biggest problem of doing business internationally?

Eileen Carter Without a doubt the main problem is trust. Take the exporter. If you send goods to a foreign country, you can never be sure that you'll be paid. So when the goods are sent by the exporter, they want to be paid immediately.

Peter Fagin But the importer has different ideas?

Eileen Carter That's right. Importers don't want to pay until the goods have been received.

Peter Fagin Is there any solution?

Eileen Carter Yes, in these cases a letter of credit is often used. That way, neither side has to take an unfair risk.

Part B

Peter Fagin Naturally, I've heard about letters of credit, but what do they do?

Eileen Carter As an exporter, you might not trust the buyer. So a letter of credit is a promise set up by a bank. This promises that the exporter will be paid.

Peter Fagin Who sets up this letter of credit, the buyer or the exporter?

Eileen Carter Usually the letter of credit is set up by the buyer. The buyer must prove that they will pay. It's set up after the order has been agreed.

Peter Fagin What does that involve?

Eileen Carter Well, the buyer's bank and the seller's bank write to each other and confirm all the details. The letter of credit states which documents need to be presented to get payment.

Peter Fagin What kind of documents do you mean?

Eileen Carter A bill of lading, for instance. This is a document which accompanies the goods all the way to their destination. Basically, it's a receipt from the carrier to the sender. It entitles the buyer to collect the goods on arrival.

Peter Fagin I see. So how does everyone get what they want?

Eileen Carter After a consignment has arrived, the documents are presented to the buyer's bank. The buyer's bank then sends payment. Then the buyer takes the proof of payment to the port and collects the goods.

Peter Fagin What a complicated business!

Eileen Carter True, but it's generally believed to be the best way of doing things. Both sides are made to think carefully before committing themselves.

9.2

1 Good morning, everybody, may I have your attention, please.
2 On behalf of Xu Silks I'd like to welcome you to our factory.
3 My name is Mei and I'm going to be your guide today.
4 As you can see we're standing in the information centre.
5 Now before we begin our tour, I'd like to tell you about the production of silk.
6 At this point I'd also like to remind you that this is a working factory.
7 So do be very careful and please keep well back from the machinery.
8 Anyway, if you'd like to gather round the display I'll tell you about the silkworms which produce it.

Unit 10
10.1

A Well, I got a mysterious phone call from an agency asking if I was interested in a job with better prospects and more money. I felt quite flattered. Anyway, so I met the person in a hotel and we discussed the proposition over a drink. Basically, she made me an offer I couldn't refuse – it was such a good job. And there was a marvellous golden hello. My old company sent instructions from on high to keep me, but that company was just a stepping stone for me. I was off!

B I guess it was expected really. My parents had always assumed that one day I would end up in their business, and so I did. I do wish that I'd worked in the wider world a bit more but working for my parents, we all share in the profits. The money doesn't go elsewhere and if I want to move on, I can.

C On the erm, grapevine, if you like. I have to go to most of the medical congresses and conferences, and eventually you get to know everyone on the circuit. So when this person I'd known asked me if I'd be interested in joining his sales team, I didn't hesitate. The company has a terrific reputation. The bonuses we get are amazing, even though the job is very demanding. It's hard to find good medical representatives, you know, and they do what they can to keep us.

D I'm part of the Indian brain drain, I suppose. It's so easy for IT professionals with the Internet. Anyway, what I did was to target ten companies that I was interested in working for, and then I found out about them from their websites and so on. Then I did a CV and emailed it to them. People were quite impressed that I'd used my initiative, and I got lots of job offers. Including my present one, which is all right, but the work's not as exciting as they made out in the interview. Good pay though: golden handcuffs – they don't want me going anywhere.

E At college I had this work placement to do as part of the course, and so they sent me here for a term last year. And they must have liked my attitude because they offered me a permanent job. It's a cool company, with really good training possibilities. I've got my foot on the first rung of the ladder and there are lots of opportunities for promotion. But you know, without the college I wouldn't have thought of applying.

F I know that some people have contacts who can pull strings for them, but I had to go through the interview process to get this job. There was an ad which said it was looking for talented people for a rewarding career and well, here I am. It isn't rewarding financially but as it's a charity, it's very worthwhile work.

10.2

1 What do you see yourself doing in five years' time?
2 How quickly do you learn new skills?
3 What was the most important thing you learnt from your placement last summer?
4 Would you rather be out and about, or office-based?
5 Do you think you could tell us about your greatest weakness?
6 Could you tell us what qualities you would bring to this job?
7 I'd like you to describe a difficult situation you handled well.
8 Would you mind telling us how much you are currently earning?

10.3

1

Interviewer What do you see yourself doing in five years' time?
Interviewee In five years' time? Uhm, I see myself running a large department, or my own business.

2

Interviewer How quickly do you learn new skills?
Interviewee Mm, that's an interesting question. I'm good at learning new programming languages.

3

Interviewer What was the most important thing you learnt from your placement last summer?
Interviewee I really enjoyed the teamwork.

4

Interviewer Would you rather be out and about, or office-based?
Interviewee I'd much rather be visiting customers than be stuck behind a desk.

5

Interviewer Do you think you could tell us about your greatest weakness?
Interviewee Well, I tend to be slow at dealing with paperwork, but I am improving.

6

Interviewer Could you tell us what qualities you would bring to this job?
Interviewee Let me think … I'm thorough and methodical, which is essential for dealing with paperwork.

7

Interviewer I'd like you to describe a difficult situation you handled well.
Interviewee Certainly. Once some important documents were lost, so I created another set.

8

Interviewer Would you mind telling us how much you are currently earning?
Interviewee I'd rather not talk about money at this stage, if you don't mind.

10.4

1

Karl I went into this huge room and there they were, lined up behind an enormous table. All six of them. One just smiled, and kept nodding all the time, so I looked at her. The worst was this guy who stared out of the window when he wasn't doodling on my CV. Finally he looked at me and asked an impossible question. My mouth went dry immediately and my mind went blank. I'd wanted the job so much – it was for a charity, a very worthwhile cause.

2

Eija It didn't really feel like an interview at all. I went from office to office and spoke to lots of different people. I've never drunk so many cups of coffee in my life – and I come from Finland, where we drink a lot of coffee! Everyone was really friendly apart from one person in Marketing. I've no idea what kind of impression I made.

3

Maria Alejandra She asked me to come in and we sat down around a coffee table. Then she fussed about with tea and biscuits and asked me some questions. She seemed embarrassed by the whole thing. I think I had more experience of interviews than she did! Anyway, she offered me the job there and then and asked if I could start straightaway!

4

Brian You know you want to do your best but you don't want to show off either. There were two people who were desperate to show that they had 'leadership potential', so they bossed everyone else around. And all the others were trying their hardest to show that they were good team players. One guy thought he was terrific, but he came over as just arrogant. I thought it was a real circus and no good at all for judging people.

Unit 11

11.1

Part A

Interviewer So, what are the advantages then, of setting up your own franchise, say?

Anthea Fowler Well, first and foremost, a franchise is the best way of going into business for yourself, without being by yourself. Lots of entirely new businesses go under in the first three years. A franchise with a tried and tested concept has more chance of survival. It's much less risky.

Interviewer How popular are they?

Anthea Fowler A third of British businesses are franchises. They're worth ten billion pounds and will shortly employ half a million people.

Interviewer How much business know-how do you need?

Anthea Fowler Not a lot. Commitment is more important, certainly until the business is up and running. Hiring and firing is difficult for people who have never been in business.

Interviewer But you don't have to be an entrepreneur?

Anthea Fowler Quite the opposite. You have to be ready to follow hard and fast rules, a business recipe if you like. A true entrepreneur wouldn't want to do this.

Interviewer Who are they best for?

Anthea Fowler Well, lately I've been working a lot with middle-aged people who have been made redundant. They feel too old to start something up from zero but have a lot of experience to build on. If you have money to invest, you can start straightaway. The other day I helped a couple find a franchise. The ink on the agreement was hardly dry before they were making plans.

Part B

Interviewer How do franchises make their money?

Anthea Fowler From the joining fee – this can vary from a few hundred to hundreds of thousands of pounds according to the opportunity. Nearly always, the system is: the bigger the business, the higher the fee.

Interviewer And then there's a percentage of your profits, isn't there?

Anthea Fowler Actually, it's usually based on turnover.

Interviewer And what do you get in return?

Anthea Fowler Training and management systems, a logo, and national advertising. Then there's back up for any eventual problem, not cash, mind: other help. Franchises have big buying power too so you can benefit from reductions. But most of all you're buying into their reputation.

Interviewer In what way?

Anthea Fowler Imagine you need new tyres. There may be a good independent tyre shop whose prices aren't as expensive, but most of us will choose a franchise operation because of the name.

Part C

Interviewer I'm not sure what sort of franchise I'd go for.

Anthea Fowler Yes, it's such a difficult choice for a lot of people. I'd choose a sector which is up and coming. Some areas are so saturated it's hard to get established. I'd also visit exhibitions, buy magazines, and talk to people who work in the real franchise environment so you can select well and wisely.

Interviewer And what should we do when we find one which interests us?

Anthea Fowler Find out how long it's been operating and talk to existing franchisees.

Interviewer And what if the franchisor asks you to sign up straightaway?

Anthea Fowler If it's too easy to join, I'd be suspicious! By and large a good franchise will have more applicants than territories. So if it's worth having, it will be you who has to convince the franchisors that you can make a success of the business, not the other way around. Being cautious may take longer, but eventually you will be better off.

11.2

Part A

James The thing is, Vicente, we need to be sure that the project is viable. We are seeking a serious return on our investment.

Vicente I can assure you that our business model is sound, and based on similar hotels in the area. It's quite viable given the tourist numbers in the area and the growth that has been forecast.

Part B

Vicente All of the figures in the report are based on detailed research by the government.

James Great. It all looks very interesting. And from talking to people in my company, we do believe that other backers would welcome the chance to invest in Venezuela.

Vicente That's great news. I should just mention that our mother company has said that they are not prepared to reveal these figures until they have had an opportunity for a face-to-face meeting with each potential backer. I'm afraid that they have to remain confidential for the moment.

James Fine. We can sort that out later.

Part C

Vicente If you don't mind, James, I'd like to put off the discussion of the layout of the hotel until later. I know it's on the agenda, but I just feel that once you've seen the site itself, you'll have a much clearer picture of how things stand.

James Perfect. I was going to suggest the same thing myself.

Unit 12

12.1

Part A

Gavin Strange We all know of companies like Mercedes and BMW who have had great reputations for years, but today I'd like to ask you about manufacturers in a different position. Once a car manufacturer develops a lousy reputation, is it possible to live it down?

Charlotte Gadsby Yes, but it takes time and commitment. Renault, which once had problems with unions and quality, managed to do it. But the most incredible example is Skoda. The Czech-built car was once very much maligned.

Gavin Strange Oh, yes, I remember the jokes. How do you double the value of a Skoda? Fill it up with petrol.

Charlotte Gadsby Yes, at one time Skodas were so notorious that it was called 'the brand from hell'. But since its takeover by Volkswagen in 1991, production has increased tenfold.

Gavin Strange How did they manage to shake off the brand's poor reputation?

Charlotte Gadsby By appealing to the buyer's rational side. It asked people to forget their prejudices and realize how trustworthy the Skoda car was, how reliable, and what marvellous value for money they represented. Advertising in the UK was very clever too: it was ironic and that appealed to many people. Skoda even sent a metal badge to its existing car owners and told them to sleep with it at night!

Gavin Strange And what effect has this had on the way that owners feel about their cars?

Charlotte Gadsby Well, in the customer satisfaction survey I mentioned, Skoda hit the headlines by coming second, just after Lexus.

Part B

Charlotte Gadsby Now, in making these changes Skoda could claim, justifiably, that it was building on its old reputation. Historically, the firm was renowned for its luxury vehicles. Its most prestigious brand, the Superb, was legendary. This all stopped when Skoda was forced to produce cars under state control for fifty years.

Gavin Strange The Skoda Superb has been resurrected, hasn't it?

Charlotte Gadsby Yes, the new Superb is based on a Volkswagen with the interior created by the eminent Spanish designer Luis Santos.

Gavin Strange And do you think it's heading for stardom?

Charlotte Gadsby A lot will depend on its market positioning. So far Skoda's revival has depended on convincing ordinary people that the cars are dependable and value for money. These consumers are less status-conscious than the typical luxury car driver. The new Superb is aimed at the upper-middle market.

Gavin Strange So?

Charlotte Gadsby Typically the people who drive more luxurious models are 'achievers': very successful professionals or successful businesspeople. There are also 'emulators'.

Gavin Strange Emulators?

Charlotte Gadsby Emulators are people who are not so successful as the achievers, but they want to copy them.

Gavin Strange OK.

Charlotte Gadsby The big question is how many of these achievers and emulators will be prepared to swap their Jaguars or BMWs for a Skoda? One of the reasons these other cars are prized is because they are status symbols.

Gavin Strange So, basically, it boils down to the snob appeal of the brand name. So, what category do the poor people who are still driving around in the pre-Volkswagen Skodas fall into?

Charlotte Gadsby They are probably what we call 'survivors'.

12.2

A

Alan So what do you think of the premises, Ms Brewer?

Sally I think they're quite nice, really. They're fairly well situated and the reception area is lovely. The offices are nice and light too. Uhm, one thing I'm worried about, though, is visitors.

Alan Visitors?

Sally Parking, specifically.

Alan I see. As you know, parking space is at a premium in this area, but you are entitled to ten spaces in the underground car park as part of the lease.

Sally Oh. As I understood it, use of the whole car parking area would be available.

Alan Only ten spaces, I'm afraid.

B

Sally Oh. The other question I had is when exactly are they available? The premises, that is. If I've understood correctly, it should be 7th April?

Alan Ye-es.

Sally Is there a problem there?

Alan Uhm, the existing tenants do have to leave by the end of the month. But there is a bit of work that needs to be done.

Sally What does 'a bit of work' entail?

Alan There's some building work, a bit of damp. The roof needs looking at. Trivial problems, really.

Sally I see. Well, uhm, thank you for your time.

Alan Yes, I hope you like it. Would you like to run through anything else before we go?

Sally No, I think I've seen everything I need to see, thanks.

Video CD-ROM

159

ANSWER KEY

1 Target markets

INTERVIEW
2 1 *15 to 35.*
   2 *make people smile or laugh.*
3 1 the key proposition (the single thought that communicates the benefit of what you are selling)
   2 They look at the product's features, not the benefits.
   3 product: saw
      features: sharp teeth and a strong wooden handle
      benefit: cuts wood more efficiently
   4 They are out socializing.
   5 SMS text messaging, the Internet, outdoor media, buses
   6 They are not loyal to one brand or service.
   7 compelling message, excellent creativity, humour
   8 the advertising of unhealthy food to children

LANGUAGE REVIEW
1 1 yes (He uses the present perfect simple to talk about results / actions that are now complete.)
   2 we don't know (He uses the present perfect continuous to talk about a process, not the end result. We don't know if the process is complete, or still ongoing.)
   3 either is possible (He uses the present continuous, he may be referring to now, or to a time in the future.)
   4 animated film for the big screen, TV adverts, company's own films, films for clients
2 (example answer) Today, I have been updating my CV, and I have written two letters.

WORDBANK
1 (collocations and example definitions)
   memorable campaign = a series of ads that people will remember
   peer group = people who are in the same age group or social group
   social responsibility = a responsibility to do things that are good for society
2 1 into   2 across   3 down

2 Triumph and disaster

INTERVIEW
2 Decisions that Tony finds difficult are: sacking people; the choice of business partner; investing. Difficult daily decisions are related to final designs and budget.

3 History of the company:

1989	Tony started his company.
1989 to 1999	It grew until they had ten employees. Made furniture for architects and private clients.
1999 to now	It became unprofitable to make the furniture themselves, so they got other people to make it, and closed the workshop.
Now	Tony designs furniture independently. It's made by himself and other people.

Qualities of a good entrepreneur: Can see a good product and decide where and for how much it should be sold.
Why start-ups often go wrong: They are based on an emotional, not a business decision, e.g. trying to make a living from a hobby.
The best start-ups: Based on a good business model, could sell anything, as long as there is a market for it.
Debt: There is a high risk of getting into debt, but this depends on how the company is run. Tony runs his company on the principle of no debt. This restricts its growth. It is all right for a company to be in debt as long as it can pay the interest on the debt.

LANGUAGE REVIEW
1 TONY: managing departments | managing small stores | managing large store | ▼ started company | Now

ROBERT: | | ▼ had idea | sitting in olive grove | Now

2 (example answers)
MARTIN: Martin sold his first business to an American company. After signing the contract, he did an interview with Wall Street, then he made a mistake: the share price had fallen by 50%, and he joked that the American team must be happy that they'd bought the company now. Nobody laughed.
TONY: Tony once had a difficult situation with a client. After he had completed a project for them, he didn't get paid. It was quite difficult to get the money, but eventually he was successful.

WORDBANK
1 (example definitions)
   create debt = borrow money
   fall into debt = find yourself in debt
   service a debt = pay the interest on a loan
2 1 down   2 from   3 in   4 for

_# Video CD-ROM answer key

3 Prioritizing

INTERVIEW
2 1 concentration 2 does not have to
3 there are often last-minute changes
3 1 three
2 She writes a list of everything she has to do that day, and then decides who is going to do what.
3 She sets a time limit.
4 To leave time for crisis management, because something unexpected always happens.
5 client, designer, project manager (Lucy), somebody from the construction team, buyer, and suppliers.
6 The meetings and the approval dates.
7 The client looks at the work that has been done, and if they like it, they sign it off (= approve it).
8 In order to finish a model that was not ready in time.

LANGUAGE REVIEW
1 1 LUCY PLAN:
put in a café, add a couple of other floors, put in departments for computer design and small model making
2 TIM ON-GOING ACTIVITY:
work on job positions
SPECIFIC ARRANGEMENT:
meet clients, interview job candidates
3 JON SPECIFIC ARRANGEMENT:
move to new house
4 LUCY ONGOING ACTIVITY:
work on film things
ACTION FINISHED BEFORE A STATED FUTURE TIME:
fantastic projects, e.g. film on big screen

WORDBANK
1 **put a hundred per cent into something** = do something using all your effort
think nothing of = do something as if it is normal, and not unusual or too hard
be everything to somebody = be the most important thing in somebody's life
move something to one side = stop something to make time for something else
2 (example answers)
1 I put a hundred per cent into *my work / everything I do*.
2 I move everything to one side when *I have an important meeting / we have a crisis*.
3 *My family / Success* is everything to me.
4 I think nothing of *getting up at five to go for a run / working till eight in the evening*.
3 1 in 2 off 3 off

4 Globalization

INTERVIEW
2 If fashions are the same everywhere, your country is more like the UK; if they vary from city to city, it is more like Germany.

3 1 **UK:** student market very strong; not diverse like Germany; Genes UK supplies about 50 shops; marketing less important than in Germany
2 **Switzerland**
3 **Germany:** has a diverse market; four times the size of the UK; different towns have different fashions; marketing, branding, professionalism, and image of label are important
4 **where they produce and why:** in the UK; to support local businesses; they need to produce good fashion cheaply and quickly
5 **globalization:** exploits the smaller people; companies like H&M, Gap, Ikea, produce quickly and cheaply all over the world; for Andy, globalization means the effect of global companies on companies like his

LANGUAGE REVIEW
1 1 always, hardly ever, usually; from time to time; generally
2 present simple and *will*
2 (example answer) I generally get up at seven and have a shower, then get dressed. Sometimes I'll have a cup of coffee if I have time, but I hardly ever eat anything until later. I usually leave the house to go to work at 7.45, but from time to time I'll sleep late and leave about 9.

WORDBANK
1 (example definitions)
have money behind you = have money available to you, for example because you are part of a large organization
the smaller people = people, companies, etc. that do not have much money or power
a small fish in a big sea = a small company in an industry in which many big, powerful companies compete
stick to what you are doing = continue doing the same thing, without changing
2 predominantly oOooo   particularly oOooo
ultimately Oooo   actually Ooo

5 Company culture

INTERVIEW
2 Jon uses *friendly, happy, picturesque,* and *relaxed*.
3 1 schools, banks, and governments
2 ●●●●● 5 directors
■■■■■■■■■■ 9 or 10 departments
⋮ ⋮ ⋮ smaller teams and project groups within departments
3 Groups at the top are more formal; groups lower down are more short-term project groups.
4 They have lunch or drinks together, and have chats between corridors and rooms.
5 Jon
6 They trust employees not to abuse the rules.
7 Employees can wear casual clothes, but if they interface with clients they would probably wear a suit.
8 Very low – people usually stay for a number of years, because they are happy there._

Video CD-ROM answer key

LANGUAGE REVIEW
2 1 working hours – In Jon's company, you do not have to start and finish at a certain time.
  2 food – In Katja's lab, you are not allowed to eat or drink.
  3 make-up – In Katja's lab, you can't wear make-up.
  4 company credit cards – In Jon's company, you are supposed to use the company credit card for equipment for company use, train tickets, etc.
3 Tim is probably giving a strong piece of advice, as a company cannot force a job candidate to follow its rules.

WORDBANK
1 **abuse rules** = ignore rules or use them in an unfair way
 atmosphere = the feeling or mood that a place has
 dress code = rules about what clothes you should wear
 environment = the place and conditions that you work in
2 1 in   2 to   3 in   4 with

6 Supply and demand

INTERVIEW
2 the cost of the product (including production, shipping, and breakages), and what the local competition is charging
3 1 … it's great to see the shop become successful, and the people of Oxford love it.
  2 … 50 cm-wide cylinder pots with a wide base … ; … England is windy and they don't blow over in the wind.
  3 … middle- and upper-middle-class people with little time, who want something of good quality in their garden.
  4 … glazed, coloured pottery from Asia; … central Italy.
  5 … keeping his fixed costs low (his chain of good contacts may help him to do this).

LANGUAGE REVIEW
1 ; 2
  1 have risen dramatically ↑
  2 there has been a slight rise ↗
  3 have gone up ; has risen ↑
  4 have been going up and up and up ↑
  5 have been stable →
  6 have neither risen nor fallen recently ; have stayed more or less the same →
  7 property prices ↑ salaries ↗

WORDBANK
1 (example answers)
 chain of contacts = e.g. suppliers, transporters
 fixed costs = e.g. salaries, premises rental
 local competition = a business which offers the same product or service in the same region as you

2
Noun	Noun (agent)	Adjective	Verb
competition ooOo	competitor oOoo	competitive oOoo	compete oO
fluctuation ooOo	–	–	fluctuate Ooo
production oOo	producer oOo	productive oOo	produce oO

7 Negotiations

INTERVIEW
2 1 The ideal outcome is one where both companies win.
  2 Tim would be flexible in the negotiation.
3 **A good negotiator:** listens; sees things from the other person's point of view; has good interpersonal skills
 Negotiating styles: aggressive; don't negotiate; consultative
 Tim's preferred negotiating style: consultative
 How Tim negotiates: adapts his style to the person he's negotiating with – if they are aggressive, he mirrors that, etc.
 Do's: listen; strike a rapport with the person; see things from their point of view
 Don'ts: argue; be aggressive; force your point of view on the other person

LANGUAGE REVIEW
2 1 If a client speaks to Tim rudely, he looks at the situation from their point of view and tries to gain rapport with them.
  2 If an experiment goes wrong, Katja repeats it.
  3 If Tim hadn't chosen his career as a headhunter, he would have started a publishing company. (Katja wouldn't have chosen any other career.)
  4 If Tim went bankrupt, he would start again. If Luke went bankrupt, he would get another job.
  5 When Tim retires, he'll probably travel.

WORDBANK
1 ; 2 gain rapport = build up a good relationship with somebody over time
 interpersonal skills = the ability to communicate well with people
 strike a rapport = find you immediately have a friendly relationship with somebody
3 1 to   2 up with   3 on; with

8 Staying competitive

INTERVIEW
2 According to Martin, a good consultant should be a good listener, a good communicator, honest, diplomatic, analytical, and good at problem-solving.
3 **(Turn to the bottom of page 163 for example spidergram)**

LANGUAGE REVIEW
2 1 In his first business, Martin *intended to sell* marketing services to engineering companies, but engineering companies weren't interested in his services.
  2 Annabel *tries to solve* a problem *by remaining* positive, *looking* at the solutions, and *working out* the best one.
  3 Ray *likes to relax by playing* chess and *drinking* wine. Annabel *likes to relax by doing* yoga and *going* for long walks.

WORDBANK
1 acquire a company   face up to problems
 change direction   win business
2 1 in   2 back   3 through   4 up to

9 International business

INTERVIEW
2 According to Katja:
1 **At work**
   Advantages: You can learn things from other countries, and get more training in your field. The more you travel, the better you get at your work.
   Difficulties: You can be expected to move even if you no longer want to.
2 **In your private life**
   Advantages: It's a very interesting experience.
   Difficulties: You eventually want to settle down and not travel any more. You have to learn a new language.
3 **Germany:** Katja is originally from there.
   France: She worked there before coming to the UK. There are a lot of permanent jobs in science, so people become less dynamic. Working hours are the same as in the UK.
   England / UK: It's good in immunology – there is lots of funding. Jobs for scientists are insecure, so people are dynamic, ambitious, and work hard.
   Oxford: A prestigious university.
   Developing countries and Asia: A lot of students from these countries are at Oxford. They are the best in their countries, and work very long hours because they want to achieve a lot in a short time.
   America: Katja travels there for work, for meetings, and to meet the people she collaborates with.

LANGUAGE REVIEW
1 1
split cells → cells make *antibodies* → *manufacture* antibodies → test by injecting antibodies into *humans*

2
create music (on computer) → *master* track → *transfer* track onto vinyl

2 (example answer)
The books are written by authors in various places, then they are printed at a printer's in Norfolk, UK. The books are then distributed to bookshops in the UK or sold all over the world over the Internet.

WORDBANK
1 **3 SYLLABLES:** dynamic oOo, insecure ooO
   4 SYLLABLES: experience oOoo, relocation ooOo
   5 SYLLABLES: collaboration oooOo, collaborator oOooo
2 1 around; to   2 down with   3 to; in

10 Human resources

INTERVIEW
2 Ray says don't ask questions purely about the salary or the holidays or what perks the job might offer. It's better to concentrate on aspects such as the training opportunities and the prospects for the company generally.

3 **Suitable job candidates:**
– have relevant qualifications
– are not over-qualified
– have experience
– are flexible
– bring useful skills to the company
Techniques used by interviewers:
A soft approach
– feels comfortable to the interviewee, but doesn't get to the real issues
– doesn't mean the interviewer is on your side
A hard approach
– involves asking aggressive questions
– can seem intimidating
– but allows candidates to shine and appear strong
CVs:
Some people exaggerate their achievements – they'll be found out at the interview stage.
Others underplay them – they may never get to the interview stage.
Advice for interviewee:
– Ask the right questions at the end of the interview.
– Learn techniques for keeping the conversation going.
– Know how to answer hard questions such as, 'What would you bring to our company?' and 'Why should we employ you rather than somebody else?'.

LANGUAGE REVIEW
1 take up; take on; keep up with; turn down; get on with; look forward to; put off
2 (example sentences)
I enjoy studying, but it *takes up* a lot of my free time.
I hope to *be taken on* by a good company when I qualify.
I read newspapers to *keep up with* world events.
If I was offered a job in the US, I wouldn't *turn* it *down*.
I *get on* well *with* all my colleagues.
I*'m looking forward to* finishing this course.
I tend to *put off* doing things that I don't enjoy doing.

WORDBANK
1 relevant qualifications   adopt an approach
  training opportunities   underplay achievements
2 1 adopts; approach.   3 underplay; achievements.
  2 training opportunities   4 relevant qualifications
3 (example answers)
sell themselves = persuade the interviewer that they are right for the job / show their strengths
shine = be impressive / make a strong impression
is on your side = is trying to help you

11 Business start-up

INTERVIEW
2 To promote one of Hilltop Publishing's books, the author went on a cycling tour to the places mentioned in the novel. On the way, he stopped at bookshops to sell the book. Catherine supported him with press and local radio.
3 **Hilltop Publishing:** small family business; publish books, some songs; started because they thought their different areas of expertise would work well together
Catherine Croydon: director; experienced editor

Luke Croydon: works for family business; manages IT; manages dance music sector; studied sound production and guitar at college
Dave Croydon: Catherine's husband and business partner; marketing expert; sold his own marketing company
Positive points of running your own business: satisfaction of choosing what is valuable and promoting it yourself
Difficulties in running your own business: finding a distributor; self-distribution is hard and time-consuming
What to do before starting a business: do a lot of research; have a good marketing plan; make sure there's a market for your product in the area where you'll be operating; don't plunge in until you're sure it's viable

LANGUAGE REVIEW
1 (example answers)
One day, Luke would like to be a politician in the House of Lords.
Some day, Catherine would like to publish a best-selling book and bring out a hit record.
In the future, Matthew would like to run a hotel or a restaurant.
Lucy's job is *not nearly as* structured as her last job.
According to Matthew, the social role of advertising is *far more* important than people think.

2 (example answers)
1 Eventually, I'd like to run my own business. / I hope to work abroad some day.
2 Many people think of Britain as a very cold country, but actually it has a mild climate.
3 I'm far less shy than I was ten years ago. / I'm not quite as fit as I was. / I don't go out nearly as often as I used to.

WORDBANK
1 ; 2 (example definitions)
level of expertise = the amount of specialized knowledge and experience somebody has
personal touch = individual attention that only a small business can give to somebody
small independents = small publishers that are not owned by a larger company
marketing plan = ideas for how to promote your company or service in the best way
3 1 to   2 in   3 with   4 in

12 Reputations

INTERVIEW
2 Annabel says that the lemons are seedless.

3 (example spidergram)

LANGUAGE REVIEW
1 1 the   4 the   7 A   10 –
   2 a   5 –   8 an 11 the
   3 the   6 –   9 a

WORDBANK
1 **have a good image** = be considered to be a good company
media training = learning the skills necessary for representing an organization in public
trade press = newspapers and magazines containing news about a particular industry
2 1 to   2 to   3 over

8 Staying competitive

INTERVIEW
3 (example spidergram)

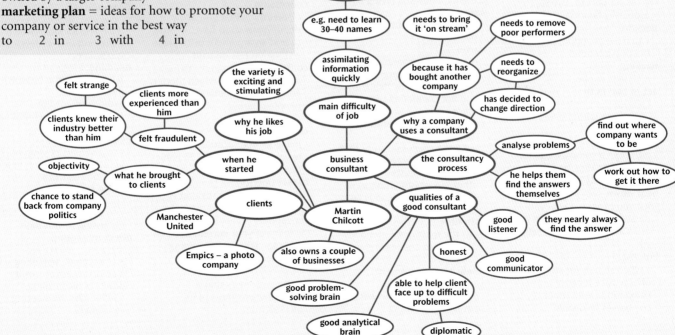

Glossary

account manager /əˈkaʊnt ˌmænɪdʒə(r)/
n an employee responsible for one or more of the company's regular customers

acquisition /ˌækwɪˈzɪʃn/
n the act of buying a company

act on /ˈækt ɒn/
v if you act on advice, information, etc. you take action as a result of it

adopt /əˈdɒpt/
v to accept and start using or selling a new product, system, etc.

appointee /ˌəpɔɪnˈtiː/
n a person who has been chosen for a job or position of responsibility

aptitude test /ˈæptɪtjuːd test/
n a test designed to show whether sb has the natural ability for a particular job or educational course

aspirational brand /ˌæspəˌreɪʃənl ˈbrænd/
n a brand which shows that its purchasers want to have more money or status than they do

authoritarian /ɔːˌθɒrɪˈteəriən/
adj in an authoritarian company culture, people lower down in the organization are expected to obey authority and rules without question

backer /ˈbækə(r)/
n a person or company that gives support to sth/sb, especially financial support

backfire /ˌbækˈfaɪə(r)/
v to have the opposite effect to the one intended

backing /ˈbækɪŋ/
n U help; support

act in bad faith /ˌækt ɪn ˌbæd ˈfeɪθ/
v to do sth with the intention of deceiving sb

bankrupt /ˈbæŋkrʌpt/
adj when a company cannot continue trading because it cannot pay its debts

beat down /ˌbiːt ˈdaʊn/
v if you beat sb down, you persuade them to reduce the price at which they are selling sth

bid /bɪd/
v when sb bids for sth, they offer a price for it in competition with other companies or people

bill of lading /ˌbɪl əv ˈleɪdɪŋ/
n a document that contains details of goods that are transported, which the buyer must show in order to take the goods when they arrive

bluff /blʌf/
n an attempt to trick sb by pretending sth is true when in fact it is not

booming /ˈbuːmɪŋ/
adj having a very successful period

brand awareness /ˌbrænd əˈweənəs/
n U the extent to which people recognize and know about a particular brand

brand-conscious /ˈbrænd ˌkɒnʃəs/
adj knowing about and recognizing a particular brand

breach of contract /ˌbriːtʃ əv ˈkɒntrækt/
n a situation when sb does not do sth that they have agreed to do in a contract

brief /briːf/
v to give sb information about sth so that they can deal with it

on the brink /ˌɒn ðə ˈbrɪŋk/
if you are on the brink of sth, you are almost in a very new, dangerous, or exciting situation

bullish /ˈbʊlɪʃ/
adj confident and hopeful about the future

business angel /ˈbɪznəs ˌeɪndʒl/
n an investor who helps new companies develop by lending them money and giving advice

cargo /ˈkɑːgəʊ/
n U the goods carried in a ship, plane, or truck

cartel /kɑːˈtel/
n a group of separate companies that agree to increase profits by fixing prices and not competing with each other

cash-and-carry warehouse /ˌkæʃ ənd ˌkæri ˈweəhaʊs/
n a large wholesale store that sells goods in large quantities at low prices to customers from other businesses who pay in cash and take the goods away themselves

cash flow /ˈkæʃ fləʊ/
n U the movement of money coming into and leaving a company

celebrity endorsement /səˌlebrəti ɪnˈdɔːsmənt/
n the use of a famous person to advertise a product

civil-engineering firm /ˌsɪvl endʒɪˈnɪərɪŋ fɜːm/
n a company that designs, builds and repairs roads, bridges, canals, etc.

clinical trials /ˌklɪnɪkl ˈtraɪlz/
n pl tests to make sure that a new drug works and is safe before it goes on sale

collapse /kəˈlæps/
n a sudden big fall in prices

colonialism /kəˈləʊniəlɪzəm/
n U the practice by which a powerful country controls another country or other countries

comfortably off /ˌkʌmftəbli ˈɒf/
adj having enough money to live a normal life

commission /kəˈmɪʃn/
n U an amount of money that is paid to sb for selling goods or services and which usually increases with the quantity sold

commodity /kəˈmɒdəti/
n a product or a raw material that can be bought and sold, especially between countries

compromise /ˈkɒmprəmaɪz/
n an agreement made between two people or groups in which each side gives up some of the things they want so that both sides are happy at the end

computer-literate /kəmˌpjuːtə(r) ˈlɪtərət/
adj able to use computers well

concession /kənˈseʃn/
n something that you allow or do, or allow sb to have, in order to end an argument or to make a situation less difficult

confrontation /ˌkɒnfrʌnˈteɪʃn/
n U a situation in which there is an angry disagreement between people or groups who have different opinions

conglomerate /kənˈglɒmərət/
n a large organization formed by joining a group of companies together

consignment /kənˈsaɪnmənt/
n a quantity of goods that is sent or delivered somewhere

consolidate /kənˈsɒlɪdeɪt/
v to make your current position stronger, without expanding

consumer base /kənˈsjuːmə(r) beɪs/
n the customers that a company gets most of its income from

consumption /kənˈsʌmpʃn/
n U the amount of a product that is used in a particular period

controlling interest /kənˌtrəʊlɪŋ ˈɪntrəst/
n enough shares in a company, often over 50%, to allow the shareholder to make decisions about what the company should do

copywriter /ˈkɒpiraɪtə(r)/
n a person whose job is to write the words for advertisements

core staff /ˌkɔː(r) ˈstɑːf/
n employees who are most essential to a business

core time /ˌkɔː(r) ˈtaɪm/
n U the hours of the day during which employees working flexible hours must be present

crane /kreɪn/
n a tall machine with a long arm, used to lift and move heavy goods

critical path(s) analysis /ˌkrɪtɪkl ˌpɑːθ(s) əˈnæləsɪs/
n U a way of examining the tasks involved in a project, showing the order in which they should be completed and how much time is needed for each

customer base /ˈkʌstəmə(r) beɪs/
n all the people who buy or use a particular product or service

at the cutting edge /ət ðə ˌkʌtɪŋ ˈedʒ/
working with the newest, most advanced technology

dead-end job /ˌded end ˈdʒɒb/
n a low-paid job in which no more progress or development is possible

deadline /ˈdedlaɪn/
n a point in time by which sth must be done

deadlocked /ˈdedlɒkd/
adj when no agreement can be reached

delegate /ˈdelɪgeɪt/
v to give part of your work or authority to a person in a lower position than you

dictate terms /dɪkˌteɪt ˈtɜːmz/
v to tell sb what to do, without discussing it with them

direct marketing /daɪˌrekt ˈmɑːkɪtɪŋ/
n U a type of marketing where a company advertises its products by emailing, telephoning, or meeting consumers

discontinue /ˌdɪskənˈtɪnju:/
v to stop selling a product

discounted /dɪsˈkaʊntɪd/
adj reduced in price

disposable income /dɪˌspəʊzəbl ˈɪnkəm/
n U income left after taxes, etc. that you are free to spend or save as you want

distribution channel /ˌdɪstrɪˈbju:ʃn ˌtʃænl/
n the way that products are made available to customers

distributor network /dɪˈstrɪbjətə(r) ˌnetwɜ:k/
n all the companies and people involved in delivering a company's products to customers

downturn /ˈdaʊntɜ:n/
n a time when an economy, industry, etc. is weaker than normal; a fall in the amount of business that is done

dress code /ˈdres ˌkəʊd/
n a set of rules that an organization has about what people must or must not wear

driving force /ˈdraɪvɪŋ fɔ:s/
n an influence that causes a big change to happen

dual income /ˌdju:əl ˈɪnkəm/
adj in a dual income family, two people earn money from full-time work

early adopter /ˌɜ:li əˈdɒptə(r)/
n somebody who is among the first to use a new product, system, etc.

egalitarian /iˌgælɪˈteəriən/
adj in an egalitarian company culture, employees are all treated equally

elasticity of demand /ˌelæˌstɪsəti əv dɪˈmɑ:nd/
n U the extent to which a change in the price of a particular product will cause a change in demand for it

emerging market /ɪˌmɜ:dʒɪŋ ˈmɑ:kɪt/
n a new market that is developing quickly and becoming important

endorse /ɪnˈdɔ:s/
v to say in an advertisement that you use and like a particular product or service so that other people will want to buy or use it

ethical /ˈeθɪkl/
adj acting in a morally acceptable way

exclusivity /ˌeksklu:ˈsɪvəti/
n U the fact of being the only company allowed to sell sth

expand /ɪkˈspænd/
v if you expand a business, you invest money to make it bigger

exploit /ɪkˈsplɔɪt/
v to treat sb unfairly by making them work and not giving them much in return; to make use of sth in order to gain an advantage

factory farming /ˈfæktəri ˌfɑ:mɪŋ/
n U farming that uses industrial methods to produce large amounts of meat, milk, etc. as quickly and as cheaply as possible

fall behind /ˌfɔ:l bɪˈhaɪnd/
v to fail to keep to the times planned in a schedule

fixed costs /ˌfɪkst ˈkɒsts/
n pl the costs that a business must pay that do not change even if the amount of work produced changes, such as rent, wages, and lighting

flat charge /ˌflæt ˈtʃɑ:dʒ/
n a fixed price

flexitime /ˈfleksitaɪm/
n U a system in which employees work a particular number of hours each week or month but can choose when they work these hours

float /fləʊt/
v when a company is floated on the stock exchange, it sells its shares to the public for the first time

flop /flɒp/
v to be a complete failure; n a complete failure

franchisee /ˌfræntʃaɪˈzi:/
n a person that has bought the right from a company to sell the company's goods and services in a particular area

franchisor /ˈfræntʃaɪzə(r)/
n a company that sells the right to sell its goods and services in a particular area

freight forwarder /ˈfreɪt ˌfɔ:wədə(r)/
n a company that arranges for goods to be transported and exported on behalf of others

funding /ˈfʌndɪŋ/
n U money for a particular purpose

GDP /ˌdʒi: di: ˈpi:/
n U Gross Domestic Product; the total value of all the goods and services produced by a country in one year

get out of /ˌget ˈaʊt əv/
v to avoid a responsibility or duty, especially one that you have agreed to in a contract

globalization /ˌgləʊbəlaɪˈzeɪʃn/
n U the process by which businesses and organizations grow and start to operate in countries all over the world

glut /glʌt/
n a situation in which there is more of sth than is needed or can be used

golden handcuffs /ˌgəʊldən ˈhændkʌfs/
n pl a large amount of money and other financial benefits that are given to sb to persuade them to continue working for a company rather than leaving to work for another company

golden hello /ˌgəʊldən həˈləʊ/
n a large amount of money or other financial benefits given by a company to new employees in order to attract good people

good faith /ˌgʊd ˈfeɪθ/
n U if you do sth in good faith then you do it honestly and without any intention to deceive

green belt area /ˈgri:n belt ˌeəriə/
n an area of open land around a city where building is strictly controlled

grey market /ˈgreɪ ˌmɑ:kɪt/
n the unofficial buying and selling of goods, especially from a cheaper to a more expensive market

hand over /ˌhænd ˈəʊvə(r)/
v when a speaker hands the audience over to sb, they allow the next speaker to begin talking

be headhunted /bi ˈhedhʌntɪd/
v be persuaded to come and work for a different company

headhunter /ˈhedhʌntə(r)/
n a person whose job is to find people who are suitable for vacant senior jobs, and persuade them to leave their present jobs

headquarters /ˌhedˈkwɔ:təz/
n the place from which an organization is controlled

hierarchical /ˌhaɪəˈrɑ:kɪkl/
adj in which people have different levels of authority, responsibility, or importance

hierarchy /ˈhaɪərɑ:ki/
n a system in which people are organized into different levels of authority, responsibility or importance from highest to lowest

higher education /ˌhaɪə(r) edjuˈkeɪʃn/
n U education and training at college and university, especially to degree level

hold /həʊld/
n the part of a ship where the goods are stored

hospitality event /ˌhɒspɪˈtæləti ɪˌvent/
n a special event, such as a sporting event or a show, that a company pays for its important customers to go to

hot /hɒt/
adj very fashionable

hot-desk /ˌhɒt ˈdesk/
v to work in a system where employees do not have their own desk, but use any that is available

HQ /ˌeɪtʃ ˈkju:/
n = headquarters

Human Resources /ˌhju:mən rɪˈzɔ:sɪz/
n U the department in a company that deals with employing and training people

ID tag /ˌaɪ ˈdi: tæg/
n a name badge that people wear so that they can be identified

Inc. /ɪŋk/
used in the names of companies in the US as a short way of writing Incorporated (= officially created as a company)

insider trading /ɪnˌsaɪdə ˈtreɪdɪŋ/
n U illegally using knowledge from your job to make a profit investing in shares

insolvent /ɪnˈsɒlvənt/
adj not able to trade because you cannot pay your debts

instalment /ɪnˈstɔ:lmənt/
n one of a number of payments that are made regularly over a period of time until sth has been paid for

intranet /ˈɪntrəˌnet/
n a computer network that is private to a company or an organization but is connected to and uses the same software as the Internet

invoice /ˈɪnvɔɪs/
n a list of goods that have been sold, work that has been done, etc., showing what you must pay

iron out /ˌaɪən ˈaʊt/
v to get rid of differences or problems

joint venture /ˌdʒɔɪnt ˈventʃə(r)/
n a new business that is started by two or more companies, often in the form of an independent company whose shares they own; the product or service that the business sells or provides

junk email /ˌdʒʌŋk ˈi:meɪl/
n U advertising material that is sent to people who have not asked for it

kick-start /ˈkɪk ˌstɑ:t/
n something that helps a process or project start more quickly

layout /ˈleɪaʊt/
n the way furniture and rooms are arranged in a building; the way text and images are arranged on a page

lease /li:s/
n a legal agreement that allows you to use a building for a period of time in return for rent

letter of acceptance /ˌletə(r) əv əkˈseptəns/
n a letter that you write to officially accept an offer, especially the offer of a job

Glossary

letter of credit /ˈletə(r) əv ˈkredɪt/
n a letter from a bank that allows you to get a particular amount of money from another bank

letting agency /ˈletɪŋ ˌeɪdʒənsi/
n a business that provides buildings usable for a period in return for rent

level off /ˌlevl ˈɒf/
v to stay at a steady level after a period of sharp rises or falls

leverage /ˈliːvərɪdʒ/
n U the ability to influence what people do

liabilities /ˌlaɪəˈbɪlətɪz/
n pl money that a company owes

under licence /ˌʌndə ˈlaɪsns/
adv if a company manufactures a product under licence, it has official permission to do so

liquidate /ˈlɪkwɪdeɪt/
v to sell sth in order to get money

loss leader /ˈlɒs ˌliːdə(r)/
n a product or service sold at a loss to encourage people to buy more profitable goods or services

make up /ˌmeɪk ˈʌp/
v if you try to make up time, you do extra work to compensate for time that you have lost or wasted

manoeuvring /məˈnuːvrɪŋ/
n U clever plans and actions that sb uses to gain an advantage

margin /ˈmɑːdʒɪn/
n = profit margin

marketing mix /ˈmɑːkɪtɪŋ ˌmɪks/
n the main factors that influence a customer's decision to buy a particular product or service

market intelligence /ˌmɑːkɪt ɪnˈtelɪdʒəns/
n U market information that a company has

market share /ˌmɑːkɪt ˈʃeə(r)/
n the amount of sales of a particular type of product that a company has, compared with the total sales

mass market /ˌmæs ˈmɑːkɪt/
n a market in which a very large number of sales are possible

matrix /ˈmeɪtrɪks/
n an arrangement of symbols, numbers, etc. in rows and columns

menial /ˈmiːniəl/
adj a menial job is not skilled or important, and is often boring

merchandise /ˈmɜːtʃəndaɪs/
n U goods that are bought or sold; goods that are for sale in a shop

merger /ˈmɜːdʒə(r)/
n the act of joining two or more businesses into one

me-too brand /ˌmiː ˈtuː brænd/
n a brand that copies another brand that is already successful

morale /məˈrɑːl/
n U the amount of enthusiasm and confidence that a group of workers has

mortgage /ˈmɔːgɪdʒ/
n a long-term loan which is used to buy a home

mother company /ˈmʌðə(r) ˈkʌmpəni/
n a company that owns or controls smaller companies of the same type

multinational /ˌmʌltiˈnæʃnəl/
n a company that operates in several different countries; *adj* operating in several different countries

negative connotation /ˌnegətɪv ˌkɒnəˈteɪʃn/
n a negative idea suggested by a word in addition to its main meaning

networking /ˈnetwɜːkɪŋ/
n U a system of meeting and talking to other people who may be useful or helpful to you in your work

network marketing /ˌnetwɜːk ˈmɑːkɪtɪŋ/
n a type of marketing where a company gives people a commission for selling a product to people they know

niche market /ˌniːʃ ˈmɑːkɪt/
n a market in which a company has an opportunity to be the only company to sell a particular product

night shift /ˈnaɪt ʃɪft/
n a period of time during the night worked by a group of workers who are then replaced by another group during the daytime

notice period /ˈnəʊtɪs ˌpɪəriəd/
n a fixed period of time that you must continue working after saying that you are going to leave your job, or after your company says that you must leave

oriented /ˈɔːrientɪd/
adj used to or adapted to working in a particular way, in a particular market, etc.

outgoings /ˈaʊtgəʊɪŋz/
n pl the amount of money that a business or a person has to spend regularly, for example every month

outlet /ˈaʊtlet/
n a shop that sells goods or food of a particular type

outstanding /aʊtˈstændɪŋ/
adj not yet paid; exceptionally good

overheads /ˈəʊvəhedz/
n pl regular costs that you have when you are running a business or an organization, such as rent, electricity, wages, etc.

overnight success /ˌəʊvənaɪt səkˈses/
n something that immediately becomes successful

overtake /ˌəʊvəˈteɪk/
v to become greater in size, importance, etc. than sb/sth else

panel interview /ˈpænl ˌɪntəvjuː/
n an interview in which several people ask you questions

paternalistic /pəˌtɜːnəˈlɪstɪk/
adj in a paternalistic company culture, people lower down in the organization are looked after well, but given very little responsibility to make decisions

pay off /ˌpeɪ ˈɒf/
v to finish paying money owed for sth

pay-scale /ˈpeɪskeɪl/
n the range of levels of pay for people within a company or profession

perk /pɜːk/
n something you receive as well as your wages for doing a particular job

piracy /ˈpaɪrəsi/
n U illegal copying of computer programs, DVDs, books, etc.

pitfall /ˈpɪtfɔːl/
n a danger or difficulty, especially one that is hidden or not obvious at first

placement /ˈpleɪsmənt/
n the service of finding suitable jobs for people; a job, often as part of a course of study, where you get some experience of a particular kind of work

plentiful /ˈplentɪfl/
adj available in large amounts

PR /ˌpiː ˈɑː(r)/
= public relations

predatory pricing /ˌpredətri ˈpraɪsɪŋ/
n U a situation where a powerful company prices a product very low in order to prevent competition and protect its market share

presence /ˈprezns/
n U the fact of making yourself noticed by a lot of people

press release /ˈpres rɪˌliːs/
n an official statement made to journalists by a company

press the issue /ˌpres ðɪ ˈɪʃuː/
v to ask more questions than sb wants to answer

prestigious /preˈstɪdʒəs/
adj respected and admired as very important or of very high quality

price-sensitive /ˌpraɪs ˈsensətɪv/
adj in a price-sensitive market, a small change in price will have a big effect on sales

production facility /prəˈdʌkʃn fəˌsɪləti/
n a factory

product placement /ˈprɒdʌkt ˌpleɪsmənt/
n U a type of advertising in which a company pays to have one of its products appear in a film/movie or television programme

product recall /ˌprɒdʌkt ˈriːkɔːl/
n a request made by a company for people who have bought a particular product to take or send it back, especially because it may have a dangerous fault

profit margin /ˈprɒfɪt ˌmɑːdʒɪn/
n the difference between the amount sb pays for sth, and the amount it sells for

projected sales /prəˌdʒektɪd ˈseɪlz/
n pl the estimated sales figures for a period in the future

proposal /prəˈpəʊzl/
n a formal suggestion

proposition /ˌprɒpəˈzɪʃn/
n a suggestion or plan for action

prospect /ˈprɒspekt/
n the possibility that sth will happen; *n pl* future possibilities; a chance of being successful in the future

protocol /ˈprəʊtəkɒl/
n U an accepted way of behaving in a particular formal situation

provisional /prəˈvɪʒənl/
adj if a job offer is provisional, it will only be definite when certain checks, tests, etc. have been completed successfully

psychometric test /ˌsaɪkəˌmetrɪk ˈtest/
n any test that measures sb's mental abilities, personality, attitudes, etc., often used when choosing sb for a job

public relations /ˌpʌblɪk rɪˈleɪʃnz/
n pl the business of giving the public information about a company in order to create and maintain a good image

pull strings /ˌpʊl ˈstrɪŋz/
v to use your influence in order to get an advantage

put off /ˌpʊt ˈɒf/
v to change sth to a later time or date; to make sb no longer want to do sth

quasi- /ˈkweɪzaɪ/
prefix (used with adjectives) partly

raw materials /ˌrɔː məˈtɪəriəlz/
n pl the basic elements, which manufacturers make into finished products

Glossary

recession /rɪˈseʃn/
n a difficult time for the economy of a country, when there is less trade and industrial activity than usual and more people are unemployed

redundancy payment /rɪˈdʌndənsi ˌpeɪmənt/
n money that you receive when you lose your job because there is no more work available

reference number /ˈrefrəns ˌnʌmbə(r)/
n a number that is used to represent a particular product, customer, etc.

refund /rɪˈfʌnd/
v to give sb their money back; /ˈriːfʌnd/ n money that you give back to sb

reimburse /ˌriːɪmˈbɜːs/
v to pay back money to sb which they have spent or lost

rep /rep/
n an employee of a company who travels around a particular area selling the company's goods to shops, etc.

repackage /ˌriːˈpækɪdʒ/
v to sell a product in a new package in order to increase its sales

reputable /ˈrepjətəbl/
adj known to be honest and to provide a good service

retail chain /ˈriːteɪl ˌtʃeɪn/
n a group of shops owned by the same company

revenues /ˈrevənjuːz/
n pl the money that is received by a business, usually from selling goods or services

rough costings /ˌrʌf ˈkɒstɪŋz/
n pl an estimate of approximately how much money will be needed for sth

rung on the ladder /ˌrʌŋ ɒn ðə ˈlædə(r)/
n one of the jobs in a series that an employee will have if they make progress in a company

run through /ˌrʌn ˈθruː/
v to quickly give or receive information about sth

sabbatical /səˈbætɪkl/
n a period of time when sb is allowed to stop their normal work in order to study or travel

sale or return /ˌseɪl ɔː rɪˈtɜːn/
n s if goods are supplied on a sale or return basis, any item that is not sold can be sent back without having to be paid for

sales lead /ˈseɪlz ˌliːd/
n information about a possible new customer, which may lead to sales if action is taken

sales literature /ˈseɪlz ˌlɪtrətʃə(r)/
n U printed information about goods or services that a company sells

saturated market /ˌsætʃəreɪtɪd ˈmɑːkɪt/
n a market in which demand for a product has been met, so no more can be sold

from scratch /frəm ˈskrætʃ/
adv without any previous knowledge or preparation

segmentation /ˌsegmənˈteɪʃn/
n U the division of a market into groups of different types of consumer

serial interview /ˈsɪəriəl ˈɪntəvjuː/
n a series of interviews that take place one after another

setback /ˈsetbæk/
n a difficulty or problem that delays or prevents sth, or makes a situation worse

settle out of court /ˌsetl aʊt əv ˈkɔːt/
v if a legal case is settled out of court, one side agrees to pay money to the other side in order to avoid going to court

shortlist /ˈʃɔːtlɪst/
v to make a list of a small number of possible markets, job candidates, etc. that have been chosen from a large number; n a small number of candidates for a job, possible markets, etc. that have been chosen from a large number

skimming (the market) /ˌskɪmɪŋ (ðə ˈmɑːkɪt)/
n the action of putting a high price on a new product in order to make a quick profit before competition lowers the price

soundbite /ˈsaʊndbaɪt/
n a phrase that sb plans to use while they are speaking, because they want it to be remembered

speculative application /ˌspekjələtɪv æplɪˈkeɪʃn/
n a request that you make to work for a company, although they have not advertised a job

stagnant /ˈstægnənt/
adj not developing or growing

start-up /ˈstɑːt ʌp/
n a new company

step down /ˌstep ˈdaʊn/
v to leave an important position and let sb else take your place

stepping stone /ˈstepɪŋ ˌstəʊn/
n a job that sb does because it will allow them to move on later to the job that they really want to do

stick to /ˈstɪk tuː/
v keep doing something until it is finished

stock /stɒk/
v to keep a particular product available for sale in a shop; n (often pl) the amount of sth that is available to be sold or used

subscriber /səbˈskraɪbə(r)/
n a person who pays to receive regular copies of a magazine, service, etc.

subscription /səbˈskrɪpʃn/
n an amount of money that sb pays regularly in order to receive a magazine, service, etc.

subsidy /ˈsʌbsədi/
n money paid by an organization to keep the cost of sth low

sue /suː/
v to make a claim against sb in a court about sth that they have said or done to harm you

superior /suːˈpɪəriə(r)/
n a person who is above you in a company

supply chain /səˈplaɪ tʃeɪn/
n the whole series of processes, companies, places, etc. that are involved in making and selling a product

take up /ˌteɪk ˈʌp/
v if you take up an offer, you accept it

team-building /ˌtiːm ˈbɪldɪŋ/
adj activities organized for employees where they work as a team, and which are often fun

tender /ˈtendə(r)/
v to make a formal offer to carry out work or supply goods at a stated price

time off in lieu /ˌtaɪm ɒf ɪn ˈluː/
n U extra time away from work that employees can have if they have worked extra hours

to-do list /tə ˈduː lɪst/
n a list of things that you have to do

token of goodwill /ˌtəʊkən əv ɡʊdˈwɪl/
n something that a company gives to a customer to show that they value their business

track /træk/
v to follow the progress of goods that have been ordered

tracking study /ˈtrækɪŋ ˌstʌdi/
n a study in which people are asked the same questions at different times, in order to find out how people's opinions, tastes, needs, etc. change over time

trademark /ˈtreɪdmɑːk/
n the product, style, etc. that a company is best known for

transaction golf /trænˌzækʃn ˈɡɒlf/
n U a game of golf played by people who hope to do business together

in transit /ɪn ˈtrænzɪt/
being moved or carried from one place to another

transport infrastructure /ˌtrænspɔːt ˈɪnfrə ˌstrʌktʃə(r)/
n the transport system in a country

trial period /ˈtraɪəl ˈpɪəriəd/
n a fixed period that you work for in a new job, during which the company judges your performance and decides whether to employ you permanently

turnover /ˈtɜːnəʊvə(r)/
n the total amount of goods or services sold by a company during a particular period of time; the rate at which employees leave a company and are replaced by other people

tycoon /taɪˈkuːn/
n a person who is successful in business or industry and has become rich and powerful

underpin /ˌʌndəˈpɪn/
v to support sth and form its basis

understaffed /ˌʌndəˈstɑːft/
adj not having enough people working and therefore not able to function well

universal benefits /ˌjuːnɪˌvɜːsl ˈbenəfɪts/
n pl benefits that are given to all employees

up-front /ˌʌp ˈfrʌnt/
adj that must be paid in advance

upgrade /ˌʌpˈɡreɪd/
v to give sb a better seat on a plane

value added tax (VAT) /ˌvæljuː ˌædɪd ˈtæks/
n U a tax that is added to the price of goods and services

vending machine /ˈvendɪŋ məˌʃiːn/
n a machine from which you can buy drinks, cigarettes, etc. by putting coins into it

venture capital organization /ˌventʃə ˈkæpɪtl ˌɔːɡənaɪˌzeɪʃn/
n an organization that invests money in new companies to help them develop

viable /ˈvaɪəbl/
adj that can be done, used, achieved, etc.; likely to be successful

voucher /ˈvaʊtʃə(r)/
n a printed piece of paper that can be used instead of money to pay for sth

wind up /ˌwaɪnd ˈʌp/
v when sb winds up a company, they stop running it and close it completely

wiped out /ˌwaɪpd ˈaʊt/
adj forced out of business

withdraw /wɪðˈdrɔː/
v to take away sth that you had offered to sb/sth; to decide to no longer take part in sth; to stop selling a product, for example because it may be dangerous

work for peanuts /ˌwɜːk fə ˈpiːnʌts/
v to work for very little money

OXFORD
UNIVERSITY PRESS

Great Clarendon Street, Oxford OX2 6DP

Oxford University Press is a department of the University of Oxford.
It furthers the University's objective of excellence in research, scholarship,
and education by publishing worldwide in

Oxford   New York

Auckland   Cape Town   Dar es Salaam   Hong Kong   Karachi
Kuala Lumpur   Madrid   Melbourne   Mexico City   Nairobi
New Delhi   Shanghai   Taipei   Toronto

With offices in

Argentina   Austria   Brazil   Chile   Czech Republic   France   Greece
Guatemala   Hungary   Italy   Japan   Poland   Portugal   Singapore
South Korea   Switzerland   Thailand   Turkey   Ukraine   Vietnam

OXFORD and OXFORD ENGLISH are registered trade marks of
Oxford University Press in the UK and in certain other countries

© Oxford University Press 2005

The moral rights of the author have been asserted

Database right Oxford University Press (maker)

First published 2005

2009 2008 2007
10 9 8 7 6 5 4 3

No unauthorized photocopying

All rights reserved. No part of this publication may be reproduced, stored in a retrieval system, or transmitted, in any form or by any means, without the prior permission in writing of Oxford University Press, or as expressly permitted by law, or under terms agreed with the appropriate reprographics rights organization. Enquiries concerning reproduction outside the scope of the above should be sent to the ELT Rights Department, Oxford University Press, at the address above

You must not circulate this book in any other binding or cover and you must impose this same condition on any acquirer

Any websites referred to in this publication are in the public domain and their addresses are provided by Oxford University Press for information only. Oxford University Press disclaims any responsibility for the content

ISBN-13: 978 0 19 457580 5

Printed in China

ACKNOWLEDGEMENTS

Video photography by Tom Dick & Debbie Productions Ltd
www.tomdickanddebbie.com

The authors and publisher are grateful to those who have given permission to reproduce the following extracts and adaptations of copyright material: p6 Adapted from 'A breath of fresh air – that will be nine quid please' by Colin Grimshaw, *The Independent* 26 March 2001. Reproduced by permission of Independent Newspapers (UK) Ltd. P8 'Generation Y' by Ellen Newborne & Kathleen Kerwin, *Business Week* 15 February 1999 © The McGraw-Hill Companies Inc. Reproduced by permission. p11 Extracts from www.adbusters.org. Reproduced by permission of Adbusters Media Foundation. p12 Information about BMW C1 from ww.bmw.co.uk. Reproduced by permission of BMW UK Ltd. p12 Review of BMW C1, Evening Standard. Reproduced by permission of Evening Standard / Atlantic Syndication. p18 'Secrets to success laid bare' by Louise Armitstead. Abridged and amended from an article originally published in *The Sunday Times*. Reproduced by permission of *The Sunday Times*. p19 'Switched on, the computer games queen' © Rupert Steiner / *The Sunday Times* 14 September 1997. Reproduced by permission of Times Newspapers Ltd. p28 'Beat the clock' © Professor Cary L. Cooper / *The Sunday Times* 5 March 2000. Reproduced by permission of Times Newspapers Ltd. p38 'China wipes the smile off Western lips' © Catherine Wheatley / *The Sunday Times* 31 October 1999. Reproduced by permission of Times Newspapers Ltd. p47 Extracts from *Riding the Waves of Culture*, 2nd Edition by Fons Trompenaars and Charles Hampden-Turner. Reproduced by permission of Nicholas Brealey Publishing. p48 Extracts from www.merck.com. © 1995 – 2004 Merck and Co. Inc., Whitehouse Station NJ, USA. All rights reversed. Adapted and used with permission of Merck and Co. Inc. p61 Extracts from *The Essential Manager's Manual* by Robert Heller and Tim Hindle. © 1998 Dorling Kindersley, text © 1998 Robert Heller and Tim Hindle. Reproduced by permission of Penguin Books Ltd. p66–77 Interview with Eric Perrot. Reproduced by permission of Eric Perrot. p68 Extract from Mark H. McCormack on Negotiating by Mark H. McCormack. Published by Arrow Business Books. Reproduced by permission of The Random House Group Ltd. p76 Interview with Bill Watts. Reproduced by permission of Bill Watts. p79 'Bull in a beer market' by Grant Clelland, *The Business* 7/8 March 2004. Reproduced by permission of *The Business*.

p89 'A simple box that changed to world' by Saeed Shah, © *The Independent* 30 August 2000. Reproduced by permission of *The Independent*. p96 Adapted from 'White collars felt in war on CV Fraud' by Jonathan Thompson, *The Independent* 10 December 2000. Reproduced by permission of Independent Newspapers (UK) Ltd. p98 'Perk practice' © Anita Chaudhuri, *The Guardian* 30 August 2001. Reproduced by permission of Guardian Newspapers Ltd. p108 'How to join the family business' © Tola Awogbamiye, *The Guardian* 30 August 2001. Reproduced by permission of Tola Awogbamiye. p117 VALS Life Style Segmentation from Dictionary of Marketing 2nd edition by A.Ivanovic and P.H Collin, 1989, 1996. Reproduced by permission of Bloomsbury. p118 'Focusing on Armchair Athletes, Puma becomes a leader' by Kevin J O'Brien © 2004 by The New York Times Co. Reproduced by permission. p130 'Internal tutorial: How the Internet works' from http:|/english.unitechnology.ac.nz. Reproduced by permission of the New Zealand Ministry of Education. All rights reserved. p130 'Anguish of telling a son he will never run family firm' © John O'Donnell / *The Sunday Times* 5 August 2001. Reproduced by permission of Times Newspapers Ltd.

Illustrations by: Claire Clements pp16, 20, 30, 56, 109; Mark Draisey pp34, 50, 66, 96; Mark Duffin pp13, 62, 81; Richard Duszczak pp 127, 133; Sophie Exton pp21, 22, 23, 52, 134; Ben Kirchner pp42, 87, 97, 100, 120; Oxford Designers and Illustrators pp48, 114; Ami Plasse p94.

The publishers would like to thank the following for their kind permission to reproduce photographs and copyright material: Adbusters Media Foundation p11(all) (Extracts from www.adbusters.org); Alamy pp6b (Butch Martin), 17l (Jacky Chapman/Janine Wiedel Photolibrary), 18cr (Tim Hetherington/ImageState), 36br (Andy Bishop), 58 (Popperfoto), 72 (Pictor International/ImageState), 82 (Pictor International/ImageState), 93b (lookGaleria), 93t (Pictor International/ ImageState), 101t (Pictor International/ImageState), 110 (Eugenio Opitz), 113b (Philip Wilkins/The Anthony Blake Photo Library), 116bl (National Motor Museum/Motoring Picture Library), 123b (foodfolio), 124 (Robert Slade); Anthony Blake Photo Library pp32 (Ming Tang-Evans), 91tl (Anthony Blake); AP Photo p102 (Jeffrey A. Camarati/Stringer); BMW pp14bl&br (Information about BMW C1 from www.bmw.co.uk. Reproduced by permission of BMW UK Ltd.), 46cr; British Red Cross p46l (The Red Cross and Red Crescent emblems and names are used with the authorisation of the British Red Cross); Chocosuisse pp91bc&c&cl; Corbis UK Ltd. pp14t (Bill Ross), 26t (Lester Lefkowitz), 28 (Bill Varie), 36tl (Yang Liu), 36tr (Jim Richardson), 38b (Walter Hodges), 38t (Randy Faris), 46b (Daniel J. Cox), 53c (BJ Formento), 53cl (Walter Smith), 53cr (Chris Carroll), 53l (Steve Prezant), 53r (Michael Prince), 57t (Michael Freeman), 68 (Dennis Galante), 80 (Bill Varie), 86r (Michael Prince), 89c (Michael T. Sedam), 89l (Hulton-Deutsch Collection), 89r (E.O. Hoppé), 90cr (Earl & Nazima Kowall), 90l (Stephanie Maze), 91cr (Fukuhara, Inc.), 91tc (Kevin Schafer), 91tr (Gilles Rigoulet/Sygma), 92 (Chris Lisle), 98 (Catherine Karnow), 101b (SIE Productions), 103bl (Paul Edmondson), 103tr (Laureen March), 106l (RNT Productions), 106r (Anne Domdey), 121 (Ben Wood); Empics p118 (Peter Robinson); Getty Images pp9 (James Muldowney/ Taxi), 33 (Romilly Lockyer/The Image Bank), 40 (Bruce Ayres/Stone), 60 (Ryan McVay/The Image Bank), 70 (Sean Justice/The Image Bank), 76b (Martin Barraud/The Image Bank), 79t (Romilly Lockyer/The Image Bank), 83 (Chabruken/Taxi), 103tl (Taxi), 111t (Antonio Mo/Taxi), 123c (Anne-Marie Weber/The Image Bank); Greenpeace Pictures p46r; Intel Corporation (UK) Ltd. p46cl; Mary Evans Picture Library pp26b, 116t; Oxford University Press pp17r, 18l, 19t, 27, 36bl, 39, 47, 49, 57b, 59, 67t, 69, 77, 78, 79bl, 86l, 88, 91bl, 97, 107, 109, 111b, 117, 119; Eric Perrot p66b, Photofusion Picture Library pp73 (Christa Stadtler), 123t (Paula Glassman/Format Photographers); Photolibrary.com pp10 (Helen Ashford), 103br (Frank P Wartenberg); Rex Features pp54 (Action Press), 113t (Nils Jorgensen); SCi Games Ltd p19b; Science Photo Library p90r (Pascal Goetgheluck); Skoda Auto p116br; Sony Ericsson UK & Ireland p76t; Still Pictures pp90cl, 91br; The Gadget Shop Ltd p18tr; The O-Company pp6tl&tr; Zooid Pictures p67b; Mark Bryan p 66c.

Commissioned photography: page 18 (gadgets) Pierre d'Alancaisez

The publishers wish to thank the British Red Cross for its permission to use the red cross and red crescent emblems and names in this publication. Inclusion of an organisation in this booklet does not signify its endorsement of any of the other organisations listed.